COMPETING
IN THE
AGE OF AI

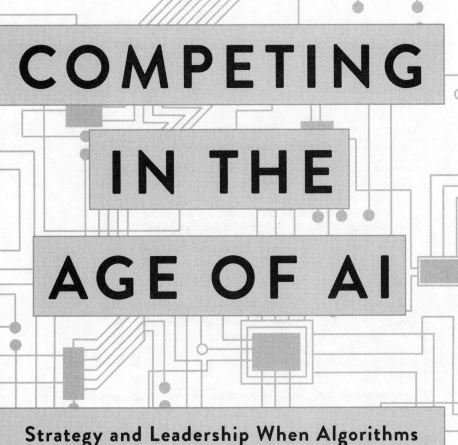

COMPETING IN THE AGE OF AI

Strategy and Leadership When Algorithms and Networks Run the World

MARCO IANSITI
KARIM R. LAKHANI

Harvard Business Review Press
BOSTON, MASSACHUSETTS

The web addresses referenced in this book were live and correct at the time of the book's publication but may be subject to change.

Library of Congress Cataloging-in-Publication Data

Names: Iansiti, Marco, 1961- author. | Lakhani, Karim R., author.
Title: Competing in the age of AI : strategy and leadership when algorithms and networks run the world / Marco Iansiti and Karim Lakhani.
Description: Boston, MA : Harvard Business Review Press, [2020] | Includes index.
Identifiers: LCCN 2019024137 | ISBN 9781633697621 (hardcover)
Subjects: LCSH: Artificial intelligence—Industrial applications. | Competition. | Leadership. | Business planning.
Classification: LCC Q335 .I323 2020 | DDC 658/.0563—dc23
LC record available at https://lccn.loc.gov/2019024137

The paper used in this publication meets the requirements of the American National Standard for Permanence of Paper for Publications and Documents in Libraries and Archives Z39.48-1992.

To my mother, Laura, my wife, Malena, and to all my amazing kids.
—M. I.

To Shaheen, Sitarah, and Doulat, the women in my life
who make it all worthwhile.
—K. R. L.

Contents

Preface
Colliding Worlds

This book defines the age of AI by the emergence of a different kind of organization, structured for a business environment shaped by digital networks, analytics, and artificial intelligence. Its defining characteristic is a distinct kind of operating architecture—one that is horizontally connected, designed to leverage an integrated foundation of data and to drive the rapid deployment of AI-powered applications, enabling exponential growth in scale, scope, and learning. The architecture departs from the traditional, siloed structure of firms, which limits growth and responsiveness, prevents agile communication and coordination, localizes decision making, and traps technology and data in isolated pockets. The new structure enables the rapid and pervasive deployment of what computer scientists call "weak AI": mostly off-the-shelf algorithms fine-tuned to very specific use cases, enabling the execution of most of the firm's most critical operating tasks.

This book examines a recurring pattern of *digital firms* colliding with traditionally structured firms in sector after sector; Ant Financial with banks, YouTube and Netflix with the entertainment industry, and Airbnb with traditional hotel companies are just three examples. In these collisions we can see what happens when an exponential system runs into a *saturated* system—one that has reached its limits. As you may recall from your high school precalculus class, exponential curves are flat at the origin and then rise at an increasing rate. As the Ant, YouTube, and Airbnb examples illustrate, the value initially provided by digital firms is limited. Incumbent competitors may barely notice, and, if they do, they often tend to minimize, rationalize, and effectively ignore the new kind of competition. As the threat continues to grow, the incumbent firms may attempt to slow it down, perhaps by marketing its disadvantages to consumers or by lobbying regulators. As it grows further, some incumbents start building operational responses, transforming and digitizing many of their own systems. In most cases these efforts come too late, and once the exponential firm reaches critical mass, the growth rate explodes and the traditional system is overwhelmed. Think of what happened with Android and Nokia, Amazon and Barnes & Noble, YouTube and Viacom, and Ant Financial and the Hongkong and Shanghai Banking Corporation of China.

When we wrote this book, we believed that the emergence of this new kind of firm was inevitable. But we also believed that the transformation of the economy would take years—enough time for most traditional organizations to take their time to respond and adapt. When we launched our book in January 2020, we did not foresee how the Covid-19 pandemic would so quickly alter the economic and social landscape and force all organizations to adapt and digitize overnight. The pandemic has made it urgently clear that the transformation must happen now for firms to confront a different kind of exponential threat: the new coronavirus.

Confronting Exponential Growth

The Covid-19 crisis is an apt illustration of what happens when a system driven by exponential growth collides with a traditional system. The early days of the pandemic fooled us as well. When we ran around the United States and Europe for our book tour in January and February 2020, we had absolutely no idea we were sitting on top of an explosive charge that was just about to go off at a global scale. We gave talks in Boston, Chicago, Los Angeles, and San Francisco and then London, Munich, Paris, and Milan. As reports from China grew more alarming, we paid little attention.

Covid-19 hit critical mass in Europe on the day one of us (Marco) flew from Paris to Milan. As the flight took off, things seemed calm. We noticed some passengers staring with concern at their phones, and a couple donned masks. But by the time Marco and his wife landed in Milan, our voice mail was blowing up. In the car from Malpensa Airport to the hotel, we listened to the messages and began to understand that a major crisis was unfolding. We learned that the number of Covid-19 cases had been increasing by an order of magnitude just in the past couple of days. The virus had overwhelmed a number of towns near Milan, which were already closing down. We hopped into another car, drove to Zurich, slept a few hours, and took a tense flight straight back home to Boston. And this is where we have been ever since, watching, horrified, as the pandemic has held us all in its grip.

The novel coronavirus wreaked havoc on global health and economic institutions, demonstrating with relentless speed how the exponential growth of infection can easily overwhelm traditional organizations like health-care systems, medical supply and technology companies, food distribution, financial services, education systems, and on and on and on. Most organizations and governments paid no attention to Covid-19 in its early days. They underinvested in the technologies, supplies, processes, and systems that could have brought it under control.

This is how collisions work.

Ignoring an exponential system until it reaches critical mass is a recipe for catastrophe. Just as we see in collisions between traditional and digital firms, the only lifesaving strategies involve a clear recognition of the threat, an immediate response, and thoughtful planning for long-term transformation. If we recognize the threat early enough, we can slow it down with tactics. In the case of Covid-19, these would have included widespread symptom tracking, quarantines, and social distancing. But we don't have to wait for the threat to hit; we can—we must—ramp up our traditional defenses as well as we can. Again with Covid-19, these tactics would have included making massive investments in testing, accumulating inventories of critical supplies, and creating ICU surge capacity in our hospitals. But beyond basic preparedness, the most effective way to handle an exponential threat is by putting an operational architecture in place designed to be equal to the challenge by enabling an agile and potentially exponential response. This is what we found when we looked at the organizations that were responding most effectively to the pandemic. Whether they were old or new, these organizations made use of a deep and integrated foundation of data to power operational decision making, with the help of software, analytics, and AI.

We can't imagine a clearer argument for swift transformation. Every organization should get to work now to digitize and structure its processes, systems, and capabilities to accelerate operational scale, scope, and learning. There is no longer any rationale for waiting. It doesn't matter if your organization is new or old. Ultimately, if the virus doesn't get you, your competitors will.

Let's look at a few illustrations.

A Different Kind of Firm

While we were busy launching this book, some organizations were already deeply engaged in fighting Covid-19. Consider what happened in just the early weeks of the pandemic.

> On December 31, 2019, the Wuhan Municipal Health Commission reported a cluster of pneumonia cases in Wuhan, Hubei Province, China.[1]
>
> On January 4, the World Health Organization (WHO) reported on social media a cluster of pneumonia cases—with no deaths—in Wuhan.
>
> On January 5, WHO published its first disease outbreak news (DONs) on the new virus. Stéphane Bancel, CEO of Moderna, a biotech firm in Cambridge, Massachusetts, took note of the report.
>
> On January 12, China publicly shared the genetic sequence of Covid-19.

On January 13, the US National Institutes of Health (NIH) and Moderna's infectious disease research team finalized the digital sequence for mRNA-1273, the company's vaccine against Covid-19.[2]

On February 7, Moderna's plant in Norwood, Massachusetts, manufactured the first clinical batch of the vaccine.

On February 24 (just as we were flying from Europe back to the United States), the first clinical batch of the Moderna vaccine was shipped to NIH for use in its Phase 1 clinical study.

On May 7, Moderna announced that the FDA review of Phase 1 was successfully completed and vaccine development could begin Phase 2. Phase 3 is expected to begin in the early summer of 2020, potentially leading to a vaccine in the early December time frame, less than eleven months after the effort was started.

Moderna's progress has been unprecedented. If clinical trials are completed successfully, this could become the fastest vaccine development effort in history.

The Software of Life

Moderna is a very different kind of biotechnology company. In many ways, the organization is purpose-built for this kind of rapid response and exponential impact.

CEO Stéphane Bancel describes Moderna as a "a tech company that happens to do biology."[3] Cofounder Noubar Afeyan launched Moderna in 2010 as a portfolio company within his biotechnology startup factory, Flagship Pioneering, to pursue the promise of messenger RNA (mRNA) technologies. Moderna is built on a different technology base from traditional biotechs. In essence, mRNA-based drug development is a software discipline that centers on the role mRNA plays in encoding what the human system needs to produce a specific protein. Thus, the technology provides software instructions for the human body to produce the right proteins to fight a specific disease.

Key to Moderna's vaccine development is embedding the mRNA instruction set into an organic vehicle that can introduce the code into human cells. This foundation is provided by DNA *plasmids*, which work as a platform that can be rapidly adapted to carry specific mRNA instructions. Producing the plasmid foundation at scale and personalizing it to the mRNA code needed for a specific vaccine are the roles of Moderna's manufacturing process. In the words of Juan Andres, Moderna's chief technical operations and quality officer, "[O]ne of our key advantages is that we have one platform that powers every application, every vaccine, [and] all our knowledge and experience goes there, and it rapidly accumulates from generation to generation." Melissa Moore, chief science officer of the company's mRNA platform, along with her team of more than a hundred scientists, keeps improving mRNA science and delivery, which enables Moderna's clinical researchers to think through how mRNA can be applied to a multitude of health problems. Moore and her team lean on the mRNA platform in the same way that app developers leverage core application programming interfaces (APIs) and software development toolkits from Apple iOS and Google Android to create new applications.

Moderna is built on what we call an "AI factory" (chapter 3). The data-centric operating model extends well outside of the R&D process to encompass every aspect of the firm. The foundations of Moderna are an integrated data platform: a single, consistent "system of record" that embeds data originating from every functional specialty. The architecture enables the data to be combined and recombined with great speed and reliability to power an infinite range of possible business and scientific applications. These applications use algorithms to drive business execution across every function, from R&D to manufacturing, and from finance to supply chain management.

The fundamental idea behind the AI factory is to industrialize the company's approach to data, analytics, and artificial intelligence.

Moderna's AI factory does for analytics what industrialization did for manufacturing more than a hundred years ago. Data is processed in a systematic, standardized fashion, cataloged and centralized, cleansed, normalized and integrated, and exposed through APIs, which are available to Moderna teams to power new business applications. The data platform forms the core of the firm, with an organization consisting of scientists and managers overseeing it and harvesting its power. Whether we are talking supply chain predictions or finance modeling, vaccine design or manufacturing scale-up, data-powered software algorithms are operating the company. The technology underlying Moderna also shapes its organizational architecture and processes. Indeed Marcello Damiani, Moderna's chief digital officer, is also its chief process excellence officer. As a member of the executive team, Damiani's brief is to drive process change across the enterprise. Damiani's view is that it makes no sense to tweak old processes to make them more efficient; as new digital and AI technologies become available, his team works with the various functions to redesign their operating processes, enabling greater speed, efficiency, and innovation.

At this point, we do not know if the Moderna vaccine will be successful. Early updates on the performance of the vaccine look quite encouraging, however, vaccine development is fraught with failure and we of course, for the sake of all humanity, wish them and other companies the best as they attempt to create treatments and vaccines. In any case, what we do know for sure is that vaccine development, and health care more broadly, will never be the same.

Colliding with the Virus

We had been planning a lot based on our modeling. We have health-care systems engineers that model with us. We've been looking at data from China, from South Korea, from many places in the world. And I would say notably from Italy, where we've had access to a great deal of data. And we've been comparing our experience at Mass General and its Partners Healthcare with both the northern Italian and central Italian experience to try and see what might be ahead of us.

—Paul Biddinger, Vice Chair for Emergency Preparedness in the Department of Emergency Medicine at Massachusetts General Hospital

In the early winter of 2020, things started changing very quickly as the coronavirus reached critical mass in many countries outside China. The United States was startled in March as contagion entered its "power law" phase: rapid growth with a doubling of cases and mortality every few days. That's when the world of work changed dramatically. During the two weeks between March 14 and March 30, 2020, the United States may have experienced more digital transformation than it had witnessed during the previous ten years. Workers representing more than half of the US economy started working from home. In the span of two weeks at our home institution, Harvard Business School, more than 125 faculty and 250 staff worked tirelessly to move education online for about 2,000 MBA and doctoral students. Some of us had believed that a change of this magnitude would take decades.

As we witnessed the near-instant transformation of work, we all watched the numbers of infections soar as the shortages of ICU beds and medical supplies became critical. Thankfully, some health-care organizations had been planning for Covid-19 for months and had worked hard to transform in preparation for the inevitable collision with the virus.

The Massachusetts General Hospital (also known as Mass General or MGH) was founded 210 years ago to take care of the poor—a mission it still takes extremely seriously. MGH embraces its deep tradition of analysis, methodological rigor, and creative but systematic innovation, which fuels an obsessive, patient-centric philosophy that underlies its crisis response and disaster management capabilities.

MGH is a lot older than Moderna and is (in many ways) a traditional organization. Much of its information technology infrastructure is dated and is limited by regulatory constraints and long-standing processes. But when confronted with a clear, existential threat, and blessed with enlightened leadership, MGH transformed on the fly to create the kind of horizontal, integrated information architecture that characterizes the most efficient digital firms.

MGH started planning its Covid-19 response back in January. The data emerging from China, and later from Italy and elsewhere, captured many characteristics of the disease and clearly outlined the kinds of pressure the hospital would face. Mass General is organized in silos, but something had to be done to rapidly build a centralized information-processing organization that could ingest data from any number of sources, check its validity, process it, and use it to predict the load on the many complex operational systems at MGH that would have to handle Covid-19 surges.

Leading MGH's response was a cross-functional, enterprise-wide team that included Paul Biddinger; members of the emergency and critical care teams; Ann Prestipino, a senior vice president and chair of emergency preparedness at MGH, who serves as MGH's coronavirus incident commander; and Lee Schwamm, who leads digital transformation efforts for MGH and the rest of the Partners organization.

As MGH planned for the pandemic, it worked relentlessly to expand capacity, responsiveness, and agility. The teams worked to create and deploy a structure that integrated and coordinated data, information, and activities across the vast organization to manage the predicted rapid growth in Covid-19 cases. This information architecture enabled MGH to work on every problem identified by the planning process, including shortages of N95 masks and ventilators and a lack of ICU capacity, to firm up the specific procedures for handling patient arrivals as they began to spike.

At the heart of the MGH crisis response architecture was its information system and data platform. The system enables centralized aggregation and accumulation of data and integrates information on clinical outcomes, planning systems, financial data, and capacity loads with usage data and supply chain forecasts. All this enabled the MGH team to rapidly develop and deploy dashboards for each department to equip clinicians with clear forecasts and predictive models as they planned for shifting demand.

Pulling the systems and efforts together, the MGH disaster management organization worked as a horizontal structure that coordinated and integrated cross-functional data and information sharing and critical operating activities related to the crisis. The organization served as an operational control tower, unifying MGH strategy and operational architecture while driving transformation across the many components of the organization.

One of the most substantial outcomes of the pandemic at MGH is the embrace and deployment of telemedicine. Once a minor part of the hospital's health-care delivery, telemedicine platforms grew quickly into the dominant mode of operation across the majority of disciplines. Virtual connections are now critical to interactions not only between provider and patient, but also between providers themselves, who now use online communities for information sharing, coaching, training, and mentoring. In the words of MGH emergency medicine attending physician and digital health fellow Kelley Wittbold, "I thought I would have to spend the next ten years trying to validate my career by haggling with policy makers and insurance payers to convince them of the value in digital health and telemedicine for care-delivery innovation. Covid-19 has done this for me in a matter of weeks."[4]

The results are impressive. MGH has saved countless lives, achieving superior performance across virtually every dimension of care during the pandemic. As Wittbold noted, "In crisis mode the whole institution really came together." In many ways, the MGH approach sets the stage for the digital transformation examples discussed in chapter 5. It was generally consistent with the principles we outline, but much faster than any of us thought possible.

The MGH response shows that in times of need, with clear focus and mission and with the right capabilities, even old organizations can turn on a dime, even under circumstances without the latest and greatest technology systems. Architecture is the key to coordinating and integrating the many different elements of a complex response with unprecedented agility. Critically, the MGH response to the pandemic also shows how a core of data-centric, scientific reasoning is essential to the deployment of analytics. Simply put, when lives are at stake, there is no room left for fake news, made-up data, and organizational politics. This motivates a specific approach to leadership, data-centric and analytics based, which is critical to create a data- and AI-centric organization. No digital operating model can work well without it.

MGH is not done yet. Even as Covid-19 subsides, the next challenge will be to internalize many of the lessons learned during the crisis and continue the transformation. MGH is not alone in this. Covid-19 has motivated many organizations to do extraordinary things, accept unprecedented change, and bypass age-old bureaucracies. Let's look across some other industrial settings.

Jump-Starting Transformation

Beyond all doubt, we finally have the answer to our most commonly asked question, Can older companies truly transform themselves? The urgency in responding to Covid-19 has already reshaped companies across all industries. Many seemingly entrenched traditional firms, within and beyond the health-care setting, have discovered that they too can transform, and do so rapidly and on the fly. Here are some examples.

Keeping the Internet Running

As social distancing transformed the nature of work, internet access and bandwidth became essential human needs. Telecom companies are accustomed to providing critical services, and they need to prepare for any sort of disruption. But Shankar Arumugavelu, global CIO of Verizon Wireless, admitted that even in one of the world's largest telecoms, there was no playbook for a crisis like Covid-19.

The first task was ensuring internet bandwidth and service continuity as usage surged. At the same time, most of Verizon's 135,000 employees would have to work from home, with access to the same tools and processes they needed to run the business. In addition, the company's more than 10,000 service technicians could no longer go into customer facilities and homes for installation or repair. So the company rapidly deployed software to enable technicians to virtually visit customers and enable them to handle installations and repairs remotely.

For the Verizon stores that remained open, the company established a contactless experience that included an app-based pre-booking system for customer appointments, remote co-browsing between retail employees and customers on product information, fully digital contract signing and identity verification, and touchless digital payment options including ways to handle cash through automated kiosks.

As with countless other organizations, Verizon is not known as the world's most nimble company. But the pandemic provided a way for all of us to enable changes and innovations that had been waiting on the sidelines to be rapidly deployed in action. And now, we cannot go back. Leaders and employees across the economy now understand and accept, as a basic fact, how much technology can do to transform an operating model. Just like many other CIOs in companies we have talked to, Arumugavelu now has the mandate to work with business units to bring in these approaches permanently.

Digitizing the Retail Experience

What do you do if you just can't redesign your business to avoid human proximity? With Covid-19, retailers who had only half-heartedly started the digital journey had no choice but to embrace e-commerce or shut down. Many went out of business, from little mom-and-pop operations to major chains like JCPenney and Neiman Marcus. For IKEA, the seventh most valuable retailer in the world, the reckoning was immediate and profound. Across the world, the vast majority of its 433 enormous "blue box" stores would need to shut down. All of a sudden, the only commerce available was e-commerce.

IKEA responded. The blue box stores became fulfillment centers for IKEA's e-commerce sites. In *one week*, under the leadership of Chief Digital Officer Barbara Martin Coppola, the company migrated thirteen different regional websites to the cloud and centralized them, consolidating and integrating all regional data. And over *three weeks*, the company's merchandising, pricing, and distribution executives learned to use technology, data, and AI to shape a fully digital retail experience that was true to the IKEA legacy. This was a profound change. Before Covid-19, IKEA's country managers had distributed authority over fifty e-commerce markets, with each region deciding on its own data strategy, pricing, and customer experience. With the pandemic, the digital transformation efforts—many planned but never implemented—had to become real.

IKEA did not stop there. The digital team enabled contactless fulfillment with "click and collect" models, yielding higher orders per customer. Online, sophisticated AI provided recommendations to online shoppers, augmenting the insights of the stores' retail teams. The customers, when presented with the most relevant options, purchased additional items, and basket sizes started exploding. Online stores experienced 3× to 5× growth in revenue, with much higher margins.

The changes demonstrated the value of rearchitecting the operating model for AI, and they are not going away when the stores reopen. The traditional walls between digital and physical at the company have crumbled. The physical retail team now sees the digital operation as a complement rather than a substitute. Coppola and her team are now moving on to supply chain optimization and operational efficiency. They are moving all of IKEA to a common data platform to spawn a variety of algorithms that enhance customer, employee, and supplier experiences. Coppola expects the company to continue embracing technologies that support IKEA's obsession with its customers, while enabling employees to augment and automate decision making in stores and online.

Helping People at Risk

For better and (sometimes) for worse, digital operating models can enable highly precise targeting at near-zero marginal cost. During a pandemic, this kind of precision can save lives. One of the most difficult challenges is that the fear of catching the virus is keeping people with other medical conditions from seeing doctors or coming to emergency rooms. With precise targeting, AI can help solve this problem, identifying patients at risk, reaching patient cohorts with tailored messages, and urging them to contact their physicians or go to the emergency room.

Novartis, a pharmaceutical company, had made progress developing sophisticated predictive models capable of diagnosing patients remotely (with appropriate and compliant de-identification methods), often years before a traditional diagnosis might have identified the problem. Chitra Narasimhachari, the lead scientist behind these efforts, focused on conditions such as multiple sclerosis and ankylosing spondylitis (a severe and chronic back pain), with impressive results.

The Novartis data sciences team worked to integrate a broad set of data flows across vendors, functions, and groups to clean, test, integrate, and normalize the data into a single platform. Similar to the Moderna AI factory, the vision was to make any relevant data visible to and usable by the right people and to rapidly deploy the data in powerful predictive models across many business functions.

When the pandemic hit, the Novartis commercial data and analytics transformation, led by Bharti Rai, vice president of commercial acceleration, was in midstream. The platform was not complete. The AI factory model was working in individual instances but had not yet been deployed as a universal operating model foundation. Data stores had not yet been fully connected and integrated. But with Covid-19, every functional group within Novartis wanted to tap into the incredible predictive power of the AI. The Novartis supply chain had to understand what to ship where, Novartis finance needed to figure out cash needs and profit forecasts, R&D needed predictive models of pharmaceutical efficacy and safety in brand new application areas, and sales needed to understand rapidly changing clinical needs and customer requirements. And, more than anything else, the Novartis team could identify patients at risk.

The Novartis team put efforts to build a scalable data platform into overdrive. Narasimhachari had already joined forces with Bharti Rai, head of the department, to make the centralized AI factory a reality and make it salient and accessible to frontline business leaders, who were now demanding more data and AI capabilities across the board. The company did not wait for every bell and whistle to be perfected; instead, the team went to work on the partially assembled platform to develop a variety of models to pinpoint urgent patient and business needs across a variety of geographic areas and disease classes. Some models highlighted which patients were at risk of medical complications and recommended, wherever possible, appropriate referrals and treatment regimes. For example, the models revealed that as many as 20 percent of patients were at risk of serious complications because they were avoiding making their regular or necessary visits to the doctor, and the system followed up by having Novartis customer teams alert physicians and health-care providers.

Covid-19 effectively put the Novartis digital transformation on steroids. Victor Bulto, president of Novartis Pharmaceuticals US, is now working with his team and the Novartis Global Digital Office—led by Bertrand Bodson—to drive the efforts forward, building on Covid-19 momentum to ensure that efforts are sustained. Bulto formed a new team—the Look Forward Office—to manage the ongoing transformation as the pandemic moves to the next phase.

Some Lessons

As we argue at length in this book, the age of AI is upon us, with the emergence of a new kind of firm. But when we wrote the book, we thought the world would have some time for the age to develop, and some time for all of us to think through its implications. And we thought we would have some time to develop a new generation of leaders that could embrace the digital world across the economy and fully understand the capabilities and ethics needed for transformation. Covid-19 took this luxury away from us. Every organization on

xxiv COMPETING IN THE AGE OF AI

the planet is now compelled to digitize whichever processes it can, and do so as quickly as possible.

The pandemic experience is proof that digital transformation can happen fast—frankly, much faster than any of us thought possible. In a few weeks, much of the global economy moved to a virtual model. Mobility came down drastically as any workers that could function by using videoconferencing software moved to adopt social distancing. Universities transitioned to an online teaching model. Healthcare systems embraced telemedicine, while insurance companies and regulators moved fast to change rules and reimbursement policies. Tech companies abandoned offices and some announced that office philosophies would change forever. Commercial real estate values collapsed, as did energy and travel industry stocks. And the virtual model was only the beginning. We have seen the rapid deployment of all kinds of AI, from chat bots at MGH to algorithms recommending products to customers at IKEA to models predicting patients at risk at Novartis.

You don't have to be a Silicon Valley-based tech company to become a data- and AI-centric organization. Even before Covid-19, we saw examples of organizations transforming to digitize their operating models and respond to competitive threats, from Comcast to Fidelity Investments. But naysayers still questioned the need for and viability of transformation for older companies. Covid-19 has put all these arguments to rest.

However, we also learned how, for meaningful transformation to occur, planning and preparation really improve the quality and impact of the actions. From MGH to Novartis and Moderna, what the organizations accomplished in the crisis was possible because they had already started piloting the approach and building its foundations. Even at Harvard Business School, previous experience in online teaching became highly valuable to transforming the entire institution. The challenge now is to sustain the transformation and shape it in a thoughtful and balanced manner.

These newer observations confirm many of the central messages of this book—most critically, that operating architecture really matters. An AI-centric firm is not defined by the sophistication of any individual algorithm it deploys, but by the structure and processes that enable the quick deployment of *many* AI solutions, each solving a real business problem. Moderna was certainly architected to make data, analytics, and artificial intelligence shine. But even with MGH, IKEA, and Novartis, we see the crisis motivating a reliance on the same kind of integrative data and organizational architecture to rapidly produce and deploy innovative and accurate analytics. Ultimately, architecture is what enables the kind of rapid, agile, scalable, and adaptable response that can catch up with an exponential threat like Covid-19 and enable rapid response to both threats and opportunities.

The examples also confirm that when deployed at scale, simple AI (or what we call "weak AI") can have a huge impact. To make a difference, AI does not require the stuff of science fiction novels. Simple algorithms, powered by the right data, can achieve critical results. Simple chat bots and basic machine learning can make a really big difference if they relieve critical operational bottlenecks or enable important predictions. This is another key theme in the book, because it underlies the importance of weak AI in transforming the economy and changing the way firms work. For example, much of the AI deployed across hospitals to help with Covid-19 involved mostly simple machine learning algorithms, which, trained by the right data, could help with critical predictions, like the supply of N95 masks at MGH. Again, it's about driving the deployment of simple, AI-based infrastructure across as many business processes as possible.

We must note that transformation has not come without its costs. Covid-19 has dramatically accelerated and deepened the impact of digital scale, scope, and learning on the world economy and society. Of most concern is perhaps the impact of Covid-19 on the *digital divide* between the haves and the have-nots—firms as well as individuals. Beyond an impact on competitiveness, productivity, and income, the digital divide now defines the difference between those who can work and those who can't, between those who can remain safe at home and those who cannot, between the firms that are still in business and those that are not. Deepening the tragedy, the divide is accentuating traditional economic and racial inequalities.

As it transforms all of us, the pandemic is amplifying every ethical issue related to digital organizations and operating processes—from fake news to bias, and from security to privacy. In doing so, it accelerates the disintegration of many governmental and social institutions and sharpens threats to civil liberties. This has not fully played out, yet, and it will be important for all of us to follow the debates closely and participate to help inform and safeguard democratic processes at both a local and a global scale.

From Data to Wisdom

It's coming back. As we sit here today, typing the final words of this preface, we face virtually unprecedented uncertainty across global health, economics, and politics. Some of us are witnessing a lull in Covid-19 infections, and the economy is starting to reopen across many countries. Still, the Covid-19 crisis is far from over. As cities reopen, the virus is coming back with renewed exponential ferocity in many countries and US states. Literally yesterday, we witnessed a new all-time high in both US and global daily infections. Just as hospitalizations come down in Boston, MGH is planning for another collision. Just in case.

As the pandemic continues, it unfortunately underscores another basic lesson: that without enlightened leadership, the best data and analytics will not lead to wisdom. It is tragic that some of the more basic insights gleaned during the first pandemic phase are being assimilated only by a part of society. For example, we now know, with statistical certainty, that masks help avoid infections and super-spreader events. And yet, even this basic analytical insight is not acknowledged, respected, or put to use by many of our leaders, effectively leading to unnecessary fatalities. And here we sit, watching in dread as our mounds of data, analytics, and artificial intelligence fail to contribute to the kind of collective wisdom that could really put this pandemic behind us.

But no matter what the future actually holds, the steps forward in the economy's digital transformation will not be undone. Awareness of digital impact is ubiquitous, proof points are being shared, and the momentum has built to a level that cannot be reversed. No matter what happens, what we do know for sure is that the velocity of transformation has dramatically accelerated, creating an immediate need for the kind of business and technology leadership that can help drive this next economic age.

To be effective, our leaders will need an appreciation for the value of rigor and analytics, a basic understanding of the technology and economics of data platforms, digital networks, and AI, and a hunger for change and transformation. But most of all, they will need a deep appreciation of the ethics of digital scale, scope, and learning and will need to deeply understand the adverse economic and social impact of getting transformation wrong. We truly hope this book may serve them as a strategic resource.

Marco Iansiti and Karim R. Lakhani
July, 2020

COMPETING
IN THE
AGE OF AI

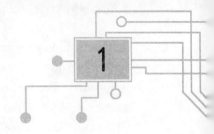

The Age of AI

"It's a Rembrandt!"

So shouted the neatly dressed, white-haired gentleman after quickly raising his hand. Several other members of the audience called out in agreement. One man, who ran a leading art museum in Australia, said he recognized the unique style of the seventeenth-century Dutch master, but he seemed puzzled that he couldn't recall this specific painting, shown in figure 1-1.

FIGURE 1-1

The next Rembrandt

Then a video began to play, and the room fell silent as the narrator described the work's provenance.[1] The portrait, it turns out, was not a Rembrandt. Rather, it was created in 2016 by a team from advertising agency J. Walter Thompson and Microsoft as a promotion for ING Group, the Dutch bank. The painting consists of more than 148 million pixels, based on 168,263 scans of Rembrandt's three hundred known paintings. A team of data scientists, engineers, and Rembrandt experts applied learning algorithms to analyze the portraits and select specific characteristics that were typical in some way of the artist's work: they determined that the new painting would feature a Caucasian male between the ages of thirty and forty, with facial hair; he would wear a hat and a white collar; and he would face to the right. More algorithms were used to assemble the components into a fully formed composition. A 3-D printer then deposited thirteen layers of paint-based UV ink on a canvas in a way that closely imitated the master's brushstrokes. Thus *The Next Rembrandt*, as the work is called, came into being via artificial intelligence—some 350 years after the artist's death.

AI is becoming a force in the arts, connecting various disciplines and media and expanding the range of artistic possibilities. With its Arts and Machine Intelligence (AMI) program, for example, Google is organizing a community of artists and engineers to explore how creative practices are being transformed.[2] The community applies the kinds of style-transfer techniques used in *The Next Rembrandt* across a broad variety of subjects and media, from film to music.

But AMI and other similar programs are taking AI even further into the realm of creation: in addition to replicating existing styles, AI is being used to create completely new works of art.[3] This endeavor transforms not only the method for crafting the work of art but also the organization and process that conceives and creates it. Ahmed Elgammal, director of the Art & Artificial Intelligence Lab at Rutgers University, is working with an art-generating algorithm called AICAN that is programmed to produce novelty without substantial help from human artists. The program starts with training data drawn from a vast assemblage of paintings dating from the fourteenth century and produces something fundamentally different: paintings "inspired" by established artistic styles but entirely new. Thus, the AI algorithms do not merely expand the range of creation and distribution methods for artists; they also model the course of art history, offering insight into art's long progression from figuration to abstraction and helping us understand processes that have been running in the collective unconscious for more than half a millennium.

This is only the beginning. If a computer, aided by a few computer scientists and some fairly basic AI, can simulate, collaborate with, or possibly even extend the work of creative genius, we can almost guarantee that no field of human endeavor will remain independent of artificial intelligence. In discipline after discipline and industry after industry, digital networks and AI are becoming pervasive, defining a new age for business and for all of us.

Competing in the Age of AI

AI is the "runtime" that is going to shape all of what we do.
—Satya Nadella, Microsoft CEO

AI is becoming the universal engine of execution. As digital technology increasingly shapes "all of what we do" and enables a rapidly growing number of tasks and processes, AI is becoming the new operational foundation of business—the core of a company's operating model, defining how the company drives the execution of tasks. AI is not only displacing human activity, it is changing the very concept of the firm.

As such, the first truly dramatic implications of artificial intelligence may be less a function of simulating human nature and more a function of transforming the nature of organizations and the ways they shape the world around us.

This book describes the profound implications of artificial intelligence for business. It is transforming the very nature of companies—how they operate and how they compete. When a business is driven by AI, software instructions and algorithms make up the critical path in the way the firm delivers value. This is the "runtime"—the environment that shapes the execution of all processes—that Nadella refers to. In a digital operating model, humans may have designed the operational systems, but computers are actually doing the work in real time: painting the digital Rembrandt, setting a price on Amazon, recommending a product on Walmart's mobile app, qualifying a customer for an Ant Financial loan—all processes that would traditionally have required human intelligence, not only to design but also to execute.

Having software shape the critical path of operational execution has substantial ramifications. Digital, AI-driven processes are more scalable than traditional processes. They enable greater scope (or variety), as they easily connect with a myriad of other digitized businesses, and they create powerful opportunities for learning and improvement, such as the ability to produce ever more accurate, complex, and sophisticated predictions and even gain fundamental understanding. In doing so, networks and AI are reshaping the operational foundations of firms, enabling digital scale, scope, and learning, and erasing deep-seated limits that have constrained firm growth and impact for hundreds of years.

We are already there, and the AI that is driving the explosive growth of firms like Facebook and Tencent isn't even all that sophisticated. To bring about the kinds of dramatic changes we're describing, AI need not be indistinguishable from human behavior, or capable of simulating human reasoning—what is sometimes referred to as *strong AI*. We need only a computer system to perform tasks that were traditionally performed by human beings, in what is traditionally referred to as *weak AI*. We don't need a perfect human replica to prioritize content on a social network, make a perfect cappuccino, analyze customer behavior, set the optimal price, or even, apparently, paint in the style of Rembrandt. Imperfect, weak AI is already enough to transform the nature of firms and how they operate.

Even with relatively basic artificial intelligence, whose applications we have seen explode over the past ten years, we are witnessing unprecedented changes. We have entered a new age in which networks and algorithms are woven into the fabric of the firm, changing how industries function and the way the economy operates. Across both new and old enterprises, digital savvy can no longer be treated as a discrete set of skills and AI can no longer be viewed as the purview of a specific job description or business function. Understanding the new opportunities and challenges has become essential to all of us. And in this new age of AI, many time-honored assumptions about strategy and leadership no longer apply.

Transforming Competition

As we enter the age of artificial intelligence, the emergence of digital operating models is transforming competition. Consider the case of photography. More than a hundred years ago, the invention of photography had a disruptive impact on the "technology" of painting by greatly reducing the demand for such work. Painters had trouble responding to this threat, but eventually they changed their approaches, inventing new techniques and styles. The important point here is that film-based photography threatened old norms and created new opportunities, but it did not dramatically transform the economy. The battle between film photography and painting resembled the pattern observed across a variety of industries, from disk drives to excavating machines, when one technological trajectory becomes disrupted by another.[4] The new overtakes the old, creating challenges for existing competitors, while the rest of the economy continues more or less as it was.

In contrast, let's look at what happened when *digital* photography came on the scene. With the invention of the first digital camera in 1975 (by Steven Sasson at Kodak), photographs could be captured as files of stored data that could be displayed and enhanced on a computer. Early digital photographs were blurry and expensive. Over time they became sharper and cheaper. Then they began to threaten traditional photography in a way at first similar to what a disruptive technology would do: undermining traditional players and creating opportunities for new businesses.

But digitizing photography did not simply provide an alternative to an older technology the way smaller disk drives disrupted the demand for larger disk drives. Digital representation completely transformed the nature and variety of activities connected to photography. It was suddenly easy and free to share pictures (benefiting from digital automation at essentially zero marginal cost), so people started snapping and sharing many more photos. No event, no activity, no meal is now too trivial to document and post on social media. This practice gave rise to a new breed of companies—Facebook, Tencent, Snapchat, Line, and TikTok are just a few of them—each of them featuring massively scalable digital operating models to help users select, shape, and share digital representations of their lives and of the world around them.

Increasingly sophisticated AI is dramatically expanding the impact of photography's transformation. Think of the vast number of photos being taken every day (now more than 10 trillion digital photographs each year, five orders of magnitude greater than the total number of traditional photographs ever taken) as a growing dataset—most of it now stored in the cloud on Google, Facebook, and WeChat, where it can be analyzed by algorithms. These troves are powering the improvement of algorithms used for facial recognition, photo sorting, and image enhancement. With the help of the additional data already available to them, and a little bit of "training," social platforms like Google, Facebook, and WeChat can automatically identify (even predict) not only family and friends but also affinities (are the people in this shot members of the same family?) and backgrounds (is this person a schoolmate?). Photo apps are already recommending products, services, and even news feeds that users might like and some are making friend recommendations—offering to "introduce" you to someone based on shared affinities or backgrounds.

When digital technology collided with traditional photography, it did not simply replace it with something cheaper, more differentiated, or higher quality. It did not merely create a new value proposition to serve customers. It enabled the emergence of a new and increasingly powerful breed of company, one that leverages a different kind of operating model and competes in different ways. In doing so, it not only changed the photography industry but reshaped the world around it. This is because when an activity is digitized (like converting a paint stroke into pixels), profound changes take place. A digital representation is infinitely scalable—it is now possible to easily and perfectly communicate the pattern it represents, replicate it, and transmit it at virtually zero marginal cost to a near infinite numbers of recipients, anywhere in the world. Moreover, digitizing the activity makes it easily connectable, also at zero marginal cost, to limitless other, complementary activities, dramatically increasing its scope. Finally, the digital activity can embed processing instructions—AI algorithms that shape behavior and enable a variety of possible paths and responses. This logic can learn as it processes data, continuously training and improving the algorithms that are embedded in it. The digital representation of a human activity can thus learn and improve itself in ways that analog processes cannot. These factors completely transform the ways a firm can (and should) operate.

Traditionally, the intrinsic scalability, scope amplification, and learning potential of technology was limited by the operating architecture of the organizations that it was deployed in. But over the past decade, we have seen the emergence of firms that are designed and architected to release the full potential of digital networks, data, algorithms, and AI. Indeed, the more a firm is designed to optimize the impact of digitization, the greater its potential for scale, scope, and learning embedded in its operating model—and the more value it can create and capture (see figure 1-2). Increasing levels of digitization, analytics, and AI/ML can dramatically improve the scalability of a business, making the value curve increase more rapidly as a function of the number of users or their engagement. As it collides with a traditional company, a digital operating model can overwhelm the status quo.

The first losers were the traditional players that could not adapt. Ultimately, Kodak was not killed by Fuji or by a digital photography startup, but by the emergence of smartphone and social network firms. Instead of focusing on industry-level tasks like film processing and marketing, Facebook, Tencent, and Google focused on connecting users and on capturing and analyzing the information that flows through their networks. These firms create value differently, capture value differently, and rely on a completely different

FIGURE 1-2

The collision between traditional and digital operating models

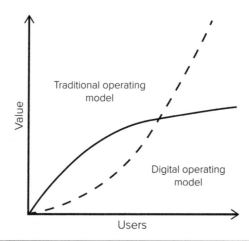

kind of operating model from Kodak's to deliver that value to their customers. The result is a fundamentally different way to compete. These companies never even considered Kodak a competitor; rather the film company was simply collateral damage in the newer companies' race to acquire users on networks that enabled photo sharing as a core service.

But the story does not end there. Just as the social and mobile platforms reached unprecedented levels of scale, scope, and learning, we began to discover that digital operating models introduced a new set of challenges while they crushed traditional competitors. Their unconstrained growth and unrestrained impact raised new risks. From privacy to cybersecurity, and from bias to fake news, the rise of the AI-driven firm is posing new kinds of threats. Traditionally, corporate leaders faced a bounded set of challenges, constrained by the relatively limited impact of their organizations on the surrounding economy, environment, and social system. Without the same intrinsic limits on scalability, scope, and impact, the new breed of digital firm requires new approaches to leadership, regulation, and even ethics.

Alexa, How Do You Transform the Economy?

Perhaps more than any other organization, Amazon embodies the way an organization can leverage a digital operating model to transform traditional industries. Amazon sells real things—goods and services we need every day—and in doing so it collides with all the businesses that have been selling those goods and services in the same way for generations. Amazon reinvents traditional business operations and puts them on digital foundations. In doing so it harvests the advantages of digital technology, analytics, and AI/ML in order to scale, extend its scope, and learn. And by colliding with traditional businesses, from books to consumer electronics to groceries, Amazon changes the rules of competition.

In a traditional business, size is a double-edged sword. As it grows, a business can usually deliver more value at a cheaper price. However, the advantages of scale tend to be limited by the firm's *operating model*, which encompasses all the assets and processes it uses to deliver the value it promises to its customers. As the firm gets bigger, its operating model becomes increasingly complex, and with complexity come all kinds of problems. Think of the long lines in your favorite retail store when there are too many customers, or the confusion that emerges when a rapidly growing firm hires too many new employees, or the quality problems that plague a manufacturing plant when demands for capacity or product variety are increased. Ultimately, complexity becomes the downfall of traditional organizations, increasing operational costs and decreasing service levels. All this despite the fact that dealing with operational complexity is the goal of many of the managerial and administrative systems developed over the past one hundred years, from the assembly line to the multidivisional company structure.

But when Amazon digitizes an operating task it embraces the advantages of *digital* scale, scope, and learning. Its digital systems scale more easily and continue to improve despite the size and complexity of its operation. When the order-taking system is fully digitized, it does not become harder to manage as more consumers use it, or as they demand more variety; it just gets better and better. As an increasing portion of the processes and tasks that deliver customer value are digitized, the advantages increase to create a much more scalable enterprise, capable of delivering an unprecedented scope of products and services, all characterized by an impressive rate of improvement and pinpointed targeting.

Take product suggestions. In traditional retail, product suggestions are made by employees in stores, but their numbers are limited by traditional recruitment and training processes along with personnel budgets. Getting the right sales expertise, furthermore, is difficult: people who are good at selling fishing rods aren't typically good at selling baby clothes. But the algorithm that creates suggestions on the Amazon website does not suffer from the same limitations. The system ingests huge amounts of data on what previous customers bought, and which product purchases were related to each other (for example, purchases that were together in the same shopping cart). The system processes all that data, factoring in product specifications and customer characteristics to suggest new, potentially appealing products. The engine learns and improves with the behavior of every relevant consumer and every relevant product—the more data, and the more scale and product diversity, the better, and Amazon's performance continues to improve. AI engines like Amazon's *collaborative filtering* algorithms do not incur human complexity costs like communication or coordination. The system does not decrease in efficiency as it grows and is thus much more scalable than a human (or organizational) learning engine. In addition, it connects easily across applications; much of what Amazon learns from a consumer's book preferences can be applied to suggestions of videos, clothing, or almost anything else.

The key to Amazon is its increasingly digital operating model. Amazon's operating philosophy centers on digitizing the best understanding of operational excellence through the broad-based application of artificial intelligence and machine learning, advanced robotics, and the instantiation of as much know-how as possible into software. In a traditional warehouse, people manage and carry out the process, with the organization suffering the same limitations we see in product suggestions. Not at Amazon. People are second-

ary in many of the most critical workflows. From demand forecast-
ing to warehouse management, and from supply chain management
to capacity planning, software and AI are increasingly running the
show. Amazon does employ many people but deploys most of them
on the edge of the digital network, doing things that computers
are not yet capable of handling (such as picking an oddly shaped
product from the warehouse shelf), while at the same time minimizing managerial complexity and maximizing the impact of digital
scalability. And many times, computers are defining what humans
should do, not the other way around, as in figuring out the optimal
path to find and pick a specific product in the warehouse.

Over and over, Amazon has collided with traditional industrial
settings and transformed them with a digitized, automated, and increasingly AI-capable alternative. Amazon's service improves with
volume, whereas the traditional business runs into complexity costs.
As Amazon grows, the traditional business loses out and the industry is transformed.

Echo, Amazon's smart speaker and microphone, extends the company's strategy to a new range of applications by utilizing Alexa, a
voice interface to the company's AI platform. Echo started by understanding simple, almost trivial commands, such as "Alexa, play
Rage Against The Machine" on Amazon's music service. The technology improved quickly as it gathered increasing quantities and
types of data and used that data to train itself. As its functionality
increases and improves over time, the Echo-Alexa duo continues
to collide with and transform many traditional tasks, from ordering vitamins to reading books, and from ordering a car service to
controlling home systems.

The Alexa service, furthermore, is designed as a true hub, with
the potential to connect the user to a virtually limitless array of
services and products. As of September 2018, Alexa had more than
fifty thousand skills (actions that it could perform via voice com-
mand) developed by a large ecosystem of third-party developers.[5] And
as Echo continues on its course, the number of human needs that
can be addressed by an Amazon-provided or -brokered solution will
only continue to increase. Every time you tell Alexa about things you
need to buy, Amazon Echo will build a shopping list and send you

the items. And every time you return and exchange items, Amazon's algorithms will keep on learning and honing its ability to predict what you need.

Amazon's model is scaling spectacularly well. The company spurred collisions between analog and digital models in industries from apparel to computing, and from consumer products to entertainment, threatening traditional stalwarts from Walmart to Comcast. In the process, Amazon has become one of the quintessential drivers of industry transformation. It has changed the way people shop across the globe and raised the expectation of personalization across the entire array of consumer products and services. As it reaches scale in more of its markets, from books to groceries, its impact and market capitalization continue to soar.

As it continues to grow and transform, Amazon is facing increasing scrutiny from communities and regulators. Given its broad reach among many traditionally defined markets, its model is not easily challenged by existing antitrust practices. Sustainable growth will hinge on Amazon leadership's ability to balance its many consumer benefits against the dislocations it might force on the rest of the economy. At the same time, Amazon's competitors are not standing still.

Becoming a More Digital Company

No industry is feeling the impact of Amazon more keenly than retail.[6] Amazon's convenience, low prices, personalization and recommendation capabilities, and software-enabled logistics infrastructure pose a formidable challenge to traditional firms. In 2017 we saw more than twenty long-standing retailers file for bankruptcy, and in 2018 even the 125-year-old giant Sears joined this list.[7] Walmart—the world's largest company by revenue—is doing all it can to avoid that fate.

Founded by Sam Walton in 1962, Walmart has not shied away from technology. For decades it set the standard in retail supply chain technology and network infrastructure, with its constantly evolving Retail Link system and its early commitment to EDI and

RFID technologies.[8] A data-rich supply chain has consistently been an important part of Walmart's operating model and a key to its impressive scale. And yet, even the most successful traditional operating models are not strong enough to confront Amazon's onslaught without substantial transformation.

To put up a credible fight with Amazon, Walmart is rearchitecting its operating model on a digital and AI-enabled foundation. Traditional siloed enterprise software systems are being replaced by an integrated, cloud-based architecture. This will increasingly expose Walmart's unique data assets to a variety of powerful new applications. This, in turn, will enable a growing number of operating tasks to be enhanced or automated by analytics and AI, and remove traditional bottlenecks to growth and transformation.

The company is also looking outside its operations for help. It has acquired a number of digital firms, including Jet.com (e-commerce) and Bonobos (an online retailer of menswear). In July 2018, Walmart announced a partnership with Microsoft, both to drive digital transformation and to access cloud capacity, technology, and AI capabilities on demand.

Walmart's online revenues have already seen substantial growth, increasing almost 50 percent year over year in 2018, and the company is waging a credible fight with Amazon. But to sustain its performance, Walmart will need to leverage data, analytics, and AI to transform its in-store experience. Stores are not going away, but the physical retail experience has to evolve both to delight shoppers and to complement the online experience. Walmart acknowledged as much in 2018 when it launched its Intelligent Retail Lab in Levittown, New York.

It's ironic that much of the effort to improve the in-store process involves learning how to apply the digital capabilities that are now routinely offered in the online world. Compared with online shopping, physical retail is often incredibly frustrating. Think about the amount of time wasted wandering a store looking for a specific item; the uncertainty of whether one is getting the best price; the lack of good recommendations, comparisons, or product choice. E-commerce has transformed consumer retail expectations, and traditional retailers have yet to evolve to match the convenience, personalization, and ease of their online counterparts. This provides an incredible opportunity.

Advanced analytics and AI can enable Walmart to bring online experiences into stores. By deploying cameras and sensors and by layering on computer vision and deep learning software, the in-store experience can acquire the convenience of online shopping. Walmart is experimenting with ways to capture customer movement and engagement patterns throughout the store, just as online retailers can track customers' journeys and clicks throughout the site. This data can be used at an aggregate level to create a heat map of customer patterns and reveal important information, such as areas where customers are converging or areas that receive little traffic. This information can help improve store offerings, product placement, store layout, or even supply chain and sourcing decisions.

Walmart and other retailers are also working on using real-time information from personal devices, such as location, integrated with past online interactions, to recognize customers and personalize the experience. Imagine a sales rep who is armed with details about your prior preferences to better recommend items or engage with customers. Implementation, however, is certainly not straightforward. Will consumers truly enjoy having a salesperson with as much information as the Amazon recommendation algorithm? How will they navigate the trade-offs between personalization and privacy? Will traditional salespeople really mediate this process, or will consumers feel better about receiving recommendations on their mobile devices?

We're already seeing dramatic changes in the store experience. Amazon Go stores, for example, have no cashiers and no lines to pay for purchases. You simply scan your Amazon app upon entry, and the store's technology tracks your movements and purchases. When you exit you are emailed a receipt. We tried to confuse the system, entering the store in a team of three, then grabbing multiple items off the shelves, putting things back in the wrong places, and exiting at various times. This stunt did not fool Amazon. We were promptly emailed a receipt with all the items everyone had in fact selected.

Without employees to hire, train, and manage, and with a sophisticated, digitally enabled supply chain, what is the bottleneck in building more stores? All that a retailer needs to do is access real estate, deploy the hardware, and install the software. The managerial cost in scaling to multiple operations is virtually nonexistent. In China, JD.com has already leveraged a less aggressive digital operating model to roll out *thousands* of convenience stores each week.[9] Walmart should pay attention.

WeChat, Xie Xie Ni . . . [10]

Lu Xiaoxue earns a living by singing to entertain Chinese tourists at the Jalan Alor restaurant district in Kuala Lumpur, Malaysia. She thanked the passerby (who happened to be one of us, Karim Lakhani) for his donation—which he'd made by scanning her WeChat QR code with his smartphone.

Thus, beggars and street performers have entered the digital age. With a few swipes and touches on her WeChat (or Alipay) app, a passerby in Kuala Lumpur (and in almost any city in Asia) can now transfer money instantly, digitally, and securely to anyone. Western visitors are often shocked to find that the cash they brought with them is virtually useless, because app-based digital systems are now the preferred mode of payment in stores, restaurants, and even with panhandlers, driving a wave of new applications leveraging the resulting data, analytics, and AI. The 7-Eleven in the luxury mall within the Petronas Towers even requests WeChat Pay *instead of* credit cards. Far away from the rarefied atmosphere of Silicon Valley, digital technology is colliding with and reshaping all kinds of businesses, professions, and applications.

One of the companies behind these collisions is China's Tencent, the maker of the WeChat app. Founded in 1998 in Shenzhen, Tencent entered the market with a PC-based internet instant messaging service for Chinese users. A few of us may remember ICQ, a messaging service launched in the early days of the commercial web (1996) that allowed users to instantly chat with friends and colleagues around the world. Realizing that most Chinese internet users had to share computers in cafes or at work, Tencent adapted ICQ functionality and centralized user data and chat histories to Tencent servers, enabling portability across computing devices. Tencent called its service Open ICQ and launched it in February 1999. The service went viral and quickly became China's largest instant messaging service and social network.

After building scale, Tencent has monetized its messaging network with advertising and premium offerings (such as special icons). Increasingly, it is extending the scope of the application by linking its users to a broad variety of complementary products and services such as avatars, games, and virtual goods. Tencent launched WeChat in 2011 as a mobile messaging application built on the Tencent messaging network. Beyond mobile access, WeChat provided a new range of functionality for its users that includes sending voice messages, sharing videos, sharing pictures and GPS locations, and sending and receiving money.

WeChat was built as an open platform, with easily accessible application programming interfaces (APIs) for software developers. These interfaces can be used to plug in to all kinds of external services and activities, from paying utility bills to setting up doctor appointments. This is how Tencent has expanded into new markets.

As Tencent continues to connect global consumers, its digital operating model is driving enormous scale and scope. At its core is a data platform enabling analytics and AI opportunities with data on social interactions, spending patterns, search trends, and even political sentiment. Mirroring the success of its arch competitor, Alipay (part of Ant Financial Services Group, in the Alibaba Group), Tencent analyzes the data through machine learning algorithms to inform and automate an expanding variety of services. In China and beyond, Tencent and Ant Financial are thus leveraging the connections they have with large masses of consumers to collide with and transform industries from financial services to health care.

In only a few years, these organizations have reached out to ten times as many consumers as the largest banks in the United States and Europe; they offer a broader range of products that are continuously improving, leveraging the rapidly increasing value that can be drawn from the network and the data it provides. Between them, Tencent and Ant Financial now claim the most widely used payment service, the largest money market fund, and one of the largest small business loan networks. And, as with Amazon, communities and regulators are starting to pay serious attention.

Today, Tencent is one of the world's most valuable companies, a crucial hub in the global economy, and on a collision course with a variety of industries (and regulatory bodies). Banks beware. Regulators beware. Amazon beware? Even street performers will never be the same again.

Understanding the New Age

When the digital Rembrandt was introduced, the reactions from the art world were truly remarkable. Some experts were intrigued by the obvious capabilities and potential of the technology, calling the efforts "spectacular" and "stunning." Others viewed it as a painful, even immoral, endeavor. Jonathan Jones, the *Guardian*'s art critic, voiced what was possibly the harshest disapproval of the project, calling it a "horrible, tasteless, insensitive and soulless travesty."[11]

If truth be told, Jones's reaction is not very dissonant with what many of us feel when we witness AI-driven processes replacing traditional activities in settings that we have long known and cherished. Remember the first time you believed a news story you read online, only to learn later that it was fake? The emergence of digital networks and AI can challenge long-standing assumptions about the nature of work, firms, and institutions—assumptions such as the importance of unique, industry-specific core competencies or the value of many traditional capabilities. AI can render skills and talents obsolete, from driving a car to managing a traditional retail establishment. Digital networks can alter and transform accepted approaches to social and political interaction, from dating to voting. The broad deployment of AI could threaten millions of jobs in the United States alone. And beyond the erosion of capability, threats to traditional skills, and other direct economic and social impact, we are increasingly vulnerable as an increasing portion of our economy and our very lives become embedded in digital networks. Not surprisingly, cybersecurity has become a central problem for organizations as different as Sony Pictures and the National Association of State Election Directors.

We cannot escape the fact that the digital and analog worlds are becoming one. We are no longer looking at some new technology, at a special kind of company, or at the "new" economy. We are looking at *the* economy—the entire economic system, every industry, every segment, and every country, across manufacturing, services, and software products. We have entered a new age that is redefining how *every* organization (and virtually any worker) in the economy needs to act to create, capture, and deliver value. Whether we like it or not, digital networks and AI are transforming business, and society.

The Promise of This Book

The emergence of digital operating models is framing a mandate for leaders, in both new and old firms. We need to better understand how to manage, transform, grow, and control our businesses in an era of virtually unbounded potential impact. That's what we hope this book will do for you.

If you are leading a digital organization, you need to appreciate its full potential, along with both opportunities and challenges. If you are leading a traditional organization, you need to understand how to leverage your existing strengths in new ways and transform your operating capabilities to support the new strategies.

Apart from well-publicized failures, from Blockbuster to Nokia, we are starting to see a number of firms find new growth and opportunity by building a new runtime, investing in AI, and changing the way they operate. Several firms, from Mastercard to Fidelity Investments, and from Walmart to Roche, are leading the charge. As Vipin Mayar, who leads these efforts at Fidelity, told us, "AI is just making us better."[12]

AI presents new opportunities—for startups, established firms, entrepreneurs and intrapreneurs, for new economic, social, and political institutions, and yes, even for artists. Startups can use the frameworks described in this book to target new processes to digitize and enable, through analytics and AI, from writing emails to interpreting X-rays. And just as the new generation of digital native firms is struggling with the downsides of their unbound scale and scope, more experienced firms can define new, better-governed models for sustained growth and transformation. AI-driven transformation not only prompts the creation of new companies but also motivates old companies to lead again, adopting the best of the new kind of operating model and appreciating the increased acceleration provided by a new, digital engine, without jettisoning traditional braking systems. Banking on past experiences and fueled by a new generation, some companies are taking the best of old and new to lead the way.

Our goal with this book is to provide leaders of organizations old and new, startups, and regulatory institutions a set of frameworks for understanding, competing, and operating in the age of AI.

Our Journey

Over the past decade, the two of us have led a broad portfolio of research projects at Harvard Business School to understand digital transformation, networks, and the impact of AI across companies. The research has encompassed hundreds of firms, in industries as diverse as financial services and agriculture, from San Francisco to New York, and from Bangalore to Shenzhen. Often in collaboration with our friends at Keystone Strategy, we have also been involved in literally hundreds of strategy and transformation efforts as teachers, consultants, experts in regulatory matters, board members, and direct participants.[13] We have engaged with organizations from tiny startups to multinational corporations, and from internet pioneers like Amazon, Microsoft, Mozilla, and Facebook to traditional organizations like Disney, Verizon, and NASA. We have also been fortunate to engage with and learn from participants in HBS's global executive education programs and through courses in the MBA curriculum.

This book is a vehicle to distill what we have learned. The implications target managers in existing firms as well as entrepreneurs.

The theories described in this book address an important phenomenon. Disruption theory defined an existential threat for traditional firms in the 1990s and 2000s, as they confronted waves of technological change. Our work describes a new observation: that a new breed of firm, characterized by digital scale, scope, and learning, is eclipsing traditional managerial methods and constraints, colliding with traditional firms and institutions, and transforming our economy. Software, analytics, and AI are reshaping the operational backbone of the firm.

But we believe this transformation is about more than technology; it's about the need to become a different kind of company. As we discuss in detail in later chapters, confronting this threat does not involve spinning off an online business, putting a laboratory in Silicon Valley, or creating a digital business unit. Rather, it involves a much deeper and more general challenge: rearchitecting how the firm works and changing the way it gathers and uses data, reacts to information, makes operating decisions, and executes operating tasks.

Our work stands on foundations built by many others. Carliss Baldwin and Kim Clark showed the dramatic impact information technology can have on the nature of industries.[14] Hal Varian and Carl Shapiro first highlighted the many changes in economic theory brought about by the nature of information businesses.[15] We are among many (Jean Tirole, Michael Cusumano, Annabelle Gawer, Geoff Parker, Marshall Van Alstyne, David Yoffie, Feng Zhu, Mark Rysman, Andrei Hagiu, Kevin Boudreau, Eric von Hippel, Shane Greenstein, and others) who have worked to explain the increasingly critical role of digital ecosystems, platforms, and communities on company strategy and business models.[16] Most recently, still others (including Erik Brynjolfsson, Andrew McAfee, Kai-Fu Lee, Ming Zeng, Pedro Domingos, Ajay Agrawal, Joshua Gans, and Avi Goldfarb) revealed how computers are taking on increasingly central roles and changing the nature of work.[17] This book extends these ideas and knits them together by describing how, when these factors are combined with the impact of software, analytics, and AI on networks and organizations, something striking happens. For the first time in more than a hundred years we are seeing the emergence of a new kind of firm, which we claim is defining a new economic age. This book describes the implications of our new age of AI for strategy and leadership, targeting managers, entrepreneurs, and society as a whole.

This book is divided into ten chapters. Chapter 2, "Rethinking the Firm," examines a new concept of the firm, driven by digital networks and AI. It dives into the nature of three digital *unicorns* (the industry term for a tech startup that reaches $1 billion in value): Ant Financial, Ocado, and Peloton. We describe each firm's business and operating model, its powerful digital components, and its striking capacity to drive scale, scope, and learning.

Chapter 3, "The AI Factory," homes in on the core of the new firm, using Netflix as the central example. The core is to create a scalable "decision factory" to systematically enable data-driven and AI-driven automation, analysis, and insights. This chapter explores three critical factory components: the AI algorithms that make predictions and influence decisions, the data pipeline that feeds them, and the software, connectivity, and infrastructure that power them.

Chapter 4, "Rearchitecting the Firm," explains why exploiting AI requires a new operating architecture. Using Amazon as a key example, we contrast traditional, siloed firm architectures, which evolved over hundreds of years, with the kind of integrated, data-centric and platform-based architectures that are enabling modern firms. We show how a new type of operating model is removing constraints on firm scale, growth, and learning.

Chapter 5, "Becoming an AI Company," examines the transformation journey of deploying a digital operating model, centered on Microsoft's transformation into a cloud and AI company. We generalize our findings by reporting on research on 350 enterprises, including the development of an AI readiness index, and show how the most advanced enterprises enjoyed superior growth and financial performance. The chapter also reports on some of the most popular and impactful enterprise AI implementation scenarios. The chapter concludes by depicting Fidelity's AI transformation.

Chapter 6, "Strategy for a New Age," examines the strategic implications of the emergence of digital networks and AI. This chapter discusses the elements of strategic network analysis, which provides a systematic way to analyze business opportunities as digital networks and AI reshape the economy. The chapter is grounded in several examples and includes a discussion of Uber's strategic options, strengths, and weaknesses.

Chapter 7, "Strategic Collisions," continues our discussion of strategic implications by examining competitive dynamics. The chapter focuses on what happens when firms featuring digital operating models compete with more traditional firms. The examples range from historical competitive settings (smartphones) to current battlegrounds (home sharing and automotive). The chapter concludes by discussing some of the broader competitive implications of the emergence of digital firms.

Chapter 8, "The Ethics of Digital Scale, Scope, and Learning," examines the new range of ethical challenges created by the combination of digital networks and AI. We look at several key issues, including digital amplification, algorithmic bias, data security and privacy considerations, as well as platform control and equity. We delineate some of the new challenges and responsibilities of business leaders and regulators.

Chapter 9, "The New Meta," describes the book's broadest implications for leaders of new and old firms, and for the governments and communities surrounding them. We lay out the new rules that are defining the new age, shaping key arenas, and transforming our collective future.

Chapter 10, "A Leadership Mandate," concludes the book by delving into the leadership challenge to shape the new AI era. We begin by identifying immediate opportunities for managers and entrepreneurs as they drive transformation and consider new ventures. This chapter examines actions that should be taken by leaders of traditional as well as digital firms, and by regulators and communities. It concludes by summarizing the most important implications for leading the increasingly digital firm and outlines actions we can take as we participate in shaping our collective future.

Your AI Journey

Ultimately, we believe that AI-powered transformation can provide opportunities for any organization if it makes the required commitments and investments. Although digital startups naturally have an easier path forward than do legacy companies, we have seen decades-old businesses adapt and thrive. Our ambition is to give readers the insight to prepare for the collisions that will inevitably affect their businesses—to deal with the threats and to identify the opportunities, and to capitalize on them.

We hope this book can provide a useful perspective on the new nature of firms, their architecture, the kinds of capabilities they require, and the structure of the new settings they compete in. This book can guide legacy companies as they seek transformation, as well as new companies as they tackle the newfound opportunities and challenges. If we all embrace and invest in understanding, deploying, and managing new strategies and capabilities, and if we confront honestly the cultural and leadership transformation this requires, the new age can lead to sustainable growth and opportunity for new and existing institutions. And rather than oppose this all-encompassing trend, we are all better off by understanding it, owning it, and, most of all, shaping it.

We begin by showing how AI is changing the way firms create, capture, and deliver value—the topic of the next chapter.

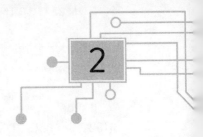

Rethinking the Firm

In June 2018, a record $14 billion fundraising and $150 billion valuation made Ant Financial[1] the largest financial technology (fintech) firm and the most valuable unicorn in the world.[2] Spun out from Alibaba only four years earlier, Ant Financial was already worth more than either American Express or Goldman Sachs.[3]

Based in Hangzhou, China, Ant Financial expanded in only a few years to deliver an unprecedented range of services to more than 700 million users and more than 10 million small and medium enterprises. Ant Financial flourished initially by focusing on financial inclusiveness, offering a comprehensive suite of products to underserved consumers and businesses in China. Ant Financial gradually expanded to the entire market, enabling an increasing range of services from bike sharing to train ticket purchases, and even charitable donations.

At the heart of Ant Financial's success is its ability to leverage data to learn about its users' needs and respond with digital services to address them. The wide adoption of its services across China and, through the Chinese tourist markets, across the rest of Asia, Australia, and Europe provides vast amounts of data, which Ant Financial uses to inform decision making on everything from fraud risk to new product features. The data is assembled into a powerful, integrated platform that uses AI to power such functions as application processing, fraud detection, credit scoring, and loan qualification.

Ant Financial is creating a new template for the twenty-first-century firm—deploying an operating model that leverages digital scale, scope, and learning to transform financial services and engage in a long-running collision with industry incumbents. Consider the operating model's efficiency: Ant Financial employs fewer than ten thousand people to serve more than 700 million customers with a broad scope of services. By comparison, Bank of America, founded in 1924, employs 209,000 people to serve 67 million customers with a more limited array of offerings. Ant Financial is just a different breed.

This chapter explores three rapidly growing examples of this new template for the twenty-first-century "digital" firm: Ant Financial, Ocado (in grocery delivery), and Peloton (in fitness). Each was created to enable new kinds of business models, with software, data, and AI as the primary operational foundation. Each is in a traditional industry, colliding with incumbent companies, reshaping how firms operate, and transforming the economy around them. The chapter concludes by focusing on Google, a more established firm that has placed AI at the core of its business and operations.

With their new approaches to creating, capturing, and delivering value to customers, these companies are leading the transformation of the economy. To understand how they are doing this, we first break down a firm into its business and operating models and analyze how it has traditionally shaped and executed on its value proposition. We then focus on how these three companies are forging a new path.

Value and the Nature of Firms

There's a well-developed understanding of the nature and purpose of the traditional firm. Economists like Ronald Coase and Oliver Williamson have declared that firms are formed to accomplish tasks that cannot be completed by individuals working through a market structure. We need firms, because coordinating each worker to engage in joint production through markets alone would require prohibitive transaction costs. Instead, firms provide long-term contracts to coordinate tasks without continually incurring the friction of continuous bargaining and negotiation and thus lower the transaction costs needed to create products and services. The value of these "bundles of contracts" is naturally shaped by the range of tasks organized by the firm—by what the firm promises to do and by how the firm actually gets it done.

The value of a firm is shaped by two concepts. The first is the firm's *business model*, defined as the way the firm promises to create and capture value. The second is the firm's *operating model*, defined as the way the firm delivers the value to its customers.

The business model thus encompasses the strategy of the firm: how it seeks to differentiate itself from competitors by providing and monetizing its unique set of goods or services. Meanwhile, the operating model encompasses the systems, processes, and capabilities that enable the delivery of the goods and services to the firm's customers. The business model defines the theory, and the operating model captures the practice—what the people and resources of the firm actually do every day. And while the business model points to the potential of the firm, in terms of the value it *could* deliver, the operating model is the actual enabler of firm value and its ultimate constraint.

Business Models

A company's business model is therefore defined by how it creates and captures value from its customers. It's important to be precise. There are two elements that come together: first, the company must create value for a customer that prompts her to consume the company's product or service; second, the company must deploy some method to capture some of the value created.

Value creation, then, concerns the reason customers choose to use a company's products or services, and the particular problem the company is solving for customers. This is sometimes known as the *value proposition* or *customer promise*. Think of the car you drive. The auto company's value creation starts with solving your transportation problem. The car allows you to move around in the world. Beyond that, the car company creates value for you by delivering quality (how reliable and safe the car is), styling (how it looks), comfort (how luxurious the interior is), ride quality (how smooth or aggressive the engine and transmission are), cost (how affordable the car is), and the brand (the image of you that it projects). Just think of the value creation differences between, say, a Kia and a Ferrari.

The factors in value creation can, of course, change. For many of us, a car's technology package and its ability to interface smoothly with our smartphone are now important considerations.

Note that the factors you consider in buying a car are very different from those you'd care about in ride-sharing. When was the last time you canceled an Uber ride because a Toyota Prius was picking you up instead of your favorite Cadillac? Value creation in ride-sharing involves the availability of drivers and the wait time, trust in the company's policies on driver certification, customer ratings of drivers, the app's ease of use, and the cost of the ride.

So although both Toyota and Uber provide mobility, the value they create is very different. One makes you buy the car, whereas the other provides you a ride on demand. Thus a company's approach to value creation requires consciously choosing the precise problem it is solving for the customer and its positioning in the marketplace. In the case of ride-sharing companies, value creation also relies on an ecosystem of drivers and riders. The greater the number of drivers available, the more value created for riders, and because drivers are independent contractors who are paid by the ride, the more riders tapping the app, the more value created for drivers.

Value capture is the other side of the coin. Naturally, the value a company captures from a customer should be less than the value it creates for the customer. In our auto company example, the value capture for an auto company rests primarily on the fact that the sales price (P) of the car is greater than the cost (C) of manufacturing the car. So the margin, $P > C$, defines the value capture for an auto company. The company may also capture additional value through its leasing operation; here the company makes money by playing arbitrage in the capital markets by having access to lower interest rates than the consumer, and adds margin by selling spare parts.

The value capture story for a ride-sharing company looks very different; it is based on consumption, or *pay-per-use*. Instead of an upfront investment by the customer, the value capture relies on a customer's choosing to use the ride-sharing service time after time; 70 percent to 90 percent of the customer fee goes to the driver, and the ride-sharing company retains the rest. Margin still matters for ride-sharing, and the price should still be greater than the cost (a point that seemed to elude both Lyft and Uber in their 2019 initial public offerings).

The new breed of digital firms is all about innovation in the business model, experimenting and recombining various aspects of value creation and value capture. In incumbent companies, value creation and capture are usually straightforward and closely intertwined: value is typically created and captured from the same source (the customer) through a simple pricing mechanism. In a fully digitized business, the options are much broader, because value creation and capture can be separated much more easily and often come from different stakeholders; most of Google's services are free to users, and the company captures value from advertisers across its product portfolio. For the digital firm, underlying all this business model innovation is a very different kind of operating model.

Operating Models

Strategy, without a consistent operating model, is where the rubber meets the air.

—Somewhat famous Italian proverb

Operating models deliver the value promised to customers. Whereas the business model creates a goal for value creation and capture, the operating model is the plan to get it done. As such, the operating model is crucial in shaping the actual value of the firm. A firm could promise to have an online retail business with nearly instant delivery; but to actualize that promise, the firm would need an impressive operating model characterized by an incredibly responsive supply chain. Devising and executing that operating model is where the real work would lie.

Operating models can be very complex, frequently including the activities of thousands of people, sophisticated technology, important capital investments, and millions of lines of code that make up the operational systems and processes that enable a company to achieve its goals. But the overarching objectives of an operating model are relatively simple. Ultimately, the goal of an operating model is to deliver value at *scale*, to achieve sufficient *scope*, and to respond to changes by engaging in sufficient *learning*. The great business historian Alfred Chandler argued that the two main challenges faced by executives are to drive economies of both scale and scope in order to survive and thrive.[4] Subsequent work in economics and management showed that a third challenge is equally important: learning—the operating capability to improve and innovate.[5] Let's review these three operating challenges.

> *Scale:* Managing scale, simply put, is about designing an operating model to deliver as much value to as many customers as possible at the lowest cost. Classic cases of improving scale involve efficiently increasing production volume or the number of customers served in, say, car production or fast food restaurants. Other examples may involve delivering products of increasing complexity in, say, completing a corporate merger or building an airport. From Ford to Goldman Sachs, firms are structured to make, sell, or provide more (or more complex) goods and services than individuals can, and to do so much more efficiently. A single person cannot efficiently manufacture an entire car in volume, nor can he produce the range of documents that are necessary to complete a complex corporate merger.

> *Scope:* A firm's scope is defined as the range of activities it performs—for example, the variety of products and services it offers its customers. Some assets and capabilities can help an organization reach economies across diverse kinds of businesses. For example, having a centralized research and

development organization can confer advantage across multiple product lines. Investing in a brand can deliver benefits for different products under the same brand umbrella. Having a centralized warehouse can achieve efficiencies across multiple product lines.

These economies of scope are important, because they enable corporations to establish multiple lines of business, perhaps managing multiple business units or creating a true conglomerate. With efficiencies of scope, firms can create and deliver a variety of goods and services efficiently and consistently. The Sears catalog operation, for example, was structured to efficiently deliver a wide variety of goods. A hospital emergency room is designed to handle a variety of emergency conditions more effectively than individual physicians can handle on their own.

Learning: The learning function of an operating model is essential to driving continuous improvement, increasing operating performance over time, and developing new products and services. From Bell Laboratories' vast R&D impact to Toyota's continuous improvement process, modern corporations have looked to innovation and learning to remain viable and competitive. In recent years, the focus on learning and innovation has increased across the board to deal with threats and capitalize on opportunities.

As firms seek to deliver value and optimize scale, scope, and learning, their operating models should match the direction set by their business models. For many years, scholars in operations strategy have argued that the performance of a firm is optimized by the alignment between strategy and operations—in other words, between business model and operating model.[6] Not surprisingly, the resources of the firm should be deployed to optimize what it seeks to do. Figure 2-1 illustrates the idea of business model and operating model alignment.

From Ford to Sears, and from Bank of America to AT&T and General Electric, there is a long history of firms achieving superior performance by designing and implementing operating models that

FIGURE 2-1

Alignment between a company's business model and operating model

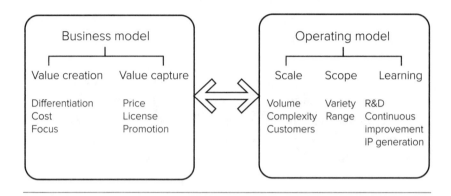

drive scale, scope, and learning objectives in alignment with their business models. Ultimately, the more the firm can drive scale, scope, and learning, the greater its value.

At the same time, however, an expansion in each of the three operational dimensions increases the complexity of traditional operating models and makes managing them ever more challenging. This, critically, creates the operational constraints that have traditionally limited the value created and captured by firms. This is exactly where the digital firm differs. By deploying a fundamentally new kind of operating model, this new type of firm is reaching new levels of scalability, achieving a vastly broader scope, and learning and adapting at a much faster rate than does a traditional firm. This is because the digital firm is transforming the critical path in the delivery of value.

When digital technology, in the form of software and data-driven algorithms, replaces labor as the bottleneck in operating activities, the implications reach well beyond the obvious consequences for the workforce. Let's take a look at how three firms are driving business model innovation by transforming operating models and removing traditional operational constraints.

On a Collision Course with Financial Services

Ant Financial is built with scale in mind. There is no way
that a human-centric approval process can be deployed here.

—Ming Zeng, Chief Strategy Officer, Alibaba

Ant Financial grew out of the success of Alipay, a payment platform created in 2004 by Alibaba, a then-nascent e-commerce platform, to facilitate payments for its shoppers and merchants.[7] Many of us now take online shopping for granted, but creating this service required Alipay to build a new kind of trust between buyers and sellers.

Many companies at the dawn of internet commerce worked hard to solve the trust problem. For Alibaba, which started as a peer-to-peer marketplace, the challenge was particularly acute: How could buyers trust the quality of the goods on offer, and how could sellers ensure that the buyers had the money to pay if the goods were shipped to them? The solution was to rely on an escrow system, wherein a third party holds payment until a contractual agreement is fulfilled. Alibaba thus invented Alipay as an escrow service for buyers and sellers on its e-commerce platform. Users connected Alipay to a bank account, and Alipay acted as an intermediary, accepting payment from a buyer, holding it until the buyer confirmed receipt of the item, and then releasing payment to the seller. This system helped alleviate the consumer distrust of online shopping and was instrumental in driving Alibaba's early growth.

Therein lies the initial business model of Ant Financial and Alipay. Value creation is related to offering a substitute for trust in the form of an escrow-based financial payment service that facilitates transactions between merchants and buyers. Ant Financial must create value for two categories of customers: consumers and merchants. Value capture occurs through the 0.6 percent transaction fee charged to merchants; consumers are not directly charged for using the service.

Alipay's growth depends on increasing transaction flow, which can come not only from having existing buyers and sellers engage in more transactions but also from increasing the number of buyers and sellers. In other words, Alipay needs to increase both the *intensive* margin of transactions (how many transactions a user makes) and also the *extensive* margin of transactions by increasing the number of buyers and sellers on the platform.

It is at this point that the second element of value creation kicks in. As the extensive margin increases, the value of Alipay increases to all its users. When the number of merchants goes up, the number of buyers goes up. More buyers, in turn, attract more sellers. And thus a positive feedback loop is created, driving increasing returns to scale. This *network effect* amplifies the value created by trust in the service.

Soon after launch, Alipay made its service available beyond Alibaba's shopping platform to all individuals and businesses in China—a move that led to exponential growth, both contributing to and benefiting from the success of Alibaba's online marketplace. Two years after launch, in 2006, Alipay had 33 million users initiating 460,000 transactions per day. By 2009, that number had grown to 150 million users and 4 million transactions a day.

By 2011, with smartphone usage skyrocketing in China, Alipay gave customers the power to purchase items without cash in person, outside the Alibaba platform, via the Alipay app on their mobile phones. To facilitate these transactions, Alibaba incorporated an established technology that did not require additional hardware, the QR code. A merchant sets up an Alipay account and displays the store's QR code in the store. Shoppers then open the Alipay app and scan the code to make a purchase, or generate their own QR code for the merchant to scan. Again, Alipay took a 0.6 percent cut of the transaction. Alipay users can use the app to buy coffee, hail cabs, pay utility bills, book medical appointments, split the bill with a friend at a restaurant, even make a donation to a street performer, as long as the vendor, or other party, also has an Alipay account.

Growth and Expansion

Alibaba CEO Jack Ma spun off Alipay because he feared possible government regulation of online payment systems. Alipay became the first product in the portfolio of the new company, Ant Financial, its name chosen carefully to represent the "little guy" the service targeted as customers. Alibaba retained rights to collect 37.5 percent of Ant Financial's pretax profits. Ant Financial's vision was to benefit society by facilitating a myriad of small transactions. Alipay and its rival WeChat Pay, launched by Tencent in 2013 (and discussed in chapter 1), grew rapidly and with no competition from the state-owned banks that dominated China's financial services, in part because they saw the internet payments market as unattractive. Use of Alipay quickly became ubiquitous in China and beyond as consumers and small and micro-enterprise merchants adopted the system. Some did away with credit card payments altogether in favor of Alipay.

Ant Financial did not stop for breath. The company took the data that it had access to and expanded the scope of its services to its clients and to the larger ecosystem. The conservative, traditional Chinese banks had created a massive opportunity for Alipay: only a small fraction of the Chinese population had access to credit, loans, or investment opportunities. Ant Financial jumped in with a sense of purpose and great speed to generate an array of services aimed at this huge market opportunity. Ant Financial extended its financial ecosystem with Yu'e Bao, an investment platform that allows Alipay users to earn interest on money in their accounts. Millions of Alipay customers can transfer pocket change from their accounts into one of Yu'e Bao's money market funds and get a 4 percent annual return. Users can participate via mobile phone, and there is no minimum deposit required, making the service accessible to a broad swath of the market.

Within the first few days after launch, more than a million people put money into the fund. Eric Mu in *Forbes* described users checking their accounts first thing in the morning to see how much wealth they had accumulated overnight: "Yu'e Bao has created hundreds of millions of ultra-lightweight investors, for whom saving and investing is no more than playing a game, and like all games, this one is slightly addictive."[8] In nine months the fund collected more than 500 billion yuan ($81 billion). By the spring of 2017 Yu'e Bao had become the largest money market fund in the world.

Along with Yu'e Bao, Ant Financial rapidly extended its roster of financial services, adding Ant Fortune, a one-stop personal investment and wealth management platform; Zhima Credit, a social credit scoring system; MYbank, an internet banking services provider; an insurance platform; and a variety of other offerings. Ant Financial launched a number of other applications, all easily accessible from its Alipay app. They included education services, medical services, transportation, social functionality, games, dining reservations, and food delivery, to name a few.

Ant Financial's broad ecosystem of features and services led to dramatic increases in its installed base and in the engagement of each user. In only a few years, Ant Financial and its Alipay services have become ubiquitous in China and beyond, as the massive amounts of data accumulated in each application are integrated, analyzed, and fed back in a relentless effort to improve knowledge about customers, personalization, and innovation.

By 2019, Ant Financial had more than 700 million users and dominated much of the Chinese financial services market even as it faced competition from Tencent. Ant Financial controlled 54 percent of the mobile payments market in China, while Tencent's WeChat controlled 38 percent. As one industry insider told Don Weiland and Sherry Fei Ju of the *Financial Times*, "These companies are like Facebook if it had a bank on top of it and everyone had a bank account [with Facebook]. There is really nothing like this in the west."[9]

In 2015, Ant Financial began to expand globally with investments in mobile payment systems in Asia, starting with a 40 percent joint stake with Alibaba in India's Paytm. From 2016 to 2018, Ant Financial continued to look for opportunities, pursuing partnerships and acquisitions that allowed the company to follow the needs of Chinese users as they traveled abroad. The company invested in South Korea's mobile payment platform KakaoPay, formed an agreement with Ascend Money (Thailand), Ingenico Group SA (a Paris-based payment system), Wirecard and Concardis (for Chinese travelers in Germany, France, the United Kingdom, and Italy), and acquired US-based biometric authentication technology company EyeVerify. Ant Financial attempted to penetrate the US market with a $1.2 billion purchase of money-transfer company MoneyGram but was thwarted by the US government due to fears about national security.

A New Kind of Operating Model

Alipay's rapidly expanding business model is built on a new kind of digital operating model. Its first foundation is a broad reliance on AI-enabled digital automation. For example, MYbank's hallmark is a 3-1-0 system for processing loans: it takes customers three minutes to apply for a loan, requires one second for approval, and involves zero human interaction. The loan approval and issuance processes rely solely on credit scores and are entirely digital and AI driven: each loan application is run through three thousand risk control strategies. Alibaba Group's Ming Zeng explains: "Our algorithms can look at transaction data to assess how well a business is doing, how competitive its offerings are in the market, whether its partners have high credit ratings, and so on." Zeng notes that Ant Financial's data analysts even feed its algorithms information on "the frequency, length, and type of communications (instant messaging, e-mail, or other methods common in China) to assess relationship quality" before approving a loan.[10] By January 2017, MYbank had served more than 5 million small businesses and individual entrepreneurs; loans averaged about RMB 17,000 and can be as low as RMB 1, with an aggregate loan volume of more than RMB 800 billion ($18 billion).

The speed and efficiency of Ant Financial's MYbank system demand a huge amount of data processing. Ant relies on cloud computing technologies to keep data processing costs low in order to scale up. The company's computing infrastructure enables it to easily handle billions of transfers per day, with a peak workload capacity of 120,000 transactions every second, and disaster recovery solutions of up to 99.99 percent in place. According to the company, it can process loans at a cost of only RMB 2, compared with RMB 2,000 at a traditional bank. With these digital systems in place, MYbank does not need physical bank locations or a large workforce.

In 2018, three years after its launch, the bank still employed only three hundred people, about the same number it started with.

The core of the operating model is a sophisticated, integrated data platform. With hundreds of millions of users making billions of transactions each day on the Alipay app, the platform collects information on everything users do, from the food they eat, to the places they shop, to the kind of transportation they prefer—not to mention how much they spend and how much they save. AI taps in to the data to drive a broad variety of functions, including personalization, revenue optimization, and recommendations, as well as the sophisticated analytics used to understand the value created by potential new products and services.

Alipay uses data and AI to ensure trust. When a user initiates a transaction, her information is passed through five layers of real-time digital checks to ensure that the transaction and the players involved are legitimate. Alipay's algorithms check buyer and seller account information for suspicious activity, look at the devices involved in the transaction, and then aggregate the data to make a decision on the validity of the transaction, much as a human might but much faster. Zeng explains: "The more data and the more iterations the algorithmic engine goes through, the better its output gets. Data scientists come up with probabilistic prediction models for specific actions, and then the algorithm churns through loads of data to produce better decisions in real time with every iteration."[11]

Ant Financial relies on data from four main sources: (1) internal consumer behavior statistics (e.g., records of relocation trends, utility bills, money transfers, wealth management, purchasing patterns on Alibaba); (2) transaction data from sellers on Alibaba's platforms; (3) public data such as government databases containing criminal records, citizen identification information, and academic profiles; and (4) data from Ant Financial's partners (e.g., merchants, hotel and car rental partners) to power Zhima credit scores. Zeng explains:

Ant uses that data to compare good borrowers (those who repay on time) with bad ones (those who do not) to isolate traits com-

mon in both groups. Those traits are then used to calculate credit scores. All lending institutions do this in some fashion, of course, but at Ant the analysis is done automatically on all borrowers and on all their behavioral data in real time. Every transaction, every communication between seller and buyer, every connection with other services available at Alibaba, indeed every action taken on our platform, affects a business's credit score. At the same time, the algorithms that calculate the scores are themselves evolving in real time, improving the quality of decision making with each iteration.

Zhima offers perks to consumers with good credit, such as favorable loan terms, whereas it requires those with low credit scores to put down additional deposits on their purchases, such as hotel rooms and bicycle rentals.

In addition, Ant Financial implemented a comprehensive, AI-driven fraud prevention monitoring system. This system can monitor hundreds of user actions, anything from a user logging in to initiating a transaction. Alipay has trained its software to identify a suspicious action and funnel it through its risk model, which can return a decision on the action almost instantly. Anything the model perceives as low risk is safe enough to proceed, but actions deemed risky require further scrutiny, including possible manual review.

Experimentation to Support Learning

Another component of Ant Financial's operating model is a sophisticated experimentation platform that runs hundreds of experiments daily, enabling the company to learn and understand the opportunities and risks provided by new features and products. Ultimately, Ant Financial's dramatic expansion came about as a direct result of focusing on the various data sources that could be amalgamated on the existing platform and rapidly recombined by agile teams driving new products and services. Ant Financial's increases in scale and scope were driven by its impressive learning capabilities, combining analytics with agile innovation.

The data and algorithms that Ant Financial deploys in its business are also useful for additional new financial services developed by agile teams. Ant relies on scenario-based prototyping (use cases) to develop new applications (solutions) or opportunities, resting and refining them while attracting a critical mass of consumers and thereby mainstreaming the technology quickly. It also leverages innovations in data mining and semantic analysis to automate customer issue resolution.

Removing the Human Bottleneck

As the Ant Financial example illustrates, the essence of the digital operating model is avoiding direct human intervention on the critical path of the product- or service-delivery process. While employees help define strategies, design user interfaces, develop algorithms, code software, and interpret data (among many other functions), the actual processes that drive customer value are fully digitized. No human organization is a bottleneck in the qualification for individual loans or the recommendation of a specific investment vehicle.

How is this done? The firm anchors these processes in a central repository of data, describing customer and operational needs in an integrated fashion. As the customer interacts with the business process, software modules gather the necessary data, extract and analyze needs, internalize their implications, and interact with the customer to deliver the value as promised. Building customer interaction processes on a centralized data architecture thus operationalizes and automates the idea of customer centricity in a clear, actionable, and scalable way.

Many new operating models, like Ant Financial's, automate data-driven actions and gradually remove human tasks from delivery bottlenecks. Take, for example, shopping on the Amazon mobile app. As the user browses through the app, offerings are being automatically selected based on data on the user's previous behavior and on the behavior of similar users. Pricing information is processed in real time (or close to it) and merged with the behavioral information to dynamically construct the page the user interacts with. A product manager eventually views aggregated data on transactions and consumer behavior, but almost every human interaction is removed from the actual critical path in service delivery. The only exceptions might be a worker helping pick the item from a largely automated warehouse, and the delivery person leaving the package at your door.

Removing human and organizational bottlenecks from the critical path has a huge impact on the nature of the company's operating model. The marginal cost of serving an additional user on many digital networks is, for all purposes, zero, apart from the small incremental cost of computing capacity, which is easily available from cloud service providers. This inherently makes a digital operating model easier to scale. Growth constraints are much less dependent on human actors, and organizational constraints are rarely a problem, because much of the operational complexity is solved through software and analytics or outsourced to external partners in the operating network.

A digital operating model also fundamentally changes the architecture of the firm. Beyond removing human bottlenecks, digital technologies are intrinsically modular and can easily enable business connections. When fully digitized, a process can easily be plugged in to an external network of partners and providers, or even into external communities of individuals, to provide additional, complementary value. Digitized processes are thus intrinsically multisided. After value is delivered in one domain (e.g., accumulating data about a set of consumers), that same process can be connected to drive value in other applications, thereby increasing firm scope and adding a multiplicative factor to the value it's delivering to the customer.

Finally, digitizing the operating model can also enable much faster learning and innovation. The vast amounts of accumulated data provide critical input to an increasingly broad range of tasks, from instant app personalization to feature innovation and product development. In addition, by digitizing many of the operational workflows, this model diminishes the overall size of the organization along with the surrounding bureaucracy. The insights provided by analyzing a rich foundation of data can thus be rapidly deployed into actions by a relatively small number of agile product teams.

Ultimately, in a digital operating model, the employees do not deliver the product or service; instead, they design and oversee a software-automated, algorithm-driven digital "organization" that actually delivers the goods. This completely changes the factors involved in management, transforms the growth process, and removes traditional operating bottlenecks constraining scale, scope, and learning in a firm.

Let's look at two more examples.

The Irresistible Digital Bicycle

We see ourselves more akin to an Apple, a Tesla, or a Nest or a GoPro—where it's a consumer product that has a foundation of sexy hardware technology and sexy software technology.

—**John Foley, founder and CEO, Peloton**

John Foley was reportedly turned down by more than four hundred investors as he was starting his next-generation fitness company, Peloton. Investors could not be convinced that a traditional product like the stationary bicycle, invented more than two hundred years ago, had a digital future. However, Foley had different ideas borne of his experience competing with Amazon as CEO at Barnes & Noble. "The top line when I got there was $500 million. I could have doubled it, and we would still have been losing $100 million," he told *Barron's* in 2014. "As a business guy, I didn't like the value proposition of that."[12] Foley realized that instead of wasting his time chasing another competitor with superior scale, scope, and AI capabilities, he needed to find a traditional category and transform it digitally.

The idea for Peloton grew out of Foley's frustration that he could not get into his favorite indoor spin classes. The studio capacities were so limited that all the choice instructors' classes were booked as soon as they were scheduled. Taking a page from Amazon and Netflix, he envisioned a new fitness company that would take away constraints of time, space, and capacity.

Founded in 2012, Peloton's main product is a sleek, high-quality indoor bicycle with an integrated 21-inch tablet to display fitness programming. Customers pay about $2,200 for the bike and then an additional $39 monthly subscription for unlimited access to fitness programming. They can choose from more than fourteen hours of daily live studio classes (from New York and London) and an ever-expanding library of more than fifteen thousand previously recorded workouts to access on demand.

Peloton's business model, built on a digital operating model, has turned the fitness industry on its head. People tend to get their exercise either in gyms (how many of us at the start of a new year have bought an annual membership?) or at home (how many of us have treadmills that have become bulky and expensive clothes hangers?). For gyms, the business model consists of making capital investments and charging customers for use through a subscription model (counting on the fact that most won't step into the place after January) and some type of pay-per-use for classes. Home fitness equipment makers sell us the equipment, so we make personal investments and hope to find motivation in working out every day. In contrast, the Peloton business model takes a traditional "analog" product and then transforms it by adding digital content, data, analytics, and connectivity to collide with a traditional industry.

Peloton's initial value creation is straightforward. Customers want the benefit and convenience of an in-home fitness experience without sacrificing access to great instructors and the community of fellow sweat hounds. Peloton brings the fitness studio to the customer's home. Value creation is enhanced by giving users access to an unlimited number of classes, including cycling, treadmill, yoga, meditation, strength training, and even outdoor walking and running workouts. Its more than one million members can binge on workouts the way Netflix subscribers can binge on shows.

Additional value creation mechanisms are the connectivity and community of Peloton members. More than 170,000 members connect through the official Peloton Facebook page, and then there are hundreds of subcommunities that have formed around Peloton instructors (who are celebrities in the Peloton world). There are countless other tribes who've coalesced around different goals, geographies, and training styles. Taking a live-streamed class is also a communal experience: members can track their performance on a live leader board, virtually high-five each other, connect with each other, and follow each other's workout progress. Instructors name-check live users, calling out their achievements and milestones and reminding them to keep their form and motivation high through the tough parts. The on-demand classes even provide connectivity with riders who might happen to be taking the class at that moment. Peloton has activated voice and video connections among exercisers to bring the fitness class experience to their home. The community also meets face-to-face through regular "home rider invasions," when Peloton members travel from across the United States, Canada, and the United Kingdom to visit the company's Manhattan studios for live classes.

The value capture model for Peloton combines product sales and subscriptions. The bike is relatively useless without a subscription, and the Peloton service has a million subscribers, with a remarkable subscription renewal rate of 95 percent. Peloton fans who don't want to buy the bike can subscribe to the company's digital content and community via the mobile app for $20 per month.

Scaling the fitness experience is at the core of Peloton's operating model. While a typical spin class at SoulCycle might have thirty or forty riders in a studio, a live-streamed Peloton cycling class may have between five hundred and twenty thousand riders sweating simultaneously. After the live class ends, it becomes part of the online library available freely to members. Peloton's leaders also realized that its members needed additional fitness options, so it expanded its scope by offering a range of yoga, strength training, and treadmill sessions (for members who've purchased a sleek Peloton-branded treadmill, of course).

Peloton is in many ways still a product-focused company, but Foley's idea was to design the iPhone of fitness equipment. Peloton built its first bike in 2013, and, in 2014, after a round of investment, it produced an improved bike that could be tested by and sold to consumers. By 2015, the bike had been perfected, and business started to take off.

The company raised around $100 million, enabling it to work closely with its manufacturer in Taiwan to increase capacity, speed up bike production and delivery, expand its software and analytics team, and dramatically increase the content delivered. The company also built its own supply chain, delivering bikes in Peloton-branded vans and dispatching employees to set up the bikes and advise customers on finding the classes and instructors to suit their tastes.

Although Peloton's success is sparked by a great product, the organization is structured more like a software company. It employs a team of more than seventy software engineers who design the company's systems for a version of Android. Peloton relies on human talent to devise, design, and produce its products and services—everything from the new treadmill to the latest "Power Zone" class. But even though humans are crucial, it is the digital service that delivers the experience in a highly scalable fashion to a rapidly increasing audience of enthusiasts.

There is no limit to the number of consumers who can subscribe to use the Peloton service (as long as its Taiwanese suppliers keep delivering the fitness equipment). As with Ant Financial, growth bottlenecks at Peloton are shifted to internal digitized systems or to resources outside the firm. Peloton, like Ant Financial, is not subject to the most significant traditional operational constraints on growth. In addition, the digital interfaces (the APIs) in Peloton's software easily expand the scope of the business by connecting to a variety of complementary apps (e.g., Apple Health, Strava, and Fitbit), social networks (Facebook and Twitter), and devices (heart rate monitors, smart watches).

Although its AI capabilities are nowhere near the level of Ant Financial's, Peloton has built a sophisticated analytics platform and digitally streamed content to transform fitness training into a new experience. The company gathers extensive data, from rider heart rate to workout frequency to musical taste, from in-studio attendance to social network engagement. It constantly analyzes the data and uses the analytics to implement a variety of improvements, from class selection and design to new product and service optimization. The analytics drive the user experience and greatly enhance engagement while increasing barriers to switching and reducing customer churn.

Unlike other exercise equipment products, loyalty to Peloton is extreme. It's easy to imagine what the company could do with its data and the type of scope expansion that is possible. For example, Peloton could connect its users to nutrition services, health-care providers, or even insurance products. The company's data stores provide it with a broad range of options to redefine what it means to be a fitness company.

Peloton has enjoyed impressive growth. Its reliance on software, data, and networks has enabled the company to scale fast, reaching more than $700 million in revenue and a $4 billion valuation on an approximately $1 billion investment.

The World's Toughest AI Business

Human beings can do everything that AI can do.
They just can't do it to scale.

—Anne Marie Neatham, COO, Ocado Technology

Online grocery delivery must be one of the most challenging businesses ever devised. Imagine promising a million people on-time delivery of more than fifty thousand of the world's lowest-margin and most perishable items through sun, rain, sleet, snow, and the Olympic Games. It is no wonder that it took many years for Ocado to win the respect of financial analysts. After going public in 2010, Ocado was roundly criticized for its business model, its operating model, and even its name ("Ocado begins with an 'o', ends with an 'o' and is worth zero," said Philip Dorgan, an analyst with RFC Ambrian Limited).[13] But in recent years the UK-based company has greatly exceeded expectations and become a darling of the financial markets.

Behind Ocado's success is a surge in AI impact on both its business and its operating model. Ocado delivers groceries, both for its own branded online and mobile service and for a variety of third parties. To do so on time, reliably, and efficiently, it has built a phenomenal foundation of data, AI, and robotics. Ocado is an AI company disguised as a supply chain company disguised as an online grocer. Its capabilities were built by necessity, over time, with painstaking conviction and deep investment.

Originally set up for browser-based commerce, Ocado introduced its first mobile app in 2009. The key to the business is Ocado's centralized data platform, rebuilt from scratch in 2014, containing unrivaled detail on its products, customers, partners, supply chain, and delivery environment. The data is accumulated in the cloud and is exposed through easy-to-use interfaces for use by agile teams deployed to optimize every kind of application, from delivery routing to robotics, and from fraud detection to spoilage prediction. All this has combined to build a rapidly growing and profitable operation with a record of 98.5 percent on-time delivery.

AI algorithms are in the driver's seat of Ocado's operational execution. Running thousands of routing calculations per second, AI makes sure the company has a highly predictable delivery model, optimized across its fleet of thousands of trucks, delivering in all weather and traffic conditions across the entire United Kingdom. The algorithms optimize truck routing in real time and make sure the products delivered are fresh.

In addition to the routing, the AI actually predicts when customers are likely to order the products in the first place, typically a couple of days ahead of the need for them. Using unusually deep customer preference data, cross-referenced with the constraints of organic farmers in Ocado's supply chain, the algorithms predict when the refrigerated trucks should arrive at Ocado's supplier network of farms to pick up meats, poultry, and produce and bring them to storage in warehouses. And the warehouses are in themselves a masterpiece of AI technology, with thousands of bots that pick, assemble, and transport the groceries; the bots are coordinated and managed by algorithms, which in turn prioritize the most crucial and timely deliveries while minimizing congestion and optimizing overall efficiency.

The warehouses (also referred to as fulfillment centers) are the jewels in Ocado's operating model. A single warehouse can be the size of eleven soccer fields and sport thirty-five miles of conveyors that move hundreds of thousands of grocery boxes every day, around ten thousand simultaneously. Algorithms route every box to avoid traffic jams and ensure freshness and delivery capacity. Other algorithms aggregate and model the entire warehouse system.

The system is flexible and can accommodate an increasing number of locations, customers, and bots as capacity expands with growth, and as Ocado's technology and operations teams continue to learn, experiment, and innovate, leading to rapidly increasing scale and scope. As COO Anne Marie Neatham notes, "Machine learning never stops. But you'll notice the common theme for the team. Visualize, trial it, iterate, iterate, iterate, iterate in volume."[14]

Over time, Ocado's AI and bot technology has collided with a range of traditional operating processes. Human labor is still used, even in the highly automated warehouses, to perform a number of tasks that bots have a hard time emulating, most notably picking certain difficult grocery items. But as you saw before, the labor is being moved off the critical path, as much as possible, to improve the scalability and reliability of the process. As Paul Clarke, Ocado's chief technology officer, put it, "For us, it's just the same journey we've been on since day one: to look for the next thing to automate, whether that's putting plastic bags in crates, or moving goods around our sheds. We start with the obvious thing and move on to automate the next thing and the next thing. You never get to the end."[15]

Ocado's deep AI and digital capabilities are enabling two different business models. Leveraging the capabilities built on its own UK-based online retail business, Ocado is also offering its technology platform to power third-party retail and delivery services; Marks & Spencer, the venerable UK retailer, is an example. Ocado is also expanding across the ocean, working, for example, with Sobeys in Canada and Kroger in the United States to set up and operate warehouses and customer fulfillment centers.

As part of the partnership, Kroger has increased its stake in Ocado to more than 6 percent and will leverage the Ocado Smart Platform's capabilities in online ordering, omnichannel integration, automated fulfillment, and home delivery. With almost $2 billion in revenue and a valuation around $7 billion, Ocado has come to the United States, and Amazon is watching closely.

Transforming Value Creation, Capture, and Delivery

Ant Financial, Ocado, and Peloton showcase three approaches to digitizing value delivery, enabling business model innovation, and driving industry transformation. In each case, we witnessed the creation of exceptional consumer value, with scale, scope, and level of innovation that is virtually unprecedented in each industry. The value capture similarities are also striking. In each case, the companies are less transactional and more invested in using digital technology to foster consumer loyalty and engagement. And as long as consumers are deeply engaged with a service, more users will join, and the monetization opportunities will multiply.

The differences among the three firms are also interesting. The three industries they originally targeted could not be more different: financial services, groceries, and fitness. While Ant Financial is exclusively a set of information-based services, Ocado delivers products with a remarkably efficient supply chain, and Peloton provides a tightly integrated product-service combination. Still, in each case, the company digitized critical operating processes, with transformative impact.

As we look closer, each company used algorithms and networks to transform its markets, but each did so in a unique way, building unique capabilities and employing unique approaches. Ant Financial built impressive capabilities in analytics and AI, and oversees a highly automated system to drive virtually unprecedented scale and scope across financial services and beyond. Ocado also features an operating model that deploys sophisticated AI, founded on an algorithmic core that drives impressive scalability, sustains an increasingly broad scope of product offerings, and enables ongoing learning and innovation. Ocado also emphasizes how its algorithms integrate with the human talent to, for example, aid drivers and product pickers. Peloton, instead, is driven more by networks and community, but it still uses data and analytics to enhance engagement and loyalty. The company takes content created by human talent and greatly amplifies its impact to a broad and expanding community of customers, who stream the service, exercise, and check progress via its increasingly sophisticated analytics. As with Ocado, human skills and labor shift into design, production, and enhancement roles, while the digital technology delivers and sustains the core experience.

Most of all, we are excited about the similarities in the operating models of these different firms. By digitizing the most critical processes, each operating model removes traditional bottlenecks and enables unprecedented scalability, scope, and learning; once the model is established, most of what these firms need for growth is additional computing power, which is easy enough to access from the cloud. Growth bottlenecks are moved to the technology layer, or to the ecosystem of partners and suppliers. Figure 2-2 illustrates the kind of digital business and operating models at the heart of these three companies.

FIGURE 2-2

Value creation and capture versus value delivery

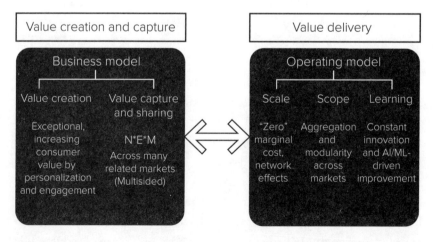

Note: N*E*M = (the number of users) * (user engagement) * (monetization)

Putting AI at the Core

On May 17, 2017, Sundar Pichai, Google's CEO, made a surprise announcement at the Google I/O conference in front of seven thousand attendees, with more than one million people viewing on live streaming. Google's strategic focus, Pichai said, was shifting from mobile to "AI first."[16]

The announcement surprised quite a few people. From its beginning, the company's business and operating models had always been driven by data, networks, and software. After all, Google commercialized the world's best search algorithm, developed leading advertising technology, and turned Android into the world's most popular software platform. The company had already invested heavily in AI, eclipsing most other firms and universities in the number of publications and patents. What did it mean for Google to be AI first?

Pichai wasn't talking about introducing a new AI-inspired product or launching a few pilots experimenting with advanced analytics. Rather, his announcement was the real deal, capping two decades of investment in developing software algorithms and AI technologies. It showed that AI had moved to the center of the company, to the core of its operating model. Increasingly, AI would be the common foundation across virtually every operating process. Pichai illustrated the approach with a variety of examples, from novel customer-facing apps (such as the innovative AI-enabled Google Assistant) to the new AI-enabled infrastructure powering Google's data centers and cloud services.

The announcement was a signal to Google consumers, advertisers, external developers, and employees that AI and its associated investments in data and analytics had become essential to the company's business and operating models. Virtually every aspect of Google was going to leverage this core. All of Google's products and services (several with billions of active users) would increase the value they delivered through conversational (speech, text), ambient (in all types of devices), and contextual (understand what you want) AI, and each process would continuously learn and adapt.

The embedded AI systems would always be trying to predict what its consumers wanted or needed, updating these models across all interactions. This predictive power would of course be hugely valuable to Google's advertisers as well. An AI-first approach meant that Google's ads would become increasingly personalized and contextualized, ultimately increasing relevance and yielding more clicks.

The Pichai announcement provided a clear message and wake-up call. For Google's employees, technical as well as business focused, this was a signal to develop an in-depth understanding of AI and drive its application across every aspect of the company's value creation, capture, and operating model. For Google's massive ecosystem of partners and developers, it was an invitation to embed AI to improve their own products and services, from exercise apps to TVs. For the rest of us who were listening, it became clear that AI had finally come of age. For literally millions of people, AI was no longer a promising set of innovative technologies; it was becoming the core of the firm.

In the next chapter, we examine how the core of the firm, like Google's, is a scalable decision factory, powered by software, data, and algorithms.

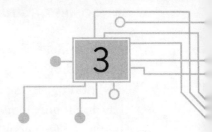

The AI Factory

Through much of history, products were painstakingly and individually crafted in artisanal workshops. That ended when the Industrial Revolution transformed the economy by spawning a scalable and repeatable approach to manufacturing. Engineers and managers became experts at understanding the processes needed for mass production and built the first generation of factories, dedicated to the continuous, low-cost production of quality goods. However, while production was industrialized, analysis and decision making remained largely traditional, idiosyncratic processes.

Now, the age of AI is manifested by companies driving another fundamental transformation. This one involves industrializing data gathering, analytics, and decision making to reinvent the core of the modern firm, in what we call the "AI factory."[1]

The AI factory is the scalable decision engine that powers the digital operating model of the twenty-first-century firm. Managerial decisions are increasingly embedded in software, which digitizes many processes that have traditionally been carried out by employees. No human auctioneer gets involved in the millions of daily search-ad auctions at Google or Baidu. Dispatchers do not decide which car is chosen on DiDi, Grab, Lyft, or Uber. Sports retailers do not set daily prices on golf apparel at Amazon. Bankers do not approve every loan at Ant Financial. Instead, these processes are digitized and enabled by an AI factory that treats decision making as an industrial process. Analytics systematically convert internal and external data into predictions, insights, and choices, which in turn guide or even automate a variety of operational actions. This is what enables the superior scale, scope, and learning capacity of the digital firm.

Digital operating models can take various forms. In some cases, they might only manage flows of information (think Ant Financial, Google, or Facebook). In other cases, operating models guide how the company builds, delivers, or operates actual physical products (think Ocado, Amazon, or Waymo). In either case, AI factories are at the core of the model, guiding the most critical processes and operating decisions, while humans are moved to the edge, off the critical path of value delivery.

In its essence, the AI factory creates a virtuous cycle between user engagement, data collection, algorithm design, prediction, and improvement (see figure 3-1). It integrates data generated from multiple sources (internal or external to the firm) to refine and train a set of algorithms. These algorithms not only make predictions but also use the data to improve their own accuracy. The predictions then drive decisions and actions, either by informing human insights or by enabling an automated response. Hypotheses about changing

FIGURE 3-1

The AI factory's virtuous cycle

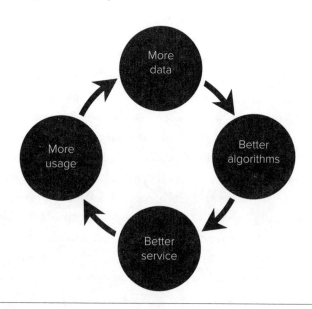

customer behavior patterns, competitive responses, and process variations are tested through rigorous experimentation protocols that enable causal identification of changes that might improve the system. Data about usage and about the accuracy and impact of the prediction outcomes is then sent back into the system for further learning and predictions. And the cycle continually repeats.

Take, for example, a search engine like Google or Bing. As soon as a user types a few letters in the search box, algorithms dynamically predict the full search term based on prior search terms and the user's past actions. These predictions are captured in a drop-down menu (the *autosuggest box*), which helps users zero in quickly on the desired search. Every user movement and every click are captured as data points, and every data point gathered improves the prediction for future searches. The more searches, the better the predictions, and the better the predictions, the more the search engine is used.

There are multiple other prediction cycles in a search engine's AI factory. During the natural search process, the search term entered by a user generates a display of organic search results, which are drawn from a previously assembled index of the web and optimized by using the outcomes (the clicks generated) of previous searches. In addition, entering the search term also starts an automated auction for the most relevant ads to match the user's intent, an auction whose results are also shaped by additional learning loops. The search-results page, which combines organic search results and relevant ads, is thus heavily influenced by data on previous search attempts. Any click on or away from the search query or search-results page provides useful data.

In addition, a product manager within the search engine operations might have some new hypothesis—for example, that showing fewer ads might improve revenues on a given page, or that highlighting search results would improve click-through rates. To provide additional fodder for improvement, these hypotheses would be loaded on the experimental machinery and tested on a statistically relevant sample of users.

Clearly there is no way all this data could be analyzed by a few analysts using manual tools, or even by casually assembled code.

The AI factory solves this problem by bringing mass production methods to data processing and analytics, thus forming the core of a digital operating model. Let's dig deeper into its nature, using Netflix to anchor the discussion.

Building and Running the AI Factory

Netflix has transformed the media landscape by harnessing the power of artificial intelligence. The core of Netflix is its AI-centric operating model: it is powered by software infrastructure that gathers data and trains and executes algorithms that influence virtually every aspect of the business, from personalizing the user experience to picking movie concepts to negotiating content agreements.

In its earliest days two decades ago, Netflix displayed movie reviews, generated recommendations based on customers' viewing histories, and shipped DVDs of new releases the day they were made available in stores. Even then, Netflix recognized the importance of using data to improve the customer experience. The company's early efforts were focused on developing a recommendation engine, which suggested movies based on a viewer's history, movie ratings, and the preferences of similar viewers.[2] Netflix not only used this data internally but also shared the reviews with movie studios. Sharing this data helped Netflix negotiate better financial terms in its partnerships with Warner Home Video and Columbia TriStar.[3]

Netflix grew rapidly, hitting eight million subscribers in 2007 when it launched its streaming service. This new offering dramatically increased the company's access to user data, which Netflix analytics teams used extensively. With its mail delivery service, Netflix could track only those titles users requested, the length of time they kept a DVD, and their rating of each title; Netflix could not monitor actual viewing behavior. With streaming, Netflix could track the full user experience—when viewers pause, rewind, or skip during a show, for example, or what device they are using. This behavioral data helped Netflix determine which movie thumbnail image to show a viewer (yes, even these are personalized based on preferences for particular genres, actors, and other such factors), predicting their likely preferences. Through more-advanced analytics, Netflix also predicted drivers of customer loyalty. With the goal of increasing subscriber viewing time and decreasing customer churn rates, Netflix used AI to launch a function that automatically queues the next episode in a series or recommends similar movies. The customization and personalization has become pervasive. As Joris Evers, then chief of communications at Netflix, told the *New York Times* in 2013, "[T]here are 33 million different versions of Netflix," meaning that each user's Netflix experience is personalized and customized.[4]

Netflix also uses data and AI algorithms to decide which content to create on its own. The company's first use of predictive analytics for this purpose was in 2013 to evaluate the potential of *House of Cards*, the fictional account of a senator's rise to the White House, in collaboration with Media Rights Capital (MRC). Cindy Holland, vice president of original content, noted in an interview, "We have projection models that help us understand, for a given idea or area, how large we think an audience size might be, given certain attributes about it. We have a construct for genres that basically gives us areas where we have a bunch of programs and others that are areas of opportunity."[5]

By 2010 Netflix was embracing the AI factory approach to systematically apply analytics and AI to the company's recommendation engine. In 2014, the company expanded the factory to improve the streaming experience by understanding user behavior, creating a personalized streaming experience for each user (based on such factors as connection speed and preferred device), and determining what movies and shows to cache on "edge servers," which are deployed closer to viewers.[6] Now Netflix has about 150 million subscribers in more than 190 countries, has amassed a content library of more than 5,500 shows, and consumes 15 percent of the global internet bandwidth.

Experience from Netflix and other leading firms underlines the importance of a few essential AI factory components (see figure 3-2):

FIGURE 3-2

AI factory components

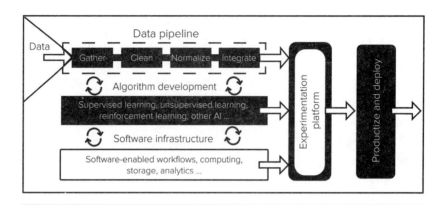

1. ***Data pipeline:*** This process gathers, inputs, cleans, integrates, processes, and safeguards data in a systematic, sustainable, and scalable way.

2. ***Algorithm development:*** The algorithms generate predictions about future states or actions of the business. These algorithms and predictions are the beating heart of the digital firm, driving its most critical operating activities.

3. ***Experimentation platform:*** This is the mechanism through which hypotheses regarding new prediction and decision algorithms are tested to ensure that changes suggested are having the intended (causal) effect.

4. ***Software infrastructure:*** These systems embed the pipeline in a consistent and componentized software and computing infrastructure, and connect it as needed and appropriate to internal and external users.

If the data is the fuel that powers the AI factory, then infrastructure makes up the pipes that deliver the fuel, and the algorithms are the machines that do the work. The experimentation platform, in turn, controls the valves that connect new fuel, pipes, and machines to existing operational systems.

Let's look first at the data pipeline.

The Data Pipeline

Data is the essential input of the AI factory. One reason for the radical advances made by AI systems in recent years is that the velocity, volume, and variety of data available for analysis has exploded. As far back as 2012, Netflix was using a broad base of data inputs. As described by Xavier Amatriain and Justin Basilico, two Netflix engineers, on the Netflix blog, the inputs are varied.

- *We have several billion item **ratings** from members. And we receive millions of new ratings a day.*

- *We already mentioned item **popularity** as a baseline. But, there are many ways to compute popularity. We can compute it over various time ranges, for instance hourly, daily, or weekly. Or, we can group members by region or other similarity metrics and compute popularity within that group.*

- *We receive several million stream **plays** each day, which include context such as duration, time of day and device type.*

- *Our members add millions of items to their **queues** each day.*

- *Each item in our catalog has rich **metadata**: actors, director, genre, parental rating, and reviews.*

- ***Presentations**: We know what items we have recommended and where we have shown them, and can look at how that decision has affected the member's actions. We can also observe the member's interactions with the recommendations: scrolls, mouse-overs, clicks, or the time spent on a given page.*

- ***Social** data has become our latest source of personalization features; we can process what connected friends have watched or rated.*

- *Our members directly enter millions of **search terms** in the Netflix service each day.*

- *All the data we have mentioned above comes from internal sources. We can also tap into **external data** to improve our* *features. For example, we can add external item data features such as box office performance or critic reviews.*

- *Of course, that is not all: there are many **other** features such as demographics, location, language, or temporal data that can be used in our predictive models.[7]*

In 2018, Netflix users had more than 5,600 movie and TV series titles to choose from. Every time users open the Netflix application on their TV, computer, phone, or tablet, the company's systems kick in to make personal recommendations and customize the interface. Virtually every aspect of a user's experience generates data, which then enables Netflix to further fine-tune the customizations it provides. (And certainly, there is much more data available now than when this post was written in 2012.) All of this data is cleaned, integrated, prepared, and used by Netflix to dynamically adapt its service to continuously improve the value it provides to its estimated 300 million users.

The depth and breadth of the Netflix data is the envy of the industry. Part of the company's data and analytics assets includes creating approximately two thousand *microclusters*, or taste communities, which connect viewers having similar tastes. Individual users can fit in to several taste communities, and they defy simple demographic profiles; a sixty-five-year-old grandmother in urban Mumbai may like the same shows as a teenager in rural Arkansas.

Netflix has "datafied" TV entertainment—a term coined by Ming Zeng, Alibaba's strategy chief and academic counsel. The idea of *datafication* refers to systematically extracting data from activities and transactions that are naturally ongoing in any business.[8] The Nest thermostat, for example, invaded a sleepy market by datafying a traditional spectrum of activities—controlling the heating, ventilation, and cooling (HVAC) systems in a home. The addition of a few electronic sensors to monitor temperature and motion in the home, along with computer-based control and Wi-Fi connectivity, enabled Nest to create a brand-new data layer that generates important new value for homeowners. The Nest device, in only a few days, can learn your habits and adjust the temperature automatically in your house, participate in energy reduction programs at your nearby utility, and enable smartphone control.

Similar datafication has happened in almost every setting, from social behavior on Facebook to fitness with an Apple Watch or Fitbit, to sleep and health tracking with the Oura and Motiv rings.[9] Increasingly, as in the Netflix example, the initial process of datafication can be combined with external data sources to provide additional value to the user. The Oura ring's app, for example, combines sleep and heart rate data with the user's activity level monitored by an Apple Watch to coach the user on the level of rest and activity needed for a productive day. Ride-sharing platforms like Uber, Lyft, Grab, DiDi, and GOJEK have built a datafication layer around transportation. The combination of their applications and the smartphone infrastructure has enabled these companies to generate data at an unprecedented level about individual transportation preferences, demand and supply needs, and overall flow of traffic in and out of urban centers. Accurate, real-time data about all this has never existed until now.

Sometimes, innovation is needed to transform traditional activities into sources of useful data. Alipay and WeChat Pay have led the way in economic transactions through their extensive use of QR codes for payments. If data is not readily available or does not exist, it may be worthwhile for a company to invest in technology and services that generate the data in the first place. Even Pitney Bowes, the hundred-year-old provider of postal equipment, has built a datafication strategy around physical addresses in the United States and is augmenting the company's business model by offering data-driven Knowledge Fabric solutions to banks, insurers, social platforms, and retailers—any organization that can use address data for marketing, fraud detection, and other purposes. The company realized that it could create and capture value beyond selling postage.

Many incumbent businesses that are attempting to build AI factories find that the data they possess is fragmented, incomplete, and often siloed within divisions and disparate IT systems. Take, for example, a typical hotel stay for a business traveler. In theory, a hotel chain should have a treasure trove of data on their customers, from home address to credit card information, to frequency of travel, airline, and mode of transportation, location of travel, class of stay, meal selections, local sightseeing favorites, and health and fitness preferences. In practice, though, the data is highly fragmented, resides in various system silos with incompatible data structures, is missing common identifiers, and may not necessarily be very accurate. Executives at many incumbent companies consistently underestimate the challenge and the urgency of the investment they face in cleaning and integrating their data across the enterprise so that they can build an effective AI factory. The first order of business facing these executives is to ensure that the appropriate investments are in place.

We emphasize that after the data is gathered, much work remains to be done in cleaning, normalizing, and integrating it. These steps are quite challenging. Data assets are most often plagued by all kinds of biases and even plain errors, and a significant investment needs to be made in ensuring that the data is checked carefully for inaccuracies and inconsistencies. Moreover, as various streams of data are integrated into a single stream to feed complex analysis, the different kinds of data must be normalized. A particular challenge is making sure that financial data is being used properly, in a way that is consistent with operational data, so that any insight that comes from analyzing the integrated dataset is accurate. For example, units should be consistent, redundancies eliminated, and variables compatible. These things often sound simple but are not, especially as the datasets reach significant size.

Algorithm Development

After the data is gathered and prepared, the tool that makes the data useful is the *algorithm*—the set of rules a machine follows to use data to make a decision, generate a prediction, or solve a particular problem.

Consider how you would analyze whether a customer is likely to leave a service like Netflix. Here the algorithm would predict customer churn as a function of variables such as usage (frequency and intensity), satisfaction, demographics, and relationships or similarities with other users. The prediction algorithm would be tuned and calibrated with data on past customers, tested for accuracy with past data or with a controlled experiment, and deployed either as an analytical tool for managers or as a step in an operational process—for example, automatically enabling a special offer to retain vulnerable customers.

Ajay Agrawal, Josh Gans, and Avi Goldfarb of the University of Toronto note that data proliferation and advances in AI algorithms have lowered the cost of making accurate predictions, increasing the scope and intensity of the usage of prediction algorithms throughout the economy.[10] Algorithms predict which Google photos include family members or friends, what Facebook content you should read next, how much revenue to expect from giving a Walmart discount to a particular customer, or when a piece of equipment at a Ford manufacturing facility will need maintenance. These kinds of predictions are vital to the success of many organizations, and the algorithms deployed should be geared to provide consistent and robust predictions.

AI algorithms can be used for a broad variety of applications, from generating relatively simple predictions (like a sales forecast) to suggesting stocks to pick for high-frequency trading, to complex image recognition and language translation tasks that may exceed human capabilities. Some of the most complex applications, such as driving a car, use a variety of different algorithms simultaneously—for example, to identify and track cars and to route a car through heavy traffic.

Although the use of applications has exploded over the past decade, the foundations of algorithm design have been around for quite some time.[11] The conceptual and mathematical development of classic statistical models such as linear regression, clustering, or Markov chains date back more than a hundred years. Although neural networks are now generating a lot of excitement, they were initially developed in the 1960s and are only now being put to use at scale with production-ready outputs. The vast majority of production-ready and operational AI systems use one of three general approaches to develop accurate predictions using statistical models, also known as machine learning. These are supervised learning, unsupervised learning, and reinforcement learning.

Supervised Learning

The basic goal of *supervised* machine learning algorithms is to come as close as possible to a human expert (or an accepted source of truth) in predicting an outcome. The classic case is analyzing a picture and predicting whether the subject is a cat or a dog. In this case the expert would be any human being who could label photos as images of a cat or a dog. The algorithms in this class of machine learning systems rely on an *expert-labeled* dataset of the outcome (the Y) and the potential characteristics or features (the Xs). The operationalization of the algorithm is called a *model*, which takes the general-purpose statistical approach and creates a context-specific instantiation of the prediction problem that needs to be solved.

The first step in supervised learning is to create (or acquire) a labeled dataset. For example, we might acquire a file containing thousands of pictures of cats and thousands of pictures of dogs, with each picture labeled appropriately. The data is then split between training and validation. The *training* dataset is used to determine the parameters of the model that generates the prediction of the outcome (whether a given picture depicts a cat or a dog). After the model is trained, the *validation* dataset is used to test the accuracy of the model. The model makes its predictions on the validation dataset; we can then compare these predictions to the expert predictions and thereby assess the quality of the model. Supervised machine learning algorithms can be used to predict either a binary outcome (for example, whether a picture shows a cat or a dog) or a numerical quantity (such as the sales forecast for a particular product).[12]

As we compare the algorithmic model's prediction of the outcome to the validated labeled outcomes, we can determine whether we are satisfied with the error rate between model prediction and expert. If we are not satisfied, we can choose a different statistical approach, get more data, or work on identifying other features that may be helpful in making a more accurate prediction. The main challenge here is to keep iterating between data, features, and algorithms until we are satisfied with the error rate between the model prediction and the expert prediction.

Examples of supervised machine learning abound. Every time we label an email as spam, we help our email provider's machine learning algorithms update its models to identify the latest clever scam. Facebook's or Baidu's ability to suggest names of friends who may appear in newly uploaded pictures is based on our prior labeling of photos. Credit card companies or payment platforms decide whether to allow a transaction based on prior purchasing habits, which automatically create labeled data. A Nest thermostat's ability to change the temperature in your living room thirty minutes before you arrive home is based on autogenerated labeled data gathered from your previous arrival and departure times, as well as your prior temperature-setting habits.

Netflix uses supervised learning in a variety of scenarios. For recommendations, Netflix has used labeled datasets made up of actions and results (e.g., movies chosen and liked) by people who are deemed by the algorithm to be similar to a given user. A large dataset of user choices, calibrated by characteristics of the user and of the decision context, can lead to effective recommendations. This kind of *collaborative filtering algorithm* is used for all kinds of recommendations, including Amazon's shopping engine and Airbnb's matching engine.

Many companies may already have vast troves of algorithm-ready labeled data thanks to their investments in systems, technologies, databases, and heavyweight enterprise resource planning (ERP) installations. For example, most large insurance companies have decades of labeled data relating to property damage and could readily implement supervised machine learning models to reduce both fraud and the time it takes to process and resolve claims— especially if the company is equipped for direct photo uploads or drone-based inspection. Similarly, health-care systems are full of labeled datasets. For example, many companies are taking medical data (such as radiology, cardiology, pathology, and EKG results) and correlating it with health diagnoses. Israel-based Zebra Medical Vision now offers technology to help radiologists make better diagnoses from X-ray, CT, and MRI scans.

Unsupervised Learning

Unlike supervised learning models, which train a system to recognize known outcomes, the primary application of *unsupervised* learning algorithms is to discover insights in data with few preconceptions or assumptions. This is what Netflix does when it discovers related groups of customers in analyzed viewing data, when it creates customer segments for marketing campaigns, or when it creates different versions of the user interface that match different usage patterns. Or think of various national security agencies and law enforcement organizations accumulating huge amounts of social media data to look for abnormal patterns and discern potential security threats. In these cases, one does not know exactly what to look for but is searching for related groups or for events that fit or don't fit established patterns.

Unlike supervised learning algorithms, where the data inputs are labeled with a given outcome, unsupervised learning algorithms aim to find "natural" groupings in the data, without labels, and uncover structures that may not be obvious to the observer. Thus the job of the algorithm is to show patterns in data, with humans (or even other algorithms) labeling the patterns or groups and deciding on potential actions. In our example of photos of cats and dogs, an unsupervised learning algorithm might find several types of groupings. Depending on how the clusters are structured, these groupings could end up separating cats and dogs, or indoor and outdoor photographs, or pictures taken during day or night, or virtually anything else. Again, an unsupervised learning algorithm does not suggest specific labels but rather establishes the most robust statistical groupings. Humans, or other algorithms, do the rest.

Unsupervised learning is useful for gaining insights from social media postings by, say, identifying customer groups and sentiment patterns that can be used to guide product development. Attitudinal and demographic survey responses by customers can be used to create customer segments. The reasons for customer churn could also be categorized through unsupervised learning. In manufacturing settings, one could group instances of machine failure or order delay.

There are three broad types of unsupervised learning. The first relates to algorithms that *cluster* data into groups. A fashion retailer may use this approach to understand how to segment its customers based on the types of products purchased, the pricing and profitability of the items, and the various channels that brought customers to the store. More-sophisticated retailers might have additional data such as social network-based graph data (whom customers are connected to) and their social media postings. All this data then can allow the company to uncover a unique set of segments, well beyond simple demographics.

Netflix microclusters—its taste communities of members with similar movie and series preferences—is a good illustration of the power of such a tool. Cluster analysis in the form of topic modeling is used extensively to find meaning in text-based data and uncover salient topics within and across texts. The technique has been used to analyze news reports, SEC filings, investor calls, customer call center transcripts, or even chat records.

The second broad category is known as *association rule mining*. A common example is the recommendations for additional products an online shopper might want to purchase based on the current set of products in the shopping cart. Amazon has made a science of association rule mining. The algorithms look for frequency and probability of co-occurrence among any set of items and then create associations that are likely to occur between various types of products. Ocado, for example, learned from its data that there was a strong relationship between diapers and beer. New parents don't get to go out much, so recommending beer and wine to shoppers when they are purchasing diapers turned out to be profitable and also increased customer satisfaction.

The third type of unsupervised learning algorithm is *anomaly detection*. Here the algorithm simply looks at each new incoming observation or datum and makes the judgment whether or not it fits prior patterns. If it does not fit the pattern, then the algorithm flags that item as anomalous. This type of application is often used in fraud detection in financial services, health care for a variety of patient data, and maintenance of systems and machines.

Reinforcement Learning

Although they are still relatively underdeveloped, the potential applications of *reinforcement* learning may be even more impactful than those of supervised and unsupervised learning. Rather than start with data on an expert's view of the outcome, as in supervised learning, or with a pattern-and-anomaly recognition system, as in unsupervised learning, reinforcement learning requires only a starting point and a performance function. We start somewhere and probe the space around us, using as a guide whether we have improved or worsened our position. The key trade-off is whether to spend more time *exploring* the complex world around us or *exploiting* the model we have built so far to drive decisions and actions.

Let's say we take a cable car up a tall mountain and we want to find our way down. It's a foggy day, and the mountain does not have any clearly marked paths. Because we can't see the best way down, we have to walk around and explore different options. There is a natural trade-off between the time we spend walking around getting a feel for the mountain, and the time we spend actually walking down when we believe we have found the best path. This is the trade-off between exploration and exploitation. The more time we spend exploring, the more we will be convinced we have the best way down, but if we spend too long exploring, we will have less time to exploit the information and actually walk down.

This is close to the way the Netflix algorithm personalizes movie recommendations and the visuals they are associated with.[13] The problem is a bit more complicated, because the Netflix team needs to figure out which movie selection to present and then which artwork to combine it with to maximize the match between user and recommendation. But in a way similar to our finding our way down the mountain, Netflix spends some time exploring options, and some time exploiting the solution offered by its models. To explore visual options, Netflix systematically randomizes the visuals shown to a user, thereby exploring new possibilities and refining the prediction model. Netflix then exploits the improved model to show the user a slew of recommendations with improved visuals.

The Netflix service continues to improve dynamically by automatically cycling between periods of exploration and exploitation, a process designed to learn the most about the preferences of a complex human being and maximize user engagement over the long term. The writer of the Netflix technology blog asked in a 2017 post, "Given the enormous diversity in taste and preferences, wouldn't it be better if we could find the best artwork for each of our members to highlight the aspects of a title that are specifically relevant to them?"[14]

The Netflix challenge is a fancy variant of a common class of models used in reinforcement learning. Known as the *multiarmed bandit problem*, it is named after imagining a gambler playing different slot machines ("one-armed bandits"), each machine characterized by a different (but unknown) reward distribution. The gambler can spend more time exploring which machine seems to give the best rewards or can focus on exploiting the one machine that seems to be the best bet so far. Any deviation from the optimal path (just cranking on the best machine) is expressed as the *regret* measure. Multiarmed bandit problems are useful in the allocation of finite resources across different processes, each associated with different reward distributions. The general idea is to maximize operating performance by minimizing regret.

Multiarmed bandit problems are vitally important to the deployment of AI in operating models. As we strive to optimize and improve operating performance across processes, managing the trade-off between exploration and exploitation is fundamental. These algorithms are used extensively to manage a variety of operating workflows, from making product recommendations to setting product prices, and from planning clinical trials to selecting digital ads. They can even guide the behavior of actual agents in imagined or real worlds, from the path of Nintendo's Mario Kart video game to the bots in Ocado's warehouses. In essence, multiarmed bandits are set up to make real operating decisions while they optimize the trade-offs between short-term impact and long-term improvement.

Reinforcement learning has captured public attention thanks to a software system called AlphaGo. Created by Google's Deep-Mind AI research team, AlphaGo has started to beat master players around the world at the ancient Chinese strategy game Go. Although computers have beaten humans at chess (remember Deep Blue by IBM), Go was thought to be too complicated for any program to master it. However, starting in 2016, this started to change as top Go masters kept losing to AlphaGo. These results were stunning—so much so that Kai-Fu Lee, an eminent computer scientist and technology investor, noted in his book *AI Superpowers* that the Chinese government declared its own "Sputnik moment" and made achieving world-class leadership in AI a national priority, with tremendous resources dedicated to achieving this goal.

That was before AlphaGo Zero came on to the scene and started beating AlphaGo at its own game. AlphaGo Zero uses the reinforcement learning approach: unlike prior versions of AlphaGo, wherein data from hundreds of thousands of games was used as input, the AlphaGo Zero system was essentially given the rules of the game and then asked to figure out the best approaches (the "Zero" stands for no external data). Reinforcement learning works by having a software agent interact with the environment and take actions within it to maximize a predefined reward. By giving the rules of the game or environment to the agent, the software system can quickly learn to maximize rewards and achieve superior performance. Google's DeepMind team has applied the lessons from Go to drug discovery and protein folding and has found that its system performs considerably better than the best scientists and their approaches.

The Experimentation Platform

To be reliably impactful, the wealth of predictions generated by data and algorithms in an AI factory requires careful validation. Google runs more than one hundred thousand experiments each year to test a vast variety of potential data-driven improvements to its service. LinkedIn reportedly runs more than forty thousand experiments each year. The experimentation capacity required by digital operating models is such that traditional, ad hoc approaches to experimentation simply cannot handle the scale and impact of what is required. A state-of-the-art experimentation platform will provide the comprehensive set of technologies, tools, and methods required to do experimentation at scale.

To use an experimentation platform, potential significant changes to the business must first be formalized as a hypothesis. Each hypothesis is then typically tested as a *randomized control trial* (also known as an A/B test) in which a random sample of users is exposed to the change (known as a *treatment*) and a second random sample of users experience business as usual (the *control*). The outcomes are then compared, and if the difference between them is statistically significant the treatment is known to actually impact the outcome, instead of just being spuriously correlated. This approach ensures that any prediction being generated by algorithms actually has a *causal* effect on the outcome.

The experimentation platform is a necessary component of the AI factory. Imagine running our algorithm to predict customer churn and learning that churn correlates with a certain age group. We still do not know whether customers in that age group are more likely to churn in general, or whether they would respond positively to some kind of special offer and continue to use our service. Before offering an expensive rebate to millions of customers, it would make sense to try an A/B test on a small fraction of users and gather statistically significant evidence on what portion of customers would remain with our service *because of* that specific offer. The same kind of logic applies to a great variety of potential business improvements recommended by an AI factory at scale.

Netflix engineers and data scientists have built an extensive experimentation platform that is fully integrated within its algorithm development and execution process.[15] Every significant product change at Netflix goes through A/B testing before it becomes a standard part of the product experience. The experimentation platform is also utilized to improve video streaming and content delivery network algorithms (the service supports hundreds of devices and a vast range of bandwidth conditions) as well as image selection, user interface changes, email campaigns, playback, and registration.

Indeed, the company tries to bring scientific rigor to all of its decision making by embracing experimentation as an integral component. The fully automated experimentation platform enables Netflix employees to run experiments at scale. The platform allows them to kick off the experiment, ensures there are no other blocking experiments or overlapping subject pools, recruits subjects from its audience, and creates reports to analyze and visualize results both during and after the experiments are completed.

Software, Connectivity, and Infrastructure

The data pipeline, the algorithm design and execution engine, and the experimentation platform should all be embedded in software infrastructure to drive the operating activities of the digital firm.

Figure 3-3 depicts an example of a state-of-the-art data platform powering an AI factory, with data flowing from bottom to top. The data platform provides a structure for software developers to build, deploy, and execute AI applications. The basic idea behind the pipeline is a *publish-subscribe* methodology for APIs (application programing interfaces). The purpose is to make clean, consistent data available to applications; think of it as something like a data supermarket.

After the data is aggregated, cleaned, refined, and processed, it is made available through consistent interfaces (the APIs), allowing applications to rapidly subscribe, sample what they need, test, and deploy. All this lets an agile development team build a new application in weeks, sometimes even days. Without these assets, a traditional IT custom-built process takes orders of magnitude more time and cost and becomes a nightmare to maintain and update. And in becoming an AI-driven company like Netflix, the idea is not to build one AI application. Rather, the idea is to build thousands,

FIGURE 3-3

A state-of-the-art data platform

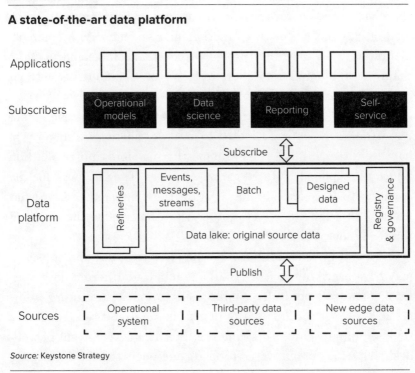

Source: Keystone Strategy

of them—indeed enough to help make as many different types of predictions as possible.

Concurrent with investments in data and software are strategic investments in connectivity and infrastructure to integrate with the data platform. As we discuss in detail in the next chapter, most enterprises, even today, operate in separate silos. Even though customers view the enterprise as a unified entity, internally the systems and data across units and functions are typically fragmented, thereby preventing the aggregation of data, delaying insight generation, and making it impossible to leverage the power of analytics and AI.

Data platforms, and the organizations that work with them, should avoid siloed structures and instead should be designed in a modular fashion. The design of interfaces is critical in ensuring modularity in both code and organization. Clear interfaces therefore allow for decentralized innovation at the module level; as long as there is a standard for the sharing of data and functionality, each module can improve its core function independently. APIs compartmentalize the innovation problem and enable independent agile teams or individual developers to focus on specific tasks without destroying the consistency of the whole.

Building a consistent (and secure!) data platform is even more important if the data is exposed to external partners. Taobao, Alibaba's online mall, is a good example, listing more than one billion items, all supplied by third-party providers. The only way for the company to satisfactorily share data with its internal and external users is through clear and secure APIs that enable the required range of functionality.

A typical internal Alibaba developer or external Taobao seller may be subscribing to more than one hundred different data platform software modules to enable them to upload inventory information, set pricing (manually or automatically), track consumer reviews, handle shipments, and the like. The development of well-designed APIs not only frees Taobao's engineers to keep developing and advancing internal systems to serve billions of users and millions of merchants but also unleashes creativity by an ecosystem of software vendors to offer a wealth of additional services.[16]

Finally, building a state-of-the-art AI factory with a well-designed data platform improves the organization's ability to focus on the crucial challenges of data governance and security. The massive amount of data that is increasingly captured from users, suppliers, partners, and employees is extremely valuable, sensitive, and private. It simply should not be stored in an ad hoc fashion. An organization needs to build a secure, centralized system for careful data security and governance, defining appropriate checks and balances on access and usage, inventorying the assets carefully, and providing all stakeholders with the necessary protection.

As part of the essential data governance challenge, carefully defining clear and secure APIs is essential to the AI factory. After all, APIs throttle the flow of data in and out of AI factory systems. Think of it as a way for the company to control all the data and functionality that it is willing to offer to internal and to external developers. As such, APIs control access to some of the most critical and private assets within the organization. They force the company to define, ahead of time, which of these critical assets it wants to make available within the enterprise and which it may be willing to offer to anyone outside the company. The data that can flow through an API can make or break a digital company. The Cambridge Analytica scandal happened because developer and manager errors apparently caused a critical hole in the Facebook platform's graph API, allowing external application developers to access much more data than may have been originally intended by the company.

Ultimately, the data, software, and connectivity underlying an AI factory must reside within a secure, robust, and scalable computational infrastructure. Increasingly this infrastructure is on the cloud, is scalable on demand, and is built using standard off-the-shelf components and open source software. In addition, it needs to be seamlessly connected to the many individual processes and activities that constitute the company's operating model. Ultimately, these are the core digital processes that shape the delivery of value, such as creating, recommending, selecting, and delivering Netflix content, billing Netflix customers, or tracking the performance of Netflix content partners.

Building an AI Factory

You don't have to be Netflix to build an AI factory. The Laboratory of Innovation Science at Harvard (LISH), where we are faculty directors, in collaboration with colleagues from Harvard Medical School and the Dana-Farber Cancer Institute, demonstrated the development of an AI system that maps the shape of lung cancer tumors based on CT image scans. Deployed in only ten weeks and on an academic budget, the system is as good as a Harvard-trained radiation oncologist.

To develop the system, we leveraged the LISH AI factory, itself built to create a data pipeline and platform architecture for solving a variety of problems, usually with the help of crowdsourced algorithm design contests on Topcoder. LISH has partnered with leading organizations like NASA, Harvard Medical School hospitals, Broad Institute of Harvard and MIT, and Scripps Research to take some of their toughest computational and prediction challenges.

Outlining a lung cancer is critical in developing an effective therapy for patients. Oncologists therefore spend much time mapping the exact volumetric shape of any tumor that is to receive radiation therapy. Correctly outlining the tumor is particularly critical so that the therapy does not miss cancer cells or damage healthy tissue. The LISH team worked with Raymond Mak, from the Dana-Farber Cancer Institute, on the possibility of automating this task, leveraging data from 461 patients consisting of more than 77,000 CT image slices.

Using Dr. Mak's data, cleaned and prepared by our lab-based AI factory, two data scientists (physicists with no background in medical imaging) designed a series of contests to find the best algorithm to outline a tumor. We embarked on three sequential contests over ten weeks and had thirty four contestants submit forty-five algorithms. We gave our contestants a "training" dataset consisting of scans from 229 patients, with the cancer fully outlined across the images by Mak. We held back the remaining dataset to see how accurate the algorithms would be in mimicking Mak's work.

The top five contestants used a variety of approaches, including convolutional neural networks (CNNs) and random forest algorithms. Surprisingly, none of our contest participants had any prior experience with medical imaging or cancer diagnostics. The solutions they developed involved both custom and published architectures and frameworks to perform the tasks of object detection and localization, with open source algorithms originally developed for facial detection, biomedical image segmentation, and road scene segmentation for research on autonomous vehicles. The phase 3 algorithms produced segmentations at rates between fifteen seconds and two minutes per scan—substantially faster than a human expert, who took eight minutes per scan. The ensemble of the five best algorithms performed as well as a human radiation oncologist (interobserver), and better than existing commercial software, as shown in figure 3-4.

FIGURE 3-4

Results of LISH analysis contest using data from the Dana-Farber Cancer Institute

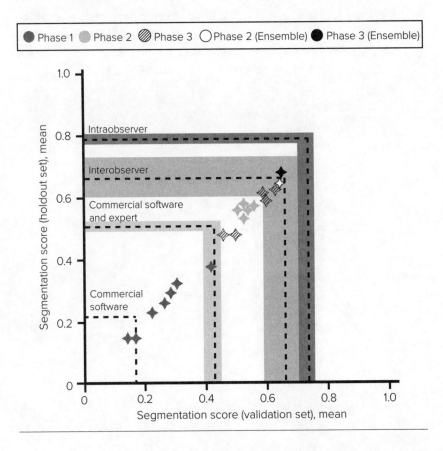

We cite this example not only because we're proud of it but also to demonstrate that an organization doesn't have to be rich in data, IT resources, or AI talent to construct an AI factory. To create ours we tapped resources that are available to everyone. And the benefit we got from it is invaluable. We shared our findings in the *Journal of the American Medical Association Oncology*—not where you'd expect to find the work of business school faculty.[17]

We admit that it's relatively easy to tap the power of AI within a small laboratory. We did not have to deal with large, siloed organizations or complex, outdated, and mismatched IT systems. As AI enables more of the operating processes in complex corporations, the way it is embedded and architected in the broader operating model becomes increasingly critical. This is why a firm's operating architecture has become a strategic consideration that should be thought through at the most senior levels. This is the topic of the next chapter.

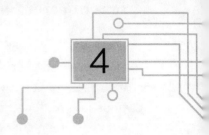

4

Rearchitecting the Firm

In 2002, when Amazon's CEO wrote this email, the online retailer had hit a wall.[1] The company was having trouble supporting its own growth. Its processes were breaking down as the software infrastructure powering Amazon's operations was cracking under pressure. Too much volume, too many products, too many different businesses—books, office supplies, electronics, apparel—were being sold on a network largely cobbled together through acquisitions and only weakly connected by a common home page. Without consistency in technology or data architecture, and without a consistent view of the customer, Amazon was coming apart at the seams.

The Bezos memo is one of the seminal documents in the digital transformation of business. In the preceding chapters, we highlight the birth and growth of a new breed of firm. The twenty-first-century firm is not only about leveraging the internet, or implementing mobile technology, or being a "digital native." Plenty of recently founded, software-intensive firms are built in the wrong way. Rather, it's about being architected differently, about being built on fundamentally different business and operating foundations.

Rather than rest on a traditional organizational model and operate through a variety of specialized and siloed organizational processes, digital firms rest on an integrated, highly modular digital foundation. Information technology is no longer merely an enabler and optimizer of traditional processes and methods; instead, software makes up the actual operating core of the firm. Replacing traditional labor- and asset-intensive organizations, fueled by a pipeline of data and powered by algorithms, software constitutes the critical path in delivering value to the firm's customers. And because of these digital foundations, the firm is capable of generating increasing returns to scale, scope, and learning—and of overwhelming traditional business models.

Even the most advanced AI factory in the world will not deliver the promised value if it is not embedded in an operating model that leverages its strengths. Bezos's intuition on this front was remarkable. In our language, he saw that the key to Amazon's sustainable growth lay in transforming its *operating architecture*, which defines the boundaries and linkages between the components of the operating model. He understood that a digital firm requires a different kind of operating model—one that is architected to take an integrated core of software, data, and AI and use it to power a new breed of organization.

To unpack the importance of the Bezos memo and its implications for the modern design of firms, we next take a bit of a detour into the history of operating models and their relationship to the architecture of organizations and technology.

Bezos and the Mirroring Hypothesis

One of the more intriguing fields of management study focuses on the relationship between the structure of an organization and the architecture of the technological systems that the organization works with. In short, the organization reflects the system, and the system reflects the organization. This simple observation carries important implications for the evolution of firms.

In 1967, a computer scientist named Melvin Conway noted that an organization is constrained to design systems that reflect the communication patterns prevalent in the organization.[2] Conway's law is based on the reasoning (supported by abundant empirical evidence) that for an integrated technology component to be designed properly, its designers must communicate frequently. Thus, it's now generally accepted that interrelated tasks are best performed by integrated teams, ideally located within a few feet of each other.[3] This is why software development projects are organized into agile feature teams rather than functional teams, and why manufacturing plants, and even financial and professional services, are organized into departments performing related tasks.

This framework is summarized as the *mirroring hypothesis*, which states that "organizational ties within a project, firm, or group of firms . . . will correspond to the technical patterns of dependency in the work being performed."[4] Well beyond design tasks, the architecture of systems mirrors the architecture of the organizations that depend on them.

These mutually reinforcing connections can become a significant asset for a firm, enhancing both quality and efficiency in the execution of work. As organizations perform similar tasks—say, designing and producing car door handles for various models and generations of vehicles—they develop productive ways of performing work. These techniques, embedded in technology, processes, and routines, enable organizations to build uniqueness and distinctiveness over time. After many years of dedicated practice, Toyota's production system (TPS) is embedded in the organization. Reinforced by incentive and performance measurement systems, these patterns serve to improve the performance of daily activities.

While making similar tasks increasingly efficient over time, these patterns can also constrain an organization, building inertia that hampers the response to change. Our Harvard colleagues Rebecca Henderson and Kim Clark argued in a 1990 paper that architectural innovations—ones that require changing the architecture between technological components—are a particular danger for established firms.[5] Their insights are relevant to many examples, including RCA's failure to rearchitect and miniaturize its tabletop radios and music devices even in the face of competition from Sony (which licensed RCA's technology!). Other examples include IBM's failure to transition from mainframe to PC, and Microsoft's failure to rearchitect PCs into smartphones. The concept of architectural inertia—the resistance to adaptation—in turn informs Clayton Christensen's disruption theory.[6] According to disruption theory, it is the architectural inertia established by the links with existing customers that prevents an organization from responding effectively to disruptive change.[7]

The bottom line in many of these perspectives and theories is similar: as organizations become good at doing something in a certain way, they develop routines and systems that reinforce each other and make it difficult to do things differently. Architectural inertia thus makes it difficult to achieve transformations that require organizing work in new ways.

Critically, architectural inertia is woven into the story of enterprise information technology over the past three or four decades. Enterprise IT has been largely deployed along traditional operating and organizational boundaries. We have general ledger systems, marketing "automation" software, customer relationship management software, product life cycle management, and enterprise resource planning, each fitting neatly into the established components of a traditional firm. Although improving efficiency on the margin, this componentization has limited the systemic impact of information technology and has constrained the scale, scope, and learning potential of the traditional firm.

In writing such a clear and provocative memo, Bezos was trying to break architectural inertia and change the architecture not only of Amazon's technology but also of Amazon's organization. Bezos was determined to transform Amazon's operating architecture and build the foundations for a software-, data-, and AI-driven firm.

Before exploring the new model, let's take a quick step back to understand the historical roots of operating models and see why traditional operating architectures look the way they do and are as entrenched as they are.

The Historical View

Long before we had information technology, firms evolved into siloed operating architectures consisting of specialized, largely autonomous functions and operating units. Dating back to at least the Italian Renaissance, operating models managed operational complexity by breaking an organization into smaller, separate units, each focused on an individual task and discipline.[8] Each unit was given a large degree of independence to maximize flexibility and minimize the load on the (excruciatingly slow) lines of communication.

One of the earliest known examples of distributed commercial operating architecture dates back to the fifteenth century. In Prato, Italy, the wool and textile trades distributed operations across many specialized production, distribution, banking, and insurance facilities.[9] This operating model functioned as a loosely connected ensemble of specialized organizations. In some cases, the relationships between organizations were established by family ties. In other cases, they were structured more formally, with joint ownership of assets among business partners, effectively creating holding companies with a multifunctional structure. These "primitive" organizations evolved a highly effective operating model and developed leading positions in Europe.

The First Firms

The first modern corporation may have been the Dutch East India Company, founded in 1602. From its inception as the consolidation of seven rival trading companies, the company achieved economies of scale by integrating various shipping portfolios and managing the considerable risk involved in individual voyages. But to manage its extensive operations, the company evolved into a multi-unit structure. By subdividing the organization into a number of specialized, geographically separate, and largely autonomous units, the company managed multinational, multidiscipline operations without drowning in communication delays and managerial complexity. Its siloed operating architecture and flexible managerial approaches worked well to accommodate the requirements of its dispersed geographic locations.

The company grew into an economic powerhouse, first monopolizing trade in spices like nutmeg, mace, and cloves from ports across Asia and Africa, and subsequently moving into silk, cotton, porcelain, and textiles. By 1670, the company was possibly the richest the world had ever seen, deploying almost two hundred ships and employing more than fifty thousand people (along with a relatively large private army) to make up a complex operating model that came to dominate global trade.[10]

Although trade and financial services continued to become more sophisticated through the seventeenth and eighteenth centuries, manufacturing processes did not evolve very much. Traditional craft methods, also known as "filing and fitting," relied on expert crafters working on one artifact at a time, producing all components and making each adjustment by hand—"filing" each part so that it would "fit" into the assembly.

The Rise of Mass Production

The Industrial Revolution transformed production techniques. From England to the United States, the emergence of mass production drove a wave of specialization and standardization. Unlike filing and fitting methods, mass production meant that each worker focused on a single component or a single stage of the production process. In this way, operating models could benefit from specialization and repetition to increase the advantage of scale and the speed of learning. This approach led to specialization within the organization by the nature or discipline of work, something that further subdivided the operating architecture of corporations.

The true icon of mass production and industrialization is found in the automotive industry—most of all, in the Ford Motor Company. Henry Ford founded the carmaker in 1903 in Dearborn, Michigan, with $28,000 in cash from twelve investors. Ford's vision was to make automobile transportation practical, affordable, and accessible to the average person. Ford sensed an opportunity to design and produce a car that could be sold at a price that met the potentially vast demand of middle-class customers.

With its introduction in 1908, the Model T (affectionately called the Tin Lizzie) was explicitly designed for mass production. Efficient, durable, reliable, and easily maintained, it was generally considered the first automobile within reach of most American consumers. Overwhelmed by the demand for its new car, Ford had to find a new way to deliver value.

Ford introduced the first moving chassis assembly line at the Highland Park Plant in 1913 and transformed manufacturing. Traditionally, cars had been assembled in fixed stalls, with workers coming to each vehicle to deliver and mount the required components. On the assembly line, vehicles would move through a series of stationary workers, with each worker performing highly specialized, increasingly narrow assembly tasks. With the help of the legendary Frederick Taylor, the Ford assembly line cut the Model T assembly time by a factor of 10, a change that in turn dramatically reduced costs. Prices came down by more than a factor of 2, and by 1918 half of all cars in America were Model Ts.

Ford had become the largest manufacturer in the United States by deploying unprecedented levels of standardization and specialization. Its operating model broke down functional specialties and associated organizational silos to the smallest, most specialized, standardized human tasks.

Twentieth-Century Operating Models

Ford's operating model led the automotive industry for decades. Over time, General Motors started to win share from Ford by offering a much broader range of cars at a broader range of prices. To increase the scope of offerings delivered by its operating architecture, General Motors created dedicated organizational units— among them Chevrolet, Buick, GMC, and Cadillac—each focused on a different product line with its own specialized assembly lines. These largely autonomous product units enabled GM to focus on the specific needs of different customer segments.[11] Now organizational silos were broken down not only by narrowly defined function but also by product.

The GM model reigned supreme through the 1950s and 1960s, until a new generation of competitors, many from Japan, introduced more efficient and higher-quality cars. Their success emerged from additional refinements in the design of operating models and operating architecture. The Toyota TPS operating model added a dedication to learning and problem solving at all levels of the organization. Toyota's model pushed back on traditional narrow specialization common in the industry, but it was notoriously difficult for others to imitate it and deploy it successfully. This remained true even when Toyota fully opened its factory floors to outsiders, wrote many books about the process, and undertook joint ventures with other auto companies.

Beyond the automotive sector, mass production took off rapidly in the twentieth century in most other manufacturing industries in the United States and Europe. As workers and organizations specialized, and as production generated more output, manufacturing operating models enjoyed increasing economies of scale, with efficiencies (and quality, as specialization improved the work) greatly increasing with the volume of the operation. Additionally, the production volumes enabled learning, further increasing production efficiencies. These economies virtually wiped out traditional crafts in a broad range of manufacturing and service industries, from weapons to textiles and from agriculture to insurance.

Over time, mass production concepts like specialization, focus, and standardization also spread widely across the service industries. Notably, the growth of supermarkets relied on significant process standardization as well as economies of scale in purchasing and delivery, and fast food franchises like McDonald's relied on highly repeatable work and scale efficiencies in both supply chain and food preparation. Specialization and standardization led to efficiencies in hotel chains and banks, energy companies and insurance providers, hospitals and airlines.

Highly specialized, siloed operating models remain essential in manufacturing and service delivery today. Take the iPhone, assembled in China by Foxconn Technology Group. Foxconn's facilities in Zhengzhou cover 2.2 square miles and can employ up to 350,000 workers, whose work is narrowly specialized, meticulously specified, and highly optimized. There are ninety-four production lines, and it takes about four hundred steps to assemble the iPhone, including polishing, soldering, drilling, and fitting screws. The facility can produce more than 500,000 iPhones a day, or roughly 350 a minute. Although modern manufacturing lines like these are enabled by information technology—tracking parts and products, analyzing problems, or enabling robotic assembly—modern operating models still drive scale by designing standard, repeatable work in both product and process development.

We emphasize, again, that the deployment of enterprise IT did not transform the trajectory of operating models. During several waves of adoption—from the mainframes of the 1960s and 1970s, to the client-server models that took off in the 1980s, to early internet-based systems deployed in the 1990s—IT systems such as Oracle financials and SAP product life cycle management improved the performance of many traditional operating processes; but these IT systems generally mirrored the firm's siloed and specialized architecture. Although often improving efficiency and responsiveness and driving additional economies of scale, scope, and learning across operating units, technology did not change the structure of the enterprise.

FIGURE 4-1

Siloed architecture

In company after company, processes, software applications, and data are still embedded in individual, largely autonomous and siloed organizational units (as sketched in figure 4-1). As we look across most major enterprises, we see that IT—and, most critically, data—are most often gathered in a distributed and inconsistent fashion, separated and isolated by existing organizational subdivisions and by generations of highly specialized and often incompatible legacy technology. Large firms often use thousands of enterprise applications and IT systems, working with a variety of scattered databases and supporting diverse data models and structures. Integrating data across different functional silos (without rearchitecting the entire system) is a long, horrifically complicated, unreliable process, requiring significant dedicated investment and extensive custom code. It's no wonder that many such projects are plagued by painful delays and cost overruns.

Traditional Operating Limits

From the East India Company to GM to McDonald's, operating models reinforced autonomy and specialization and led to new levels of productivity and innovation. In each case, there is evidence of great success. However, there is also clear evidence of limits, as the complexity of expanding operations eventually outpaced the capacity of every organization and opened opportunities for competition. Traditional operating architecture created serious constraints to firm growth and value. Ford's mass production methods ran into problems when confronted by General Motors' product variety and differentiation and Toyota's process improvement and quality mindset. Even the Toyota production system had a hard time handling rapid growth and increasing complexity, as demonstrated by its many product recalls during the mid-2000s.[12] Ultimately, as traditional organizations grow, they suffer *dis*economies of scale, scope, and learning.

When organizations expand, they become increasingly complex and difficult to manage, so they build bureaucracies and inefficiencies, and they embed norms, incentives, and rewards—and each of these fosters inertia. With too much scale, too much scope (variety), or too much demand for learning and innovation, any managerial process will eventually stop working well, leading to inefficiency and even failure. Plants reach an optimal size and then become unwieldy to organize and manage. Restaurants reach a maximum size and scope, as their customers and menus begin to overwhelm the staff's capabilities and systems. Even R&D organizations and product development teams can grow too big, and their productivity and innovativeness are known to suffer as a result. These considerations shape the maximum efficient scale of an organization and impose overall limits to its growth.

Notably, traditional information technology has not significantly loosened these constraints. As a traditional enterprise creates ever more functional silos, it deploys a myriad of IT systems, from CRM to general ledger software, each meeting the demands of the specific function to which it is assigned. Integrating and aggregating various applications and connecting potentially valuable data is a long and painful endeavor, as disparate disconnected legacy systems need to be carefully pieced together through custom software, which, over time, will itself cause its own inertia and resistance to change.

In a nutshell, firms are shaped and limited by their operating models. These models help manage complexity and growth—but only up to a point. Traditional functional structures and operating silos have also caused firms to hit limits and diminishing returns to scale, scope, and learning. Despite several generations of widespread improvements in management and operations, and even despite the

FIGURE 4-2

A traditional organization's ability to deliver value faces a curve of diminishing returns

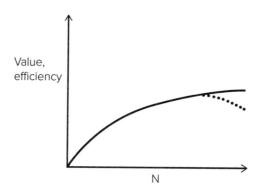

N is a parameter that stands for a variety of variables, such as the number of users or the number of complementors on a platform.

extensive deployment of enterprise IT, the complexity of operating models has constrained the value that can be delivered by the traditional firm, as depicted in figure 4-2.

A Critical, Difficult Transition

Before Bezos wrote his memo, Amazon was starting to look like a traditional firm. Its organization, data, and technology had evolved into silos, with disparate retail focus areas largely contained in separate, disconnected units. Connections between silos were haphazard and often unpredictable, motivated by meeting immediate needs and fighting fires. Amazon was dealing with limits on the scalability and scope of its business. It needed a major architectural change.

Bezos knew well that in the software business, working with multiple versions of the same code is a nightmare. Also, scattering data across systems and functions prevents aggregation, destroys the integrity of any data pipeline, and hampers the development of a comprehensive view of the customer. His brilliant insight was that while supporting traditional operating tasks (e.g., supply chain, retail op-

FIGURE 4-3

An Amazon time line

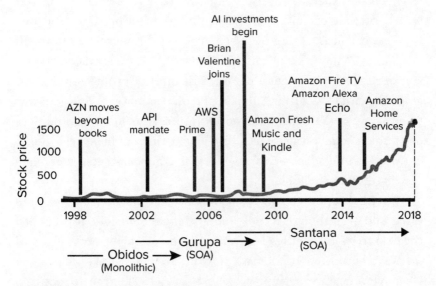

The curve depicts the Amazon stock price. Obidos, Gurupa, and Santana are the systems Amazon built to enable its operating capability and to meet its scale, scope, and learning objectives.

erations) Amazon could rearchitect those tasks, starting with the software. His vision was to build the best software- and data-driven operating model in order to expand his retail operations to unprecedented levels of scale, scope, and learning. But he also realized that to scale a software- and data-driven organization, he had to break organizational and technological silos. Figure 4-3 traces the progress of the transformation.

Bezos sought to rearchitect Amazon's technology and organization at the same time. Recognizing that software capabilities were now sophisticated enough to run significant parts of Amazon's operating model, Bezos rebuilt Amazon's retail operation on top of a software platform, which gradually evolved to embed a state-of-the-art AI factory. The organization was simultaneously transformed according to the new architectural boundaries, with emphasis on the broad deployment of agile teams working within clearly established interfaces.

Starting in the early 2000s, Amazon's transformation produced as many challenges as successes. When the first platform redesign did not meet expectations, the company brought in Brian Valentine, then a software executive at Microsoft. Valentine brought deep platform experience, having overseen successful releases of Microsoft Exchange, Windows 2000, and Windows XP. It is significant that a software platform leader—not a traditional IT professional—was charged with rebuilding Amazon's IT infrastructure. The goal was to go from siloed, disconnected IT into a true software and data platform, a common set of building blocks that could be deployed to drive scale and scope economies across Amazon's rapidly expanding roster of businesses.

The third version of the Amazon platform was code-named Santana, and even though it took a long time to complete, it propelled the firm to its current leadership position. Valentine created a real software platform, with a central, standardized set of services and clear APIs for interacting with those services. This shift required Amazon to rewrite virtually all of its e-commerce services, and the new platform, while vastly superior, took longer to build and implement than originally expected.[13]

With the redesign of its retail platform, Amazon's development organization evolved into a modular, distributed structure. Sharing a common foundation in the Santana technology, "two-pizza" agile teams (to cut down on pointless meetings, Bezos decreed that they never be so big that two pizzas wouldn't feed the entire group) can work independently while respecting clear architectural rules that enable teams to share common code and aggregate data across applications. The Amazon structure thus preserves common foundations and, crucially, aggregates the data that fuels machine learning and artificial intelligence, all while preserving the agility of small teams.

Santana enabled Bezos to get to the next stage and rapidly build data pipelines and a slew of world-class AI applications. From its recommendation engine to Amazon Echo and Alexa, the company has become a powerhouse in deploying AI across its enterprise. Although Amazon never led the pack in basic AI research (Google and Microsoft were ahead), the company has become expert in deploying the latest advances across all aspects of its business and deriving enormous operational impact.

Amazon's not-so-secret secret weapon on the AI front is its cloud services division, Amazon Web Services (AWS). Serving a million-plus customers, AWS has a mission to democratize access to information services, including compute, storage, and database, and the AI toolkit is heading in the same direction. In 2015, AWS began offering Amazon machine learning to its customers and quickly used innovations from Alexa to offer voice recognition, text-to-speech services, and a natural language processing interface.

In no time, its customers—large organizations like NASA and Pinterest, along with multitudes of startups—started to deploy AI tools on their own problems and made advances across the board. The company is now offering SageMaker, a software toolkit that enables its customers to go from data to insights by using prepackaged Amazon-developed systems, algorithms, and tools. The scope of the AI reinvention is so broad that Amazon's own internal machine learning conference has gone from hundreds of attendees to many thousands and is on track to become the largest internal company event.

The Amazon transition in operating architecture was among the first in a much broader trend across the economy. From Ant Financial to Google, a generation of AI-driven firms is being designed with this kind of operating model, driving scale, scope, and learning by aggregating software, data, and analytics and driving agile teams to focus on specific applications across the organization. These operating models depart radically from hundreds of years of corporate evolution and exhibit a profoundly different architecture, posing an existential threat to traditional firms.

Architecture for an AI-Powered Firm

How do you construct an organization founded on code instead of human labor? We must first remember that unlike humans, a digital system (let's call it a digital "agent") can communicate at zero marginal cost with a virtually infinite number of other digital agents performing similar tasks, anywhere in the world. Moreover, the same digital agent can be easily connected to the complementary activities of many other agents, providing a huge number of potential combinations. Finally, digital agents can embed processing instructions—algorithms that not only can execute logic but also might learn and improve themselves—as they process data.

Digital agents may not (yet) be as smart or as creative as humans. However, unlike humans, digital agents have no need of autonomy or isolation to reduce perceived complexity or scale, or to limit the variety of interactions. As long as digital systems use a well-designed, common interface they can connect and combine capabilities, dramatically enriching the range of possibilities.

We are not talking about a few connections but potentially a limitless set. Think of the World Wide Web, connecting untold numbers of websites through an extremely flexible and general set of networks and interfaces. Many of the websites interact frequently with each other, in ways their original designers never dreamed of. Similarly, the iOS and Android platforms connect millions of disparate apps and services, from health and fitness to financial services. The aggregate functionality they deliver is virtually boundless. Digital operating architectures thus have little need of isolated functional silos or hard separations between individual subunits. They instead benefit from unlimited connectivity and data aggregation, driving increasingly powerful analytics.

With a digital operating model, the organization should be designed to unleash the potential of the digital technology it is built on, as shown in figure 4-4. This means creating a foundation (or platform) encompassing data and technology, a platform that can be deployed easily and rapidly to create or connect to new digital agents in the form of applications that address any of a broad variety of use cases.

The ideal is to have a common foundation of data inputs, software technology, and algorithms, all provided by an AI factory, as described in chapter 3. This foundation provides easily accessible (but carefully designed and secure) interfaces that teams developing individual applications can use. The applications connect the foundation to enable operating tasks, from customer relationship

FIGURE 4-4

Operating architecture for an AI-powered firm

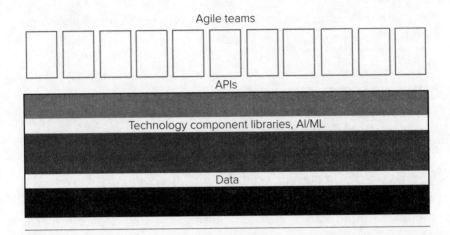

management to supply chains. The process used to develop these applications is driven by small, agile teams equipped with data science, engineering, and product management capabilities. Agile processes and digital operating architectures go hand in hand.

Modern operating models are also characterized by a relentless focus on improving performance through learning. Although some of that learning happens in real time—for example, as data fine-tunes algorithms for suggestions and pricing—much learning also happens on dedicated experimentation platforms, as described in chapter 3. Every day, employees might engage in hundreds, or even thousands, of A/B tests or randomized controlled trials to understand how various tweaks to the service prompt action by consumers, increase satisfaction, and ultimately lead to more revenue. While the data is centralized, the company's experimentation capability is highly decentralized; almost anyone with a hypothesis can launch a live experiment and use the results to implement meaningful changes.

Finally, digital operating models should promote modularity and reuse of the software and algorithms that are developed to perform various operating tasks. This requires adopting consistent frameworks for building functionality, such as React for user interfaces or Apache Storm for data processing. Interestingly, much of the software can be drawn from (and contributed to) the open domain, because the competitive advantage will move to the data that is accumulated by the firm. With this new breed of firm, we go from a focus on proprietary technologies and software to an emphasis on shared development and open source.

Breaking Traditional Constraints

In a digital operating model, the employees do not deliver the product or service; instead, they design and oversee a software-automated, algorithm-driven digital "organization" that actually delivers the goods. This transforms the growth process by removing the traditional operating bottlenecks constraining the scale, scope, and learning potential of a firm.

Removing human interaction from the critical path has a crucial impact on the operating model. The marginal cost of serving an additional user by digital agents becomes negligible, transforming the process of increasing capacity and making it much easier to scale. Furthermore, much of the operational complexity is solved through software and analytics or is outsourced to the external nodes of the firm's operating network. Algorithm-driven operating models are thus almost infinitely scalable, as long as you can continue to add computing and storage capacity to the technology infrastructure (which is now predominantly cloud based and available on demand) and add data to the AI factory pipeline.

Digital technologies are also intrinsically modular and can easily enable many more business connections. When fully digitized, a process can readily plug in to an external network of partners and providers or even into external communities of individuals to provide additional, complementary value. Digitized processes are thus intrinsically multisided and can greatly increase the scope of the operation. After value is delivered in one domain (e.g., accumulating data about a set of consumers), that same process can be connected to drive value in other applications, adding a multiplicative factor to the number of services and overall value it's delivering to the customer. This is how Ant Financial and Amazon work.

The value created by a digital operating model can also grow rapidly as learning effects lead to increasing returns to scale. This is where analytics and AI can shine. AI and ML thrive on data, and as machine learning models have evolved, the amount of data they can learn from has increased quickly. As they accumulate data by increasing scale (or even scope), the algorithms get better and the business creates greater value, something that enables more usage and thus the generation of even more data. The impact of machine learning on digitally enabled businesses, such as Amazon Echo or the Facebook ad network, effectively turbocharges the way a business delivers value to its users.

Finally, this new breed of organization transforms the role of management. Management as supervision, especially of employees performing routine tasks, is finally over. In an AI-powered operating model, managers are designers, shaping, improving and (hopefully) controlling the digital systems that sense customer needs and respond by delivering value. Managers are innovators, as they envision how these digital systems will need to evolve over time. Managers are integrators, as they work to connect disparate digital systems and identify new connections between the firm's operating model and the customers it serves. And managers are guardians, as they work to preserve the quality, reliability, security, and responsibility of the digital systems they control. Digital, AI-centered operating models challenge virtually every traditional managerial and operational assumption, forcing us to fundamentally rethink the nature of firms and of their management teams, their ability to grow, and the constraints on their impact and power.

But despite the massive business potential of the data-centric operating architectures driving AI-powered firms, many traditional firms hesitate. Their impulse is to protect capabilities, routines, and organizational boundaries, sometimes built over decades. They either do not see their architectural problem or are not willing to fully commit to the organizational transformation that is required to solve it. Frankly, the technology is the easy part. As many others have noted, organizational change is really hard.

The next chapter examines what it takes to become an AI company.

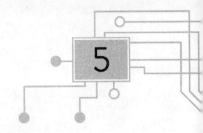

Becoming an AI Company

Balance conviction with patience.

—Satya Nadella

It was early evening on February 9, 2011, and Satya Nadella was just coming to the end of his first day running Microsoft's Server and Tools group. As it happened, one of us (Marco) was walking by Nadella's office with friend and colleague Greg Richards, who had just led a key meeting with a group of Server and Tools product managers.[1] They thought they might stop by and say hi. When they peeked into his office, Nadella waved them in.

The three of them got into a discussion of the future of the business. At that moment, Server and Tools had more than $15 billion in revenue, almost all of it from two products: Windows Server and SQL Server, both traditional, "on-premise" software. The question was, How big a bet would Nadella place on Azure—Microsoft's cloud service—which at that point had been on the market for two years but was widely considered an abject failure. Greg and Marco were skeptical. But Nadella was filled with conviction: "The cloud is our future, and we have fundamentally no choice. We will make it work." Nadella was committed.

Three years later Nadella succeeded Steve Ballmer as CEO and led Microsoft's transformation into a cloud software company—including both infrastructure like Azure (which had already been fundamentally redesigned and installations of which were doubling every quarter) and cloud-based applications like Office 365. In the first three years of Nadella's CEO tenure, Microsoft's stock price tripled in value.

It was time for another jolt. On March 29, 2018, Nadella sent an announcement to the company and the press titled "Embracing Our Future: Intelligent Cloud and Intelligent Edge." Echoing his friend Sundar Pichai, who had recently made Google's "AI first" announcement, Nadella laid out plans for Microsoft's next transformation:

Over the past year, we have shared our vision for how the intelligent cloud and intelligent edge will shape the next phase of innovation. First, computing is more powerful and ubiquitous from the cloud to the edge. Second, AI capabilities are rapidly advancing across perception and cognition fueled by data and knowledge of the world. Third, physical and virtual worlds are coming together to create richer experiences that understand the context surrounding people, the things they use, the places they go, and their activities and relationships.

These technological changes represent a tremendous opportunity for our customers, our partners—everyone. With all this new technology and opportunity comes a responsibility to ensure technology's benefits reach people more broadly across society. It also requires that the technologies we create are trusted by the individuals and organizations that use them.

Today's announcement enables us to step up to this opportunity and responsibility across all our Solution Areas.[2]

These paragraphs were followed by a series of more specific announcements describing organizational changes and new leadership roles. Microsoft's second major operating model transformation in less than ten years was under way.

Microsoft's twofold transformation is dramatic but by no means isolated. Just about every technology company that has survived for longer than a few years has gone through at least one full-on transformation of both operating model and business model. Amazon, Google, Alibaba, Netflix, and Tencent have all reinvented themselves multiple times.

But these days the need for ongoing transformation extends well beyond tech businesses; it's becoming as necessary as the need to embed digital technology. For traditional firms, becoming a software-based, AI-driven company is about becoming a different kind of organization—one accustomed to ongoing transformation. This is not about spinning off a new organization, setting up the occasional skunkworks, or creating an AI department. It is about fundamentally changing the core of the company by building a data-centric operating architecture supported by an agile organization that enables ongoing change.

This chapter focuses on what it takes to transform into an AI company and on the value of the transformation. We first focus on Microsoft's efforts, and describe the process the company went through to drive changes in both business and operating model. We highlight some of the key lessons by summarizing five principles, drawn not only from observations about Microsoft but also from our research on hundreds of other companies. The last part of the chapter focuses on other insights from this research, benchmarking the transformation process and broadening our conclusions on the impact of transformation across firms. We conclude by describing the transformation at Fidelity Investments.

Transforming Microsoft

When Nadella took over as CEO, Microsoft was a tired company. After a period of wild growth putting DOS, Windows, and Office on every desktop, the company had faced a range of competitive threats spawned by the internet and had run into serious antitrust scrutiny. As Bill Gates gradually stepped into the background, Steve Ballmer's Microsoft had lacked the spark of innovation. From problems in shipping Windows Vista to the failure of the Zune music player, and from disappointments with Windows 8 to the disastrous Nokia acquisition, there had not been much to celebrate.

Microsoft had lost its way. Perhaps most worrisome was its tumble into irrelevance with the software community. Microsoft's ecosystem of developers had been central to the company's success. When Bill Gates and Paul Allen launched Microsoft in a tiny office in Albuquerque, they built compilers for the first generation of microcomputers. It is often forgotten that when you turned on the earliest Apple computers, what you got was Microsoft BASIC. Over time, the company spawned a thriving ecosystem of DOS and then Windows developers, enabling millions of people to write PC applications and turning the personal computer into a ubiquitous platform. At the time, the developer community was considered Microsoft's most important asset.

When he became CEO, Nadella understood that Microsoft had lost its developer focus and technical edge. Its platform status was fading as the Microsoft developer community shrank, with developers moving to Linux and other open source alternatives. The world was being rebuilt on a foundation of software, data, and AI, and Microsoft had lost its way as the platform of choice. The company needed not only a new strategy but also a new mission.

A New Mission and Strategy

In framing Microsoft's new mission and strategy, Nadella went back to the origin of the company. He explained to us, "First and foremost we needed to renew our sense of purpose and identity."[3] Once again, Microsoft would become a technology company aimed at driving the productivity of its ecosystem. Its new mission is not only bold but also consistent with the company's origin: Microsoft is, as Nadella also told us, "a technology company whose mission is to empower every person and every organization on the planet to achieve more."

The mission gave rise to a new strategy. Across each of its product lines—Office 365, Microsoft Dynamics (enterprise resource planning and customer relationship management [CRM] software), and the portfolio of Azure services—Microsoft is becoming the productivity platform for the age of AI. Microsoft leaders highlight an unwavering commitment to mission and strategy and the importance of shifting to a services-based "consumption" orientation (the more you use, the more you pay) backed by a cloud-based architecture, all increasingly enabled by AI capabilities.

Becoming a leading cloud provider also meant a fundamental evolution in software architecture. The Windows developer ecosystem had experienced a steady decline since the 1990s. Meanwhile, the most innovative companies were being built on an open source foundation, often provided on demand by Amazon's AWS cloud service. Starting in the fall of 2014, after an intense day of startup visits up and down Route 101 in Silicon Valley, Nadella, along with Scott Guthrie (the Azure lead at the time), decided that it was time for Microsoft to embrace open source. Soon thereafter, Nadella appeared at a Microsoft developer conference wearing a button reading "Microsoft (heart) Linux." Since then, Nadella and his team have been consistent as Microsoft ramped up its efforts on open source projects, investing heavily and contributing much of its own software into the open domain.

The strategy gained traction with Microsoft's acquisition of GitHub in 2018. GitHub provides software project management tools and has become the most popular repository for open source projects. Microsoft is now having an impact at the very center of the open source community.[4]

Not everyone at Microsoft was on board with Nadella's strategy, but he did not hesitate. Bringing the new strategy to life necessitated significant transitions, and an exodus of experienced leaders followed. But the remaining team, bolstered with crucial new hires and promotions, developed a laser focus on the new strategy. As Takeshi Numoto, Microsoft's corporate vice president in charge of Azure, explained to us in early 2019, "There has been amazing clarity within the company on the importance of the cloud and AI. There is no plan B. Nadella has been there for around seven years. Ever since then it's been clear. We have spent five or six billion dollars a year just in CAPEX building our cloud."

Rearchitecting the Operating Model

Creating alignment around the mission and strategy may have been the easy part. It is hard to envision the kinds of operational challenges Microsoft has gone through in becoming a cloud and AI company. Microsoft's classic software business was about shipping software CDs. In contrast, a cloud business requires massive investments in infrastructure: buying, moving, and assembling literally *billions* of dollars' worth of servers, routers, and data centers.

All this is managed and organized through a complex supply chain, at a scale comparable to that of the largest hardware companies in the world. This required a relentless, dedicated capability-building effort, a variety of new processes and systems, constant problem-solving efforts, and a major transition in the management team. Microsoft had to deploy an efficient and responsive supply chain, one good enough to compete with Amazon, possibly the best supply chain company in the world. This required years of painstaking work to bring in experienced managers and consultants, map existing processes, prototype improvements, and engineer state-of-the-art digital operational systems.

After years of challenges and significant losses, Microsoft's relentless investments are paying off. Operational capabilities are running much deeper, lead times have shrunk dramatically, and new systems are instrumenting and tracking the supply chain, providing clear, nearly real-time information on problems and delays.

In return, cloud-based architectures have a number of operational benefits. A cloud provider hosts the software and controls the services, which can be improved on a continuous basis based on constant feedback from users. Because cloud consumption of a Microsoft product can increase only if the product is actually used, customer alignment is imperative.

The cloud's level of customer intimacy opens all kinds of opportunities for analytics. Anonymized product usage informs Microsoft quickly if a customer project is working (or not) and highlights which features are most effective (or ineffective). The consumption data flowing back from customer projects is tracked religiously and provides crucial telemetry feedback on product improvements. These data assets are integrated into increasingly sophisticated Microsoft data platforms, which input the data, protect it, process it to ensure quality and usability, and enable a variety of increasingly powerful analytics. The insights, in turn, generate essential improvements. "Once you are in the consumption business, you are part of your customer's operations. The responsibility is super real,"

Numoto told us. "We cannot let [our systems] go down, all the way from elections to mission-critical systems in airline operations."

Transforming the Core

In 2011, before Nadella was promoted to lead the Server and Tools business, Azure had been run as a separate, autonomous organization. The structure had caused all kinds of challenges for Microsoft. Azure had been conceived as a new platform, to be offered as a service but disconnected from Microsoft's other product lines. Moreover, the Azure team was often at odds with the rest of the server and tools group, as Azure continued to build incompatible software and fought for resources and status.

One of Nadella's first moves was to bring Azure into the fold. He put the Azure team under an experienced Microsoft executive, Bill Laing, who had previously led Microsoft's traditional Windows server business. The idea was to move Azure from the fringe of Microsoft to the center, to transform the core of the company. Laing had seen firsthand a variety of traditional software businesses come tumbling down because of their inability to change, and so he understood the mandate.

Much effort went into redesigning Azure to make it easier to use and compatible with traditional Microsoft products. In a clear departure from Azure's early focus, and to build on Microsoft's existing advantages, Azure would make it extremely easy to port traditional enterprise software to the new platform. In addition, Azure was redesigned to run Windows and Linux workloads. Microsoft also added substantial incentives for customers to move some of their applications to Azure. Nadella understood that the key to changing Microsoft's core was the transformation of Microsoft's own installed base of customers.

Leading the effort with Laing on Azure was Scott Guthrie, a highly respected engineering leader. One of the first things Guthrie did in his new role was to get the other leaders in the Server and Tools organization to actually install Azure—driving home the point that the software was really difficult to use. Guthrie made it his mission to make the platform more user friendly and much easier to deploy with Microsoft's traditional customers.

Guthrie eventually succeeded Laing in running the Azure business and pushed through change after change to make the service increasingly powerful, business friendly, and compatible with other Microsoft products. Guthrie transformed the Azure organization's structure and processes, and even its value system. He restructured the hardware and the software development teams that formed the center of the engineering organization, breaking traditional silos. He integrated all of Azure software under Jason Zander, hardware under Todd Homdahl, and later Rani Borkar, with advanced hardware engineering led by Mike Neil.

Additionally, Guthrie directed the entire organization to adopt agile methods and restructured the product teams around cohesive, business-focused goals. Rather than drive technical features, each team was asked to identify and address specific customer pain points and use cases. Most of all, the engineering organization had to dramatically improve its level of responsiveness to operations. The good news in having a cloud business is getting constant feedback from usage that highlights problems and motivates improvements. The "bad" news is that the engineering organization must react to this in real time, or as close to it as possible.

Putting AI First

As the cloud transformation continued to build steam, Microsoft entered its second transformation: layering sophisticated machine learning and AI capabilities across its operational infrastructure as well as its products and services. After announcing the transition, Nadella consolidated the company's engineering efforts into two main groups, with Guthrie as the executive vice president leading the Cloud and AI group, and Rajesh Jha leading the Experiences and Devices group.

When Nadella communicated the shift to embrace AI at the core of Microsoft, the organization was ready to go. Truth be told, Microsoft had been focused on building a strong AI capability since the early

2000s under the leadership of Harry Shum, executive vice president of AI and Research. Engineering groups were already working closely with the research team to embed AI technologies in each Microsoft product line. Azure Machine Learning, for example, had been offered as a service since 2014. The Nadella announcement made it real, accelerating AI technology development and product introductions. But even more than investing in AI-related projects, Nadella's announcement was about transforming the way Microsoft itself operated.

The Microsoft developer ecosystem is at the center of the company's AI strategy. Azure infrastructure makes Microsoft's powerful AI easily accessible to developers at startups as well as enterprises. Azure Machine Learning was introduced as part of the Cortana Intelligence Suite. The Azure team also introduced a variety of AI-driven services: search, knowledge, vision, language, and speech APIs. In mid-2018, Microsoft introduced Azure Data Factory, which embeds powerful functionality to rapidly manage and monitor data integration projects and build the foundations of a data-centric operating model on demand.

Driving Microsoft's Transformation

Microsoft's AI transformation required reshaping internal operations. The transformation of Microsoft's data assets, internal IT, and operations teams was led by Kurt DelBene. DelBene was a Microsoft veteran with many key product assignments, including being president of the Office business, before he took a leave from Microsoft to fix healthcare.gov (a vital component of the Obama administration's implementation of the Affordable Care Act). In 2015 Nadella convinced DelBene to come back to Microsoft. Although DelBene's first assignment was to run corporate strategy, he also took over the IT and operations organizations, now grouped under Core Services Engineering and Operations, and became Microsoft's chief digital officer. It is an important point that Nadella chose someone with extensive product experience to run IT and help build Microsoft's own AI factory as the new foundation of its data- and software-centric operating model.

A lot had to change. Traditionally, Microsoft IT had run in reactive mode, as with most other IT groups. IT organizations have long focused on deploying and maintaining systems, from installing CRM, to working the help desk, to keeping the enterprise network secure. But as digital technology moves to the center of the firm and begins to shape, drive, and automate critical operating tasks, IT must be able to build and deploy the software foundations of a fundamentally different operating model. Culture, capabilities, processes, and systems need to change.

To build Microsoft's new digital operating infrastructure, DelBene had to transform IT at Microsoft. Under DelBene, Microsoft IT went to proactive mode, led by a clear vision of success. Integrating IT with operations and strategy emphasized its fundamental role in how the company operates. "Our product is the process," DelBene told us in a 2019 interview. "First, we are going to articulate what the vision should be for the systems and processes we support. Second, we are going to run like a product development team. And, we are going to be agile based." DelBene changed the name of the organization from IT to Core Services Engineering and reduced its reliance on outsourced development and contractors. The organization also gained budget responsibility, instead of working on the usual "cross-charge" model. Additionally, he brought in handpicked leads from the product functions to help shape the new orientation and build capability. They, in turn, hired many more engineers from the product groups to replace contractors and build the new development culture.

DelBene explains: "We can identify where all the data in the company is. Once we figure out where all the data is, we assemble data catalogs for all the different data sources. From the catalogs, we can take the data and mash it up into lakes, so we can build ML [machine learning] models. We especially leverage AI to know when things are starting to behave in unexpected ways. The best we could do in the past was react as fast as possible; now we can preempt things, from bad contracts to cyber breaches." As Ludo Hauduc, general manager of the Core Platform team, describes it:

We can now build AI and ML models on top of everything. We can search across the entirety of our data sets and do analysis on them. We provide the components that our organization can use to build the processes that run the whole company. We are structured as a horizontal platform. This is a critical departure from the previous operating model in IT where many apps and services were siloed with little sharing, and many versions of similar capabilities. When I talk to a candidate and draw the shape of Core Services, I start drawing vertical pillars for the company, and draw my own organization as a horizontal slab across everything ... In addition, the Core Services engineering org is increasingly partnering with internal product teams at Microsoft to fill in gaps and fix issues directly. These codevelopment engagements are a fundamental departure from the way the previous IT organization operated. It helps inject the deep expertise that Core Services has gained by running the Microsoft enterprise back into its own products, and in turn making Microsoft products more complete, enterprise-ready, and valuable to Microsoft's customers.

Core Services is at the center of Microsoft's transformation, working to rebuild traditional silos on a common digital foundation. This operating foundation connects the enormous organization to a common software component library, algorithm repository, and data catalog, which can be used to rapidly digitize, enable, and deploy digital processes across the entire company. This technology stack has thus become the foundation of Microsoft's operating model, enabling processes across sales, marketing, and product groups. In addition, the efforts provide an important operating model foundation that can be deployed across Microsoft's customer base.

Governance

As part of its transformation, Microsoft has also confronted some of the broader implications of AI. In September 2015, Nadella promoted Brad Smith, Microsoft's longtime general counsel, to be Microsoft's new president, with explicit responsibilities not only to run Microsoft's corporate, external, and legal affairs (CELA) but also to tackle fundamental issues of privacy, security, accessibility, sustainability, and digital inclusion across the company. Smith had been an unusual general counsel, providing vocal support for many of these initiatives. More recently, in collaboration with Harry Shum, Smith championed the release of a book, *The Future Computed*, describing Microsoft's perspective on AI, its impact on society, and the role that technology companies should play.

The collaboration between Microsoft research and CELA goes well beyond working on a book. CELA and research work together to set the tactics, strategies, and policies that govern Microsoft's use of AI. As described by Tim O'Brien, Microsoft's general manager for AI programs, "It's an interesting marriage of two cultures within the company that couldn't be more different."[5]

The efforts took on an increased sense of urgency by the experience with Tay, an AI-powered chat bot, introduced in 2016 on Twitter. Tay was designed to personalize interactions with users while answering questions or even mirroring users' statements back to them. But as it learned from and responded to community tweets and chats, the bot tweeted a series of offensive and racist statements. Tay was shut down in a few hours, and Microsoft faced significant backlash.

The collaboration between CELA and the research team is shaping new policies across the organization, especially when it comes to AI interactions with users and customers. In addition to creating clear guidelines for designing "responsible bots," Microsoft has identified six "AI principles": fairness; reliability and safety; privacy and security; inclusiveness; transparency, and accountability.[6] The policies are making a difference on the organization as CELA team members are integrated into a variety of activities, from development to sales. Microsoft is learning from the industry's experience to manage the clash between engineering-driven (and sometimes risk-prone) innovation cultures and the potentially adverse impact of AI on society.

Five Principles for Transformation

The Microsoft journey shows that transforming an operating model is never easy, but it can be done and can produce important results. In fact, many traditional enterprises—such as Nordstrom, Vodafone, Comcast, and Visa—have made important inroads, digitizing and rearchitecting key components of their operating models and building sophisticated data platforms and AI capabilities.

We wanted to highlight five guiding principles that characterize an effective transformation process. These are drawn not only from Microsoft but also from what we have seen in a variety of organizations, from our research, and from active engagement in transformation efforts.

One Strategy

The first essential principle in transformation is to develop strategic clarity and commitment. The goals should be stated clearly, as in building an integrated data platform or organizing as agile teams. There is plenty of interest in digital transformation. But to operationalize a new strategy, especially one involving transformation, it's imperative that there be no doubt as to the seriousness of the effort, its sustaining power, and the clarity of the end goal. Aligning the organization around a fundamental transformation is difficult enough. If the leadership is not truly committed for the long term, it's probably time to call a headhunter.

One key element of the transformation is the idea of bringing unity to the company while changing it. This is not about spinning off an autonomous group, carving out an AI division, or setting up a skunkworks. Rearchitecting the company's operating model requires rebuilding the company on a new, integrated foundation. As we saw at Microsoft, a clear, compelling vision is essential, aided by constant reinforcement to drive alignment across an integrated, multifaceted effort, including sales, marketing, engineering, research, IT, HR, operations, and even the legal team. Coordination becomes increasingly essential as interactions across the business multiply. Data knows no functional boundaries, and refocusing the company on a foundation of analytics and AI requires close, multifunctional collaboration to improve results while reducing risks. What better reason can you have to get rid of organizational silos that have hampered the business for years?

As alignment across functions begins to gel, the potential for dramatic business model innovation can explode. The combination of networks, analytics, and AI opens all kinds of opportunities for value creation and capture, across a variety of new network and learning opportunities. Microsoft's own business model has expanded dramatically through its cloud and AI orientation, as have those of many other companies mentioned in this book.

Architectural Clarity

Second, it's critical to bring clarity to the technical goals of the transformation. Everyone must understand what you want your future operating architecture to look like. A strong focus on data, analytics, and AI requires some centralization and much consistency. Data assets must be integrated across the range of applications for an organization to realize the full benefit of the transformation. In addition, fragmented data is virtually impossible to safeguard consistently for privacy and security. If the data is not all held in a single centralized repository, then the organization must have an accurate catalog of where the data is, clear guidelines for what to do with it (and how to protect it), and clear standards for how to store it so that it can be used and reused by multiple parties. The importance of standard policies, components, and architecture is even greater as an organization works to deploy increasingly sophisticated AI to power its operating model.

This is where things can start to become exciting in dealing with the owners of a firm's old architecture. One of our biggest surprises in transformation efforts (maybe obvious in retrospect) is the frequent resistance of the CIO and of the IT organization. Many enterprise IT organizations were designed for a different purpose: to operate a complex IT back office, making sure everything works effectively and securely. Traditional IT charters have not included innovation and transformation, and traditional IT skill sets rarely include analytics, let alone AI. Additionally, IT was typically rewarded for being reactive to and working within existing company silos, which promoted additional fragmentation and inconsistency. Even at Microsoft, driving the new data-centric architecture required an important shift in the charter, structure, culture, and capabilities of the IT organization.

Agile, Product-Focused Organization

Developing a product-focused mentality is essential to an AI-centered operating model. The teams deploying AI-centered applications must embed a deep understanding of the application settings they are designed to enable, as with any product-focused effort. That's why at Amazon and Microsoft, highly experienced engineering leaders who'd run major product businesses were tasked with building the software necessary to rearchitect each company's operating model.

At the heart of it, building an AI-centric operating model is all about taking many traditional processes and embedding them in software and algorithms. Ultimately, the AI-centric firm, with its vast variety of AI-driven processes, is the actual "product" of a modern, transformed, core services organization.

Agile methods go hand in hand with a transformed, data-centric operating architecture. Gone are the days of massive, custom-built applications, each hardwired to specific datasets, executed by armies of consultants, over years of effort. After data, models, and technology components are made easily available in conjunction with the company's AI factory, applications can be built very quickly, especially if the teams involved know enough about the downstream settings and if they work in a rapid, agile fashion.

Clearly, beyond a new approach to architecture and organization, transformation requires a major cultural shift. Digitizing the operating model really does mean developing a software culture and mindset. It is not about opening a Silicon Valley location but about transforming the way the organization feels, from the dress code to reward systems, and from recruiting to compensation. This is not a pilot or a research effort. The focus is on changing the core.

Capability Foundations

The most obvious challenge in building an AI-centered firm is to grow a deep foundation of capability in software, data sciences, and advanced analytics. Naturally, building this foundation will take time, but much can be done with a small number of motivated, knowledgeable people.

More challenging may be the realization that the organization needs to systematically hire a different kind of person and build an appropriate career path and incentive system. If the organization is serious about transformation, traditional practices will need to be changed, because the market for this kind of talent is hot. However, experience from Microsoft to Fidelity has shown that with the right process and incentives, analytics groups can be built and motivated quickly.

One less obvious, but equally important, skill set to hire and groom for is the data and analytics product manager. As enterprise data starts to consolidate in brand-new AI factories, enterprises will need to groom and grow the people who can identify important use cases and lead teams in developing the new range of applications. This is where individuals with business backgrounds and experiences should feel an advantage. Additionally, this role of data and analytics product manager will expand as leadership challenges will, increasingly, require the same combination of skills and capabilities. This may signal the emergence of a new generation of business leader, one who drives a deeper analytics and software mindset across the firm and is fully sensitive to the impact of AI—both helpful and harmful.

Clear, Multidisciplinary Governance

As AI becomes increasingly important to each firm, the challenges created by its broader impact on society will only continue to multiply. We have already seen some of this: What if Ant Financial's social credit score system updates dynamically as users message with friends about problems at work? Clearly, the power of AI-driven services can create a host of benefits but can also unleash unintended consequences. In addition, the challenges of privacy and cybersecurity are motivating crucial investments as well as debates and regulation. These challenges have become the real bottlenecks of the AI-driven firm and leave it susceptible to sudden, often catastrophic, failure.

Digital governance should therefore involve a collaboration across disparate disciplines and functions. In doing so, it rejuvenates the role of legal and corporate affairs, whose people can be involved in product and policy decisions and not only participating in litigation and lobbying activities. AI requires deep thinking about legal and ethical exposure, and these activities should be actively staffed and supported.

Finally, beyond building strong in-house governance processes, an organization should reach well outside the firm to engage with its ecosystem of partners and customers, as well as the communities surrounding them. Amplified by the networks it connects to, AI's challenges require an extensive, dedicated governance effort, one that explicitly considers and engages with the many stakeholders across the economy and society.

Data, Analytics, and AI in the Enterprise

Microsoft's appetite for digital transformation is not unusual. We have researched the development of analytics and AI capabilities in hundreds of firms. Over the years, we have studied companies through qualitative case study methods and analytical surveys. In this section, we talk about a systematic study of more than 350 enterprises, performed with a team at Keystone Strategy, in which we assessed the data, analytics, and AI capabilities of each organization and correlated the results to business performance.[7]

The results show that even though there is a broad range across firms, the number that have already developed important new capabilities is significant. Moreover, those firms that have deployed analytics and AI capabilities are indeed enjoying superior business performance, which is an encouraging finding.

We operationalized our research by tracking around forty major business processes across firms and examining the extent to which these were informed by basic analytics or enabled by more-sophisticated AI. We also checked for the deployment of foundational technology, data infrastructure, analytics, and AI capabilities. Finally, we evaluated the architecture of information technology and data infrastructure. The individual findings were assembled into an AI maturity index.

The research focused on enterprises in the manufacturing and service sectors with a median of six thousand employees and $3.4 billion in revenue. Firms represented include most major companies in the areas of manufacturing, consumer packaged goods, financial services, and retail. Our AI maturity index results should be interpreted as a general measure of capability in data analysis, advanced analytics, and AI.

We found important differences among firms. Firms at the bottom of the sample used traditional and rudimentary means; we saw many organizational silos containing scattered data assets, often embedded in Excel spreadsheets. In contrast, firms in the top quartile were sophisticated, gathering internal and external data into an integrated data platform and leveraging AI and ML for important operational automation and business insights.

Benefits of an AI-Enabled Operating Model

Our research showed that AI maturity leaders realized substantial benefits from their data and analytics investments in a variety of business functions. We found data being used both to automate decisions and to aid in making complex decisions with a comprehensive understanding of market dynamics, customers, company operations, workforce capabilities, and product and service performance.

Let's dig into some of the specifics. The top organizations consolidated data to develop a single version of the truth about their business. In addition, the top enterprises used business intelligence tools and analytical models within their systems to develop tailored customer experiences, mitigate the risk of customer churn, anticipate equipment failure, and enable all kinds of process decisions in real time. Leading firms also used data to better understand the market, acquire new customers, and optimize advertising effectiveness. Data gathered from across the customer life cycle helped these enterprises make informed decisions, present customers with tailored offers and experiences, and mitigate support issues— all this by using a 360-degree view of their customers across all channels and touch points.

The best firms also used data and analytics across engineering, manufacturing, and operations. Many of them consolidated information across the product development life cycle and supply chain. They acted on the information frequently, and in an automated fashion. The data was analyzed to understand the drivers of operational efficiency and product quality, anticipate equipment or operational downtime, and drive process compliance and improvement across distributed facilities.

Increasingly, the top companies used internet of things technologies to instrument their products and services with connected sensors that gather telemetry on equipment and product usage. This data in turn allowed them to optimize manufacturing and service operations and transform the ways they delivered value to and captured value from their customers.

Finally, supporting all these capabilities, the best companies had built sophisticated data platforms. This easily available data was used by agile teams to rapidly deploy applications, typically increasing business performance and responsiveness or improving the customer experience. In addition, these companies used data to develop forecasts and recommendations across a spectrum of supporting functions, from optimizing business strategy to automating the creation of individual development plans for employees. Table 5-1 shows the financial impact of investments in AI capability, with a comparison of the laggards and leaders in the AI maturity index.

TABLE 5-1

Financial performance of AI maturity index leaders and laggards

	Laggards (bottom 25% of enterprises)	Leaders (top 25% of enterprises)
Three-year average gross margin	37%	55%
Three-year average earnings before taxes	11%	16%
Three-year average net income	7%	11%

Stages of Operating Model Transformation

Our research shows that the best-performing firms are investing heavily in developing data, analytics, and AI-centered capabilities. Many are driving a change in their operating models, accompanied by a substantial cultural shift to fully understand and embrace the opportunities and challenges presented by AI. Let's focus for a moment on how these changes evolve over time.

There appears to be a natural sequence of stages in the journey to become a state-of-the-art AI factory: from siloed data, to pilots, to data hubs, to AI factory (see figure 5-1).

Stage 1 is where organizations usually begin: with siloed data. We rarely see much in the way of barriers before the pilot stage (stage 2), because demonstrating the value of analytics-based decision making can be done without big organizational and cultural shifts and is often done largely by vendors and consultants.

But as we get to the data hub stage (stage 3), the organization must rearchitect itself to aggregate data from many siloed sources and use it to identify companywide opportunities. This is the point when substantial investment is needed and when the organization starts to understand that it will need to change. Not surprisingly, this is also when we see organizational resistance.

Most important (and often most challenging) is the adoption of a clear, single source of truth to guide decisions on market opportunity, pricing, planning, and operational optimization. The consistent approach to data and analytics is most often associated with

FIGURE 5-1

Four stages of digital operating model transformation

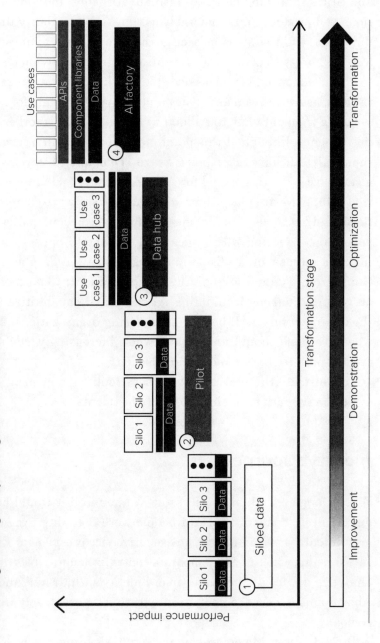

the creation of a centralized organization devoted to data sciences and analytics, frequently deployed across applications, products, and SBUs in a hub-and-spoke fashion. Although individual functions and product units inevitably ask for some flexibility to adopt unique capabilities and approaches, the data sciences team must not lose the ability to connect its organization to the individual groups to bring back insights and needed changes, keeping the centrality of the data assets (as well as privacy and security) first and foremost.

Going from data hub to AI factory (stage 4) takes another major investment, although at this point much of the architectural shift should already have taken place. Stage 4 companies have developed a standard operating model for AI. And beyond including centralized data, powerful algorithms, and reusable software components, the operating model also includes an emphasis on clear policies and governance, dealing with issues from privacy to bias. This stage includes intense, cross-disciplinary, capability-building activities. Going from a data and analytics company to a true AI factory is an ongoing journey in building AI skills and capabilities across the organization—well beyond engineering organizations. This is when everyone should understand what, increasingly, shapes the critical path to the customer and to society.

To illustrate these observations, let's look for a moment at the evolutionary path taken by Fidelity Investments.

Fidelity's Journey

When Google—and later Microsoft—announced it would become an "AI first" company, several people were listening. Among the most intent was Vipin Mayar, an executive vice president at Fidelity Investments, who ran the company's centralized data, insights, and analytics group. At the same time, Fidelity's Chairman and CEO Abby Johnson saw the need to integrate AI more deeply into the company.

In 2011, Vipin Mayar was charged with leading a new AI Center of Excellence with the portfolio of projects under the initiative governed by Fidelity's senior leadership team. Mayar launched the center's work with a series of small group sessions, organized by business unit and function, to produce a list of key AI initiatives, use cases, and goals. As Mayar recalled, "There was no shortage of applications of AI and business use cases. It was clear we had to put together some serious capabilities."[8] Applications for AI at Fidelity were viewed as essential in literally every facet of the business and Fidelity clearly needed to anticipate future needs and prioritize its AI strategy.

Fidelity was ready to go. It needed to hire top data scientists and expanded its recruitment efforts to talent that is drawn to technology companies or Silicon Valley. "Our use cases, culture, and data were a big draw for this talent, and we have now built a world class team here," says Mayar, adding, "It helped that this was a top initiative for Abby." In addition, the company encouraged the emergence of a new type of skill for the company: data- and AI-focused product management, wherein experts looked across functions with a keen eye for the business impact of analytics, and led the agile teams in the identification and deployment of new applications.

The team could now expand its data and algorithm factory and build AI as a core capability for Fidelity. In 2012, the company embarked on devising an integrated data strategy. Fidelity invested in centralizing strategic analytics data assets, starting with assembling a 360-degree view of the customer, which was stored in a secure location and made accessible to Fidelity analytics. The team put together its own analytics software stack, providing Fidelity software developers and data scientists with the tools to build, train, and deploy machine-learning models quickly.

Fidelity's data platform tracked and integrated over 36 million user profiles, interactions, and digitized voice calls. The data was mined to provide customer insights, improve Fidelity services resulting in a more integrated end-to-end experience, and provide more value to clients.

Perhaps more important than the technological changes were the organizational and cultural shifts toward the adoption of agile methods in order to offer a company of Fidelity's size the agility and decision-making speed of a smaller one. Building on these enviable integrated data assets, the organization was learning to break down traditional silos and work together on agile teams to rapidly deploy new applications. The teams worked in two-week scrums to develop applications tracking customer satisfaction, churn, and typical problems; estimating risk profiles; and developing sophisticated investment recommendation systems. Each of the new applications was repeatedly tested on Fidelity's experimentation platform to make sure it worked reliably before deployment. At the same time, Mayar launched a comprehensive education effort, with hundreds of business leaders learning the basic algorithms and attending classes to drive this capability more broadly and deeply across the firm.

Fidelity has set three priorities for its AI efforts. The first is customer experience. Fidelity makes sizable AI investments to better understand customer preferences and recommend more effective, highly personalized investment strategies. In addition, Fidelity AI investments will focus on revenue growth, finding opportunities to optimize existing operating processes, making the company more scalable, and enabling new opportunities for additional services across businesses. Finally, a set of initiatives is also aimed at generating fundamental business insights, such as devising better investment strategies, or understanding reasons for customer service calls.

Fidelity teams are now driving its increasingly data- and AI-centric operating model across its multiple lines of business, working hard to enable a huge range of processes, from portfolio analysis to customer service. As we look across the board, the impact of traditional constraints is decreasing, as more of the work is shifting to software and algorithms. While Fidelity will never entirely lose its human touch—its investment advisers remain a vital part of the business—AI is playing more of a role in improving the company's performance and delivering an exceptional customer experience. As this evolves, we are also seeing much more explicit, dedicated investments in governance, driving cross-functional policies around AI usage and impact, as well as cybersecurity and privacy. As Mayar told us, "AI is just making us better in all aspects of our business."

Fidelity is not alone. As we write this book, many firms are actively engaged in operating model transformation. Many efforts are showing promise, even across older firms, driving new capabilities, improving performance, and powering a new range of business opportunities. A new, AI-enabled kind of firm is taking off, not only with tech companies like Microsoft and Google but also across the most capable traditional enterprises. What these firms need now is a new way to approach strategy.

As new opportunities begin to emerge from the deployment of digital operating models, firms are confronted with a new breadth of strategic options to shape their business models. But as digital transformation reshapes the economy, eclipsing traditional boundaries across industries and driving new sources of competitive advantage, evaluating these options requires a new lens. Firms can connect to a variety of economic networks, drive new value from network effects, and experience important gains from data and learning effects. Now that we have examined the challenge of operating model transformation, we are ready to look at the implications for strategy and business model transformation.

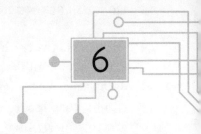

6

Strategy for a New Age

In the late 1990s, when physicist Albert-László Barabási and colleagues were analyzing the structure of the World Wide Web, they observed that the number of connections among network nodes evolved constantly and grew over time. They also observed that a small fraction of the nodes in the network were becoming much more connected and hublike and therefore more important than others. The web was following the principle of *preferential attachment*: the more-connected nodes attracted more new connections, and thus they became increasingly important and attractive to new connections.[1]

When one of us (Marco) drew an analogy between the web and the business networks resulting from digital connections in *The Keystone Advantage,* he argued that some firms (known variously as *keystones, platform firms, superstar firms,* or *hub firms*) would emerge as much more connected and powerful than others.[2] Although the book was essentially correct in its prediction, the authors did not realize how much that power would be amplified by the value of the data carried by the networks and processed through analytics and AI.

The strategic dynamics of AI and networks go hand in hand. As collisions between digital and traditional firms transform industries, and as firms develop increasingly digital foundations, the architecture of the economy is being reconfigured into a huge, all-encompassing, AI-powered network consisting of an array of subnetworks—social networks, supply chain networks, and mobile app networks, to name a few.

These networks have at least five things in common. They are made up of digital connections between network nodes, they carry data, they are shaped by increasingly powerful software algorithms, they ignore traditional industry boundaries, and they are growing increasingly important to our economy and social system.

Competitive advantage is increasingly defined by the ability to shape and control these networks and harvest the volume and variety of the transactions they carry. Competitive advantage therefore moves toward the organizations that are most central in connecting businesses, aggregating the data that flows between them, and extracting value through powerful analytics and AI. From Google to Facebook, and from Tencent to Alibaba, these network hubs are accumulating data and building the analytics and AI necessary to create, sustain, and grow competitive advantage across disparate industries.

Still, today, many businesses ignore network and data dynamics, focus on specific industry segments, and behave as if they were largely separate from the rest of the economy. As they collide with companies with digitized operating models, such conventional strategies are becoming ineffective.

The implications for strategy are important. Instead of focusing on isolated industries, each exhibiting unique properties and characteristics, strategic analysis should turn its focus to the structure and importance of the connections a firm creates across industries—from the firm to the rest of the economy—and on the flows of data through the networks the firm connects to. It used to be that strategy expressed itself in the way a firm managed internal resources. Now strategy is shifting to the art of managing the firm's networks and leveraging the data that flows through them. Just as *industry analysis* dominated strategy over the past few decades, we believe that *network analysis* will increasingly shape strategic thinking in the future.

This chapter examines these new strategic considerations and offers guidance on conducting network analysis, drawing heavily from the research of our HBS colleague and frequent coauthor Feng Zhu, whose work has shed truly important light on the subject.[3] We follow a specific logical thread designed to help the reader navigate through a complicated argument.

After a brief overview of the argument, we look from the firm outward to its economic networks and map the most critical interactions between a business and the rest of the economy. Then we analyze how each of the networks around a business can shape the dynamics of value creation along with the largely separate dynamics of value capture. This chapter continues with an example that integrates the dynamics of value creation and capture to present a systematic analysis of an existing business. We conclude by summarizing the key implications of network analysis for business strategy.

The Essence of the New Strategic Problem

This is a complex chapter, and it is worthwhile to spend a moment capturing the essence of the new strategic problem. We spend the rest of the chapter unpacking these ideas and illustrating them with examples.

While traditional industry analysis focuses on specific, isolated industry segments, *network analysis* involves understanding the open and distributed connections across firms, with each firm connected to a large number of networks across disparate industries.[4] As firms link to each other and to different networks, and as they aggregate various data flows, firms accumulate both network and learning effects.

Network and learning effects are not the same thing.[5] *Network effects* describe the value added by increasing the number of connections within and across networks, such as the value to a Facebook user of having connections with a large number of friends, or access to a broad variety of developer applications. *Learning effects* capture the value added by increasing the amount of data flowing through the same networks—for example, data that may be used to power AI to learn about and improve the user experience or to better target advertisers. In both cases, generally speaking, the

FIGURE 6-1

The value of network and learning effects

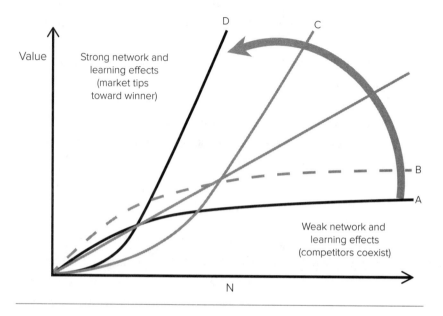

more the better, but there is a lot of nuance involved in defining how much better.

In figure 6-1, we illustrate the value created by different businesses as a function of scale. The scale is represented here by a single parameter, N, which can stand for a variety of variables, such as the number of users, the engagement of these users, or the number of complementors on a platform. Curve A, typical of a traditional business, shows the typical diminishing returns to scale. Even small network or learning effects can amplify the value provided, as shown by the dotted curve (curve B). Stronger network and learning effects can even exhibit increasing returns, as shown by curves C and D. The general idea in strategic network analysis is to find ways to increase the value created at scale and to capture the value created—effectively ratcheting up the value curve, as shown by the arrow.

To increase the value created at scale (and the resulting competitive advantage), you would try to move from curve A toward curve D in figure 6-1. Typically, traditional businesses exhibit strong diseconomies of scale. But as the impact of network and learning effects increases on a business, the value curve can change shape. Usually, little value will be delivered at first, with small networks and little data. But as scale increases, the value created and captured can increase, and do so more sharply, as you see in curves B, C, and D. The stronger the network and learning effects, the sharper the increase in value with scale. Critically, this logic can work not only for classic technology companies like Microsoft, Facebook, and Google, but also for businesses in traditional sectors.

Let's examine an example from the health-care sector.

Mapping Business Networks

Network analysis begins by mapping the most important economic networks connected to a business and examining the flows of valuable data and the opportunities that exist to gain advantage through AI. Let's walk through an example featuring a traditional firm.

A leading pharmaceutical company recently introduced a new drug focused on managing Parkinson's disease. Leveraging the power of digital networks, the company decided that rather than simply target its traditional channels (physicians and hospitals), it would expand its reach via a broader disease management strategy based on an app designed for patients to use at home. The company would track the progression of the disease through the application's daily patient questionnaire coupled with agility and coordination tests.

The information captured in the app would be used in managing the evolution of the patient's disease and optimizing the treatment. But beyond its core application, the data and access enabled by the app could also be valuable to providers of related services—for example, pharmacies, insurers, and physicians. In addition, the app could be used to create connections among patients and among service providers.

Figure 6-2 shows how a traditional product or service can be steered to impact environments beyond its traditional core applications. Strategic analysis should examine the nature and potential of all applications to discover what uses may be made of complementary networks, considering the full variety of possible

FIGURE 6-2

Network-based value creation for a disease management app

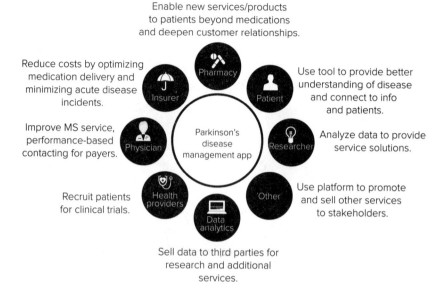

Enable new services/products to patients beyond medications and deepen customer relationships.

Reduce costs by optimizing medication delivery and minimizing acute disease incidents.

Use tool to provide better understanding of disease and connect to info and patients.

Improve MS service, performance-based contacting for payers.

Analyze data to provide service solutions.

Recruit patients for clinical trials.

Use platform to promote and sell other services to stakeholders.

Sell data to third parties for research and additional services.

Source: Keystone Strategy

network interactions. The intrinsic value created on one network may be realized (and captured) across any of a multitude of other networks the business can now easily connect to.

Many of these connections can provide great synergies with the company's core business—in this case, pharmaceuticals. For example, the app creates opportunities to dramatically increase patient engagement. This can improve the efficacy of the new drug, deepen the loyalty of the consumer base, and gather data that is useful for a variety of complementary applications that could enhance the value the company delivers to patients. Another possibility—reaching out to the patient network and enabling patient-to-patient interactions—can also foster relationships as patients turn to each other not only to gain insight and comfort but also to share their own innovative approaches for dealing with a debilitating disease.[6] In addition, connecting directly with the networks of insurers, physicians, and health providers can establish an important base of support and amplify the impact of new data-driven insights, thus improving the overall effectiveness of the treatment. Various networks can also generate new opportunities for monetization from insurance providers or, potentially, advertisers. As the opportunities increase, the value curve will increase more rapidly, as shown by the arrow in figure 6-1.

Value creation and capture opportunities for virtually any business may multiply across the networks the business may now be plugged in to. To understand the possibilities, you should first analyze each network separately, because each will have different properties and structure as well as offer different learning opportunities, willingness to pay, and level of competition. But as the analysis works its way around the various value networks, it is important to follow up by analyzing the interactions and potential synergies across the networks. We consider these factors in the next sections.

Value Creation Dynamics

The starting point of our analysis is to focus on how the business model dynamics of value creation and value capture are impacted by the network structure. We first examine the main factors influencing value creation dynamics, followed by an analysis of factors driving value capture. We then summarize the interactions across both and return to the Parkinson's app to develop the example in detail and systematically analyze its learning and network-based opportunities.[7]

Network Effects

The most important value creation dynamic of a digital operating model is its network effects. The basic definition of a *network effect* is that the underlying value or utility of a product or service increases as the number of users utilizing the service increases.

Let us take you back to the era of the fax machine (all the way back to the 1980s and 1990s) to help explain network effects.[8] The first buyer of a fax machine basically bought the dream of being able to send documents anywhere in the world through a regular phone call. The first fax machine was otherwise pretty useless. However, as more businesses adopted fax machines, the value of all fax machines climbed. The increasing connectivity increased the value of the fax network for all users. Similarly, the value of a social media platform or an internet messaging service is also a function of the number of users. Facebook would be lonely if no one else were on it. However, as our friends and colleagues join Facebook, its value to us (and them) also increases.

Precisely how much the value increases as a function of the number of users (often referred to as N) is dependent on context and is subject to much debate. For example, Metcalfe's law for communication posits that the value of a network is the square of the number of users, N^2. Others have noted that not all nodes in a network are equally valuable and that the value increase may be less steep and be modeled as $NLog(N)$. Still others simply state that the value of a network may be a linear function of N. Regardless of the shape of the value curve, the main element to take away is that a network's intrinsic utility increases as it adds users.

Traditional products do not typically generate network effects. Think about the pen you are carrying with you. The pen's value to you is the same and is fixed, no matter how many people also have a pen or even precisely the same pen. The economics of pen production may get better if increasing the volume of pens produced makes them cheaper to make and buy. But the underlying value of the pen for the tasks you do with it remains the same for you. So in our fax example, the stand-alone or even networked photocopier in every office does not exhibit network effects, but the fax machine does. Note that most modern photocopiers now incorporate fax functionality, thus giving them access to the worldwide fax network.

Generally speaking, the more network connections, the greater the value; that's the basic mechanism generating the network effect. The most basic underlying operating model of a platform hosting a network is to enable a match between users, and thus capture the value generated by network effects.

There are two main types of network effects: direct and indirect. Fax machines, messaging applications, and social networks exhibit *direct* network effects, meaning that the users value the presence of other users.

Indirect network effects exist when users in one category—say, sellers—value the presence of users in some other category—say, buyers—on a network. Uber and Airbnb are two examples of networks that exhibit indirect network effects. Riders on Uber like to have many drivers available so that their trip request is fulfilled instantaneously, and vacationers and renters want many short-term rentals available in their preferred cities. In these instances the indirect network effect is two sided: the value created by Uber increases as the number of riders increases, and that in turn increases the number of drivers, which then increases the number of riders, and so on. So, too, with content platforms like YouTube, where creators are looking for consumers and vice versa. Other examples include gaming console platforms like Microsoft Xbox and Sony PlayStation 2, where gamers and game creators value each other greatly.

In some cases, indirect network effects can be one sided, wherein only one side values the presence of the other side. On Google, Baidu, and Facebook, users are not looking for advertisers, but advertisers are surely looking for users who may be interested in the products they're selling. More specifically, users value the speed, accuracy, and comprehensiveness of the search index built by Google or Baidu (which, incidentally, improves with more use); meanwhile, advertisers value the presence of more users, because as the volume and variety of information increase in search engines, the information sharpens the targeting power of each ad.

Companies have also learned that the presence of one type of network effect (direct or indirect) can be leveraged to generate the other type. For example, although most users are on Facebook to interact with their friends and colleagues (a direct network effect), the company quickly realized that content creators, gaming providers, and website logins also wanted easy access to the same users and that this was mutually complementary. Hence, Facebook, through its API access, enabled a two-sided indirect network effect.

Similarly, makers and platforms of gaming consoles initially had a two-sided indirect network effect business, with players valuing games and game makers valuing players, but they added value when they created multiplayer functions and enabled communication among the players—thus linking previously separated network nodes to reap indirect network effects.

Although it's generally true that the larger the network, the greater the value, the actual relationship between network scale and value is much more complex, and the actual extent to which networks can increase in value as they grow differs widely. It is easier to start businesses that rely on weak network effects, but any advantage gained in the short term is less sustainable in the long term.

A premium content streaming business like Netflix, for example, can reach value very quickly, as it procures and distributes a critical mass of movies and TV shows. But over time, it attracts competitors (Amazon, Apple's iTunes, and Disney, to name a few examples) that can follow the same path without much disadvantage. Even though Netflix may have exclusivity arrangements with some content providers, there's little reason for viewers not to sign up for more than one service. In contrast, a community of content creation and distribution like YouTube enjoys much stronger network effects, and the vast majority of tiny, independent content producers has little incentive to post on any other site.

For a business to exhibit strong network effects, the value delivered must continue to increase sharply as the size of the network expands. As a rule, businesses that rely on weak network effects are characterized by many competitors, whereas those that engender strong network effects have fewer competitors and increased market concentration and therefore can claim a more substantial competitive advantage.

Learning Effects

Learning effects can either add value to existing network effects or generate value in their own right. With Google's search business, for example, the more searches conducted by users, the more (and more quickly) Google's algorithms can figure out common search patterns, and the better the service will become. These learning effects are crucial to the value provided by the search engine. As it tried to compete with Google, Microsoft's Bing partnered with Yahoo! to attract more users and advertisers, in an attempt to increase its user base and resulting scale. However, it rapidly realized that even with the greater scale, its search advertising business was not competitive with Google's because it didn't benefit from the same learning effects. Google had had years to learn and experiment with a high flow of incoming data—experience that provided an unbeatable advantage in optimizing its algorithms and delivering not only better search results and engagement but also higher monetization.

Learning effects can reinforce competitive advantage largely because they're dependent on scale. Generally, the more data used to train and optimize an algorithm, the more accurate the algorithm's output and the more complex the problem that the algorithm can be applied to solve. Figure 6-3 shows how a selection of prediction algorithms will improve with the size of the dataset. As operating models grow to embody a multitude of algorithms—each requiring large, diverse, and current datasets—learning effects will amplify the impact of scale and scope on the value created by a firm. The bigger the user base, the greater the scale, the more data that is available, and the greater the value. (All this assumes, of course, that the firm has the right operating model and the capabilities to implement the right algorithms.)

The extent to which data can have an enduring impact on competitive advantage differs from application to application. There are a number of reasons for this. First, the accuracy of most algorithms rises with the square root of the number of data points, at least for a while, and then levels off as the algorithm is fully trained. The square root law is an approximation, and in the case of algorithms that operate in isolation, accuracy does not improve that quickly, because most data points gathered are not uncorrelated. But when more than one algorithm drives a business, the combined value of their learning effects can compound. In the Netflix example, a number of both user-centered and back channel algorithms are at play simultaneously.

FIGURE 6-3

Impact of dataset scale on performance

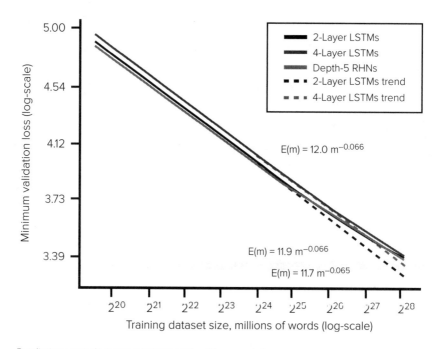

Prediction error decreases significantly with more data.

Source: Baidu Research

Other factors in competitive advantage include the type of algorithm in use and the uniqueness and scale of the data required. For a relatively simple algorithm—say, detecting the difference between images of cats and dogs—the size of the required training set will be limited, and the data required to train the algorithm may be broadly available. A business built on recognizing cats from dogs is not likely to develop a sustainable competitive advantage.

On the other hand, an algorithm that recognizes a unique type of tumor might be more defensible, because the system will require more, and more unique, data. An even more extreme example is the type of algorithms involved in driverless vehicle technologies; they are varied and complex, and they can require an extensive amount of real-time mapping and traffic data. As a result, an autonomous car business will generate considerably more moats and barriers to keep competitors away.

Learning and network effects can work hand in hand. Generally speaking, the larger a network (that is, the greater the number of its connections), the greater the value of the connections, the greater the flow of data, and the greater the opportunities for AI and overall learning. Any connection in a network can be a useful source of data, and this data can be used to learn, to train algorithms, and to amplify any advantage provided by network effects.

Clusters

The structure of the network also has an important impact on how a network's value increases with its size. Consider Airbnb and Uber. While Airbnb offers what is essentially a global service, Uber's network is highly clustered around specific urban areas.

In a research project with Feng Zhu, Xinxin Li of the University of Connecticut, and Ehsan Valavi of Harvard Business School, we modeled Uber and Airbnb to understand how network clustering affects the sustainability of network-based business models. We found that clustering makes a big difference. Travelers do not care much about the number of Airbnb hosts in their home cities; instead, they care about the number of hosts in the cities they wish to visit. Hence, the network is global. Any serious challenger to Airbnb would have to enter the market on a global scale. It would need to create global brand awareness to attract critical masses of travelers and hosts in a sufficient number of cities to build a liquid marketplace, where many bids, offers, and participants can easily enter and exit at low cost. Thus, entry into the home-sharing market carries a high price. Indeed, there's only one successful competitor to Airbnb at scale: HomeAway/Vrbo, which entered the market with a different business model.

In general, global networks are more concentrated around a small number of critical hubs. Barriers to competition typically are high, and sustaining profitability is relatively easy for the dominant player. (Marriott's decision to compete directly with Airbnb

FIGURE 6-4

The difference between local (left) and global networks

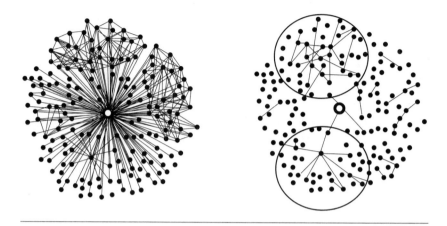

and HomeAway will provide insight into how well incumbents can devise and execute a network-effects strategy.)

In contrast to Airbnb's network, Uber's network is highly clustered, grouped around individual urban locations (see figure 6-4). Drivers in a Boston neighborhood will care only about the number of riders available in that same neighborhood, and the same is true for riders. Moreover, except for relatively rare frequent travelers, riders in Boston will not care much about the number of drivers and riders in, say, San Francisco.

This means that Uber's overall scale of more than a million drivers globally does not matter much to the value it can deliver locally. Therefore, the more a network is fragmented into local clusters, the less the impact of scale and network effects, and the easier it becomes for challengers to enter. Clustered networks are thus typically highly competitive. (And even with locally strong network effects, the impact of scale is effectively capped at the level required to serve the local cluster.) Any competitor with local scale can achieve similar efficiencies.

This kind of clustered network structure makes it easy for a competitor with less scale to reach critical mass in a local network and to take off through a differentiated offer or a lower price. Indeed, in addition to Lyft at the national level, Uber faces a number of local competitors in major cities. In New York, for example, it's getting strong competition from Gett, Juno, and Via, as well as from taxi operators. Likewise, DiDi—China's largest ride-sharing company—having driven Uber from its home market, now faces competition from local car companies worried about becoming commoditized by ride-sharing platforms.

Clustered networks are not limited to ride sharing. Similar structures can be observed for group buying sites such as Groupon, and food delivery platforms such as Grubhub. Moreover, the clustering is not always geographic. In many medical networks, patients are clustered around disease classes, such as diabetes or specific kinds of cancer. Sports networks are clustered around teams. In each of these cases, the firms involved are vulnerable to competition. Any focused competitor, specializing in a given cluster, geographical region, or specialty, will have a shot at a business. Typically, global hubs do not emerge in clustered networks.

The phenomenon of clustering applies to the value of data and AI as well as network structure. Consider, for example, whether data acquired in Boston will be relevant to the Uber passenger experience in San Francisco, or in Paris. Geographic differences usually limit the value of aggregation across locations.

Evolution of Network and Learning Effects

Finally, because networks change continuously, the strength and structure of network and learning effects can and will change over time. Changes can either strengthen or weaken the value creation curves, making markets more or less competitive. Microsoft Windows provides one of the more interesting examples. In the PC's heyday, during the 1990s, most of the applications that a PC used were client based, meaning that they actually lived on the PC. This defined the relevant local network of Windows developers, whose applications would connect with Windows and drive much of the value of a PC. At its peak, during the late 1990s, there were around six million dedicated developers writing applications exclusively for Windows, and Windows was entrenched as a dominant platform.

Around this time, economists rightly made the argument that Windows-based network effects were strong, because the value of a competitive platform would be highly dependent on assembling a comparable number of dedicated developers. In addition, the fact that applications written for DOS/Windows were not compatible with the Apple operating system (or even on non-Intel processors like the DEC Alpha) made it difficult for app developers to work with non-Microsoft platforms. Microsoft's technological lock-in created a formidable barrier to entry.

However, as internet usage exploded, and as the power of internet-based applications and services took off, the relevant business networks changed. Most of the relevant functionality moved away from PC applications to web-based and mobile applications, which were open and typically worked across different operating systems. Not surprisingly, we see extensive Android, Chrome, and iOS operating systems on both PCs and tablets, and even the resurgence of Mac personal computers, especially at the high end of the market. Mac shipments increased more than fivefold during the mid-2000s. When the strength of a network effect decreases, affected markets become less concentrated.

Value Capture Dynamics

In recent years, because of the ease with which digital networks can connect various types of users and businesses, options for value capture have grown dramatically.[9] Optimizing the value captured by a business can be a significant undertaking, drawing on economic analysis, strategic thinking, and technological capabilities. Digital value capture technologies allow for careful usage metering, sophisticated pricing algorithms that react to product inventory conditions, and even outcome-based pricing models.

However, even with sophisticated pricing approaches, not all the value created for a user network will be captured. The *appropriability of value* (that is, the ability to capture value) on any digital business network is a function of a number of important considerations, such as the existence of competitive solutions and the customer's willingness to pay. When several options are available—such as working with a multisided platform business or network hub—you can adjust pricing to charge the side or network having the least competition and the greatest willingness to pay. This is why search engines do not charge end users and instead charge advertisers for an exclusive opportunity to reach a user who clicks on a specific search term. Often, the search term is an indication of a commercial need, and access to the click is therefore valuable.

The key here is to realize that network effects open new types of value capture options. Take, for example, a system that has direct network effects; some companies may find it useful to charge customers for the value the companies are generating by giving customers access to the network. Xbox and PlayStation 2, for example, have opened monthly subscription access to their platforms so that players can directly connect with other players and enjoy multiplayer games.

Companies that have two-sided indirect network effects have more options for value capture, because they can find multiple ways to monetize their services by charging each side separately, depending on each side's willingness to pay. For example, Ant Financial can make money from consumers and merchants in multiple ways, and Airbnb charges both the renters and the hosts for each stay. Alibaba and Amazon have discovered that advertising fees from merchants are becoming a lucrative revenue source above and beyond the transaction fee they collect from the merchants.

Multihoming

The first and most important force shaping value capture is multihoming. *Multihoming* refers to the viability of competitive alternatives, specifically to situations wherein users or service providers in a network can form ties with multiple platforms or hub firms ("homes") at the same time. If a network hub faces competition from another hub connecting to a network in a similar way, the first network hub's ability to capture value from the network will be challenged, especially if the switching costs are low enough for users to easily use either hub.

The more or the fiercer the competition, the lower the value cap- tured by a network hub. For example, many smartphone app develop- ers multihome across the iOS and Android operating systems. This makes it hard for these platforms to make money on the developer side of their market. However, even though multihoming is common on the developer side, the vast majority of consumers single-home to either iOS or Android phones and continue this practice over sev- eral phone generations, something that enables Apple and Android to extract significant profits from the consumer side of the market.

When multihoming is common on each side of a platform, it be- comes almost impossible for the platform to generate a profit from its business. In the ride-hailing industry, for example, many drivers and riders use multiple platforms to their advantage. Riders can compare prices and wait times, and drivers can reduce their idle time. Not surprisingly, Uber, Lyft, and other competitors constantly undercut each other as they compete for riders and drivers.

Airbnb also experiences serious multihoming on both sides of its platform, because other home-sharing sites present a similar value proposition. Homeowners can easily list the same property on multiple sites (e.g., HomeAway and Vrbo) at the same time with- out much of a barrier, although the fee structures and models may be different. On the other side, renters can search all available sites looking at properties to rent. Multihoming thus hinders profitabil- ity in both ride- and home-sharing services.

Incumbent platform owners can try to reduce multihoming by at- tempting to lock in one side of the market (or even both sides). For example, Uber offered drivers the option to lease cars through part- nerships with car manufacturers with affordable payment plans; this arrangement would lock drivers into driving with Uber only, because drivers would be expected to serve a sufficient number of Uber rides to maintain their eligibility for the loans. Uber and Lyft also offer rate discounts for drivers who drive a large number of miles on their respective platforms, again encouraging drivers to become exclusive. In addition, both companies provide the next ride request to a driver during a ride in progress to encourage another pickup very close to the current drop-off location, reducing a driver's idle time and hence the incentive to use other platforms. Both of these platforms have also introduced usage-based rewards programs for their riders to drive stickiness and reduce multihoming.

Similar approaches have been more successful at Airbnb. For example, it offers tools and advantages exclusively to power users, which provide value but also increase switching costs across platforms. But because of the low adoption cost of multiple platforms, multihoming is still common and profitability is limited.

Firms have developed a number of other approaches to try to avoid multihoming. Video game console makers such as Microsoft and Sony have signed exclusive contracts with game publishers. On the player side, the high prices of consoles and their associated subscription services, such as Xbox Live and PlayStation Plus, reduce players' incentives to multihome. In a similar vein, Amazon provides fulfillment services to third-party sellers and charges them higher fees when their orders are not from Amazon's marketplace to incentivize them to sell exclusively on its platform. It also uses Amazon Prime, a paid subscription service for free two-day shipping for most of its products, to retain customers and reduce their tendency to multihome.

Disintermediation

Disintermediation, wherein nodes in a network can easily bypass the firm to connect directly, can also be a significant problem for capturing value. Take Homejoy, a home services marketplace that shut down a few years ago. After the original match was made between service provider and homeowner, there was little incentive for customers to continue to work through the hub, and disintermediation was common. Homejoy's transaction-based value capture model was doomed, and the service was shut down. This problem is a frequent one, especially for marketplaces—from Homejoy to TaskRabbit—that provide only a connection between network participants. After the first connection is made, most if not all of the value created is delivered, and it's difficult to hold a user accountable to the network hub for ongoing rents.

For better or worse, hubs have used various mechanisms to deter disintermediation, including requiring terms of service that demand users conduct all transactions on the platform or blocking users from exchanging contact information, at least before payment is confirmed. For example, Airbnb withholds the exact locations of hosts and their contact information until payments are made. These kinds of strategies, however, are not always effective. Anything that makes the hub more cumbersome to use can make it vulnerable to a competitor offering a more streamlined experience. Airbnb's substantial scale advantages are in this case defending the hub from competition.

A more honorable way to discourage disintermediation is to enhance the value for users of conducting business through the hub. Hubs may facilitate transactions by providing insurance, payment escrow, or communication tools; resolving disputes; or monitoring transactions. These services, however, can become less valuable to users after they build strong trust among themselves.

Grace Gu, a doctoral student at Harvard Business School, and Feng Zhu examined an online freelance marketplace to understand the relationship between trust and disintermediation. They found that as the network hub improved the accuracy of its reputation system to foster stronger trust between its clients and freelancers, more disintermediation did in fact occur, which offset revenue gains from better matches. After sufficient trust is established between a user and a service provider, services such as payment escrow and dispute resolution are no longer valued—and the need for the platform is diminished.

A more effective way to reduce disintermediation is to reduce transaction fees and make up the revenue on different market sides. The Chinese outsourcing marketplace ZBJ, launched in 2005, had a business model wherein the company charged a 20 percent commission, but it has estimated that as much as 90 percent of revenue was lost because of disintermediation. In 2014, the company discovered that a large number of new business owners used the site to get help on logo design. Typically, the next task these clients would need is business and trademark registration, services the platform started to provide. Recognizing the opportunities, the company started offering complementary services and now is the largest trademark registration service provider in China—an offering that generates more than $1 billion in annual revenue. The platform has significantly reduced its transaction fees and focuses resources on growing its user base instead of fighting disintermediation. The company is now valued at more than $2 billion.[10] If disintermediation is a threat, providing complementary services can work a lot better than charging transaction fees.

Network Bridging

Although multihoming and disintermediation are the enemies of network-based profitability, network bridging can improve and even rescue a firm's business model. *Network bridging* involves making new connections across previously separate economic networks, making use of more-favorable competitive dynamics and different willingness to pay. Network participants can improve their ability to both create and capture value when they connect to multiple networks, bridging among them to build important synergies.

The classic example here is Google search. If Google charged users directly for search—for example, on a per transaction basis—users would use it much less. Google bridged the search business with a network of advertisers who were willing to pay handsomely for access to Google's users by matching their search intent to a relevant advertisement. Payment is another classic example. Traditionally, payment systems have not been big money makers, but access to users and small businesses, as well as the accumulation of data, has made it more than worthwhile for companies to invest in payment networks.

It is worth emphasizing that data-based assets are almost inevitably useful across many scenarios and across multiple network sides. Firms that succeed in building critical mass in users can use this asset to capture value on new and different networks. This is the fundamental reason that hub firms like Amazon and Alibaba move into many different markets.

Alibaba successfully bridged e-commerce platforms Taobao and TMall into financial services by leveraging its payment network, Alipay. Alibaba took advantage of transaction and user data from

Taobao and TMall to launch new services through its financial-services arm, Ant Financial—including a credit system for merchants and consumers based on their transaction data. Using this system, Ant Financial was able to issue short-term loans to consumers and merchants with very low default rates. The loans from Ant allowed consumers to purchase more products on Alibaba's e-commerce plat-forms and provided merchants with funds for inventory purchases.

These networks mutually reinforce each other's market position and help sustain each other's scale. Indeed, even after its rival, Tencent, offered a competing digital wallet service, WeChat Pay, through its popular social networking app WeChat, Alipay remains an attractive digital wallet in part because of its tight bridging with Alibaba's other services. As the most successful network hubs connect across markets, they can be increasingly effective in driv-ing connections across previously disconnected industries.

Strategic Network Analysis

In the previous sections we discuss factors that can strengthen or weaken value creation and capture in networks. Let's now put to-gether the implications and distill them into a consistent approach to strategic network analysis across the multiple networks that connect to a business. We use Uber as an example.

Mapping the Networks

The first step in strategic network analysis is to list the major net-works a business is connected to. Uber, for example, is primarily connected to riders and drivers. A more minor network makes con-nections with food providers to power Uber Eats. Additionally, in March 2018 Uber launched Uber Health, a service that makes connections with health-care providers and lets clinics, hospitals, rehab centers, and other health-care institutions book rides for pa-tients. Uber Health is one of several efforts Uber has under way to

FIGURE 6-5

Networks connected to Uber's core business

partner with different organizations to increase value creation and capture opportunities, including grocery delivery.

Figure 6-5 sketches out the many networks connecting with Uber's operating model. The number of networks will likely grow as Uber searches for additional value capture opportunities. We have seen the company try out UberKITTENS (users pay to cuddle with kittens) and even Uber ice cream delivery.

Network Value Creation and Capture Factors

The second step is to evaluate the potential of each major network in the business for value creation and capture at scale. Table 6-1 includes a checklist of network properties that will strengthen and weaken value creation and capture.

Overall, Uber's situation is difficult. Let's go through the checklist in sequence.

Uber's main businesses do not have direct network effects. There is no value to a rider if other riders are also taking Ubers. Similarly, drivers receive no value from the presence of other drivers. Possibly, there is even a negative impact, because the more riders who exist in close proximity, the more competition there is for a ride

TABLE 6-1

Evaluating Uber's strategic networks

Strengthen value creation and capture	Weaken value creation and capture
• Strong network effects	• Weak network effects
• Strong learning effects	• Weak learning effects
• Strong synergies with other networks	• No synergies with other networks
• No major network clusters	• Important network clusters
• No (or single-sided) multihoming	• Extensive multihoming
• No disintermediation	• Extensive disintermediation
• Extensive network bridging opportunities	• No network bridging opportunities

and the lower the Uber quality of service. (One exception is Uber-Pool, which we discuss in more detail later.)

Weakening network effects further is the geographical clustering of the Uber networks. Having a critical mass of riders and drivers is crucial, but it must be done location by location. Having a high density of drivers in San Francisco is not helpful to users in Detroit. This means that any service with local scale can be competitive to Uber's service, and it implies that the profitability of its core service will always be challenged by inevitable, low-cost competitors.

Uber does have important learning effects, and its businesses benefit from the accumulation and analysis of the extensive amount of data it collects. The learning effects help it adjust pricing due to traffic conditions and other factors, predict supply and demand to make sure that it can offer the right quality of service, and per-form a number of other useful analyses that optimize the value created by its service. It is not clear whether these learning ef-fects are massive enough to ensure sustained profitability for the company.

However, Uber's ride-hailing app suffers from extensive multi-homing problems on both rider and driver networks. A large pro-portion of both riders and drivers have more than one ride-hailing app and regularly check to make sure they are using the most economical service.

Disintermediation of Uber is not a common problem. In part, this is because the company has put in place many measures to enhance the stickiness and convenience of its service for riders and drivers, and in part it stems from the significant penalties the service threatens drivers with who disobey the rules.

The bottom line is that clustering and disintermediation open the door to extensive competition for Uber across all of its core geographies, and the profitability of these services is by no means assured. Absent massive learning effects, Uber's core business will likely remain unprofitable for the foreseeable future.

However, despite its challenged core business, Uber does show promise in the many additional networks it can connect to its core networks of drivers and riders. Uber's future profitability will hinge on its ability to bridge its highly engaged riders and drivers into a growing variety of additional networks. These are starting to provide a variety of other options for value capture, which may enable the company's long-term profitability and viability.

Mapping Uber's Opportunities

Uber has a variety of bridging opportunities enabled by the intrinsic value of its core service, as shown in figure 6-6. Generally speaking, as long as intrinsic value is there, Uber should be able to find a way to bridge the business and make some money. Uber's core service should enable additional value creation, and especially the value capture of being a gateway to additional networks.

One kind of bridging opportunity concerns connecting the driver network with other business networks. Grocery delivery, Uber Eats, and Uber Health are all examples of this class of network bridging opportunities. Uber's driver network is thus plugged in to a variety of other providers, some less local (e.g., Walmart or Kaiser Health). The idea is to foster more enduring, global connections to differentiate Uber from other providers who are fiercely

FIGURE 6-6

Mapping Uber's value creation and capture opportunities

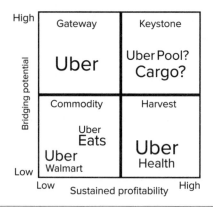

competitive on a local level because of network clustering and multihoming. Will these opportunities be profitable? Clearly it depends on the nature of deals that Uber can seal with providers. Grocery deals are quite competitive because alternatives exist, and Uber's trial with Walmart was suspended because the numbers did not look good. Uber Health seems to have brighter prospects.

Uber Eats is another interesting option. It involves building a new network of connections with local and global restaurant providers. Although certainly providing another shot at goal, this strategy does not ensure sustained profits because again it suffers from extensive competition and local clustering challenges. Apparently, Uber Eats is profitable in some locations but generally unprofitable.

Other interesting Uber opportunities include UberPool and Cargo Systems. UberPool is a service that attempts to drive additional economies by sharing rides across multiple users. The interesting thing about UberPool is that the network effects are much stronger than in the regular Uber service. In fact UberPool adds *direct* network effects to Uber's traditional indirect network effects business. Suddenly, the more riders Uber has, the more the value to riders increases. With UberPool at scale, it is much less likely that a competitor could provide a similar service. The chance that a smaller service provider could find two random passengers starting from a close location and ending up at a similarly close location is extremely small. Unfortunately, the chances are small even at Uber's current size, and the service has been plagued by profitability and dissatisfaction problems. If UberPool ever reaches scale, however, it might truly contend for the keystone category, because it will harvest significant profits while having the same bridging potential of traditional Uber ride-sharing.

One additional interesting idea is Cargo, which was started by serial entrepreneur Mark Pincus of Zynga and Support.com fame. Cargo connects the rider network with a variety of retail opportunities by offering a convenient way to sell products to riders while they are a captive audience in a ride-sharing vehicle. Cargo advertises that drivers can make hundreds more dollars each month. This is sheer profit for drivers (and for Uber), which could make a material difference to Uber's profits.

Ultimately, the intrinsic value embedded in Uber is real and offers a myriad of bridging opportunities, but achieving a stable valuation as a public company will require work—and perhaps more modest expectations.

Strategic Questions

We now summarize our arguments into a set of questions. These are questions entrepreneurs and executives should ask about their own businesses as they develop strategies and envision the potential value creation and capture opportunities in the networks the business could connect to. For a concrete example, let's go back to the Parkinson's app introduced at the beginning of the chapter.

What is the core service delivered?

As with most traditional strategic analyses, the best way to start is to go back to the most essential way the business creates value. In the case of a cool AI startup, for example, what is the specific process your firm is digitizing and enabling through AI? In the case of an advanced business, what is the most basic value proposition?

With the Parkinson's app, the core value is in improving the effectiveness of treatment by gathering data on the daily progress of the disease.

What networks are key to providing that service, and what are their characteristics? Do they have strong learning or network effects? Are they clustered?

This next step is a systematic assessment of the characteristics of the core network the business is plugging in to. The most critical network for the Parkinson's app is its patient network. Its most essential dynamic is the learning effect, because the app's patient data should be highly useful in carefully monitoring the progress of the disease in a way that has previously been impossible. There are many ways to gather useful data, from basic coordination tests taken by the patient, to a simple daily survey. Given the complexity of the disease and its many rare forms, the tail of the distribution in disease characteristics is quite long, and the potential for the data to be increasingly useful at scale is very high. The learning effects are thus strong, which is both good and bad news for the app. The bad news is that it will take many deployments before the data is truly useful. The good news is that after it reaches critical mass, the app should be able to sustain a significant competitive advantage.

If network and learning effects are weak, how do you strengthen them over time? How do you increase the value delivered?

As the business grows, one should consider the potential to ratchet up value created by driving additional learning and network effects. Learning effects are already strong in the Parkinson's app, but they could be bolstered over time by providing additional functionality to promote additional significant network effects. If functionality is added to the app to encourage interaction among the participants, for example, it could engender significant exchanges, in the form of mutual support, coaching, and advice on fighting a difficult disease. These direct network effects could help further sustain the app's competitive advantage.

If the network effects are strong and there is very little value delivered until critical mass, how do you get there?

This is the classic chicken-and-egg problem. Any company depending on strong network and learning effects needs a way to bootstrap its business until it acquires enough scale for the learning and network effects to kick in. This is true of the Parkinson's app: its scale is still too modest to deliver much in the way of learning and network effects.

To kick-start growth, we could try several tactics. We could load the app with content to attract users. We could provide treatment advice and best practices, even invest in making live help available to answer treatment questions. We could also gamify the experience, making the app more entertaining and engaging. The Peloton app, for example, leveraged the Facebook network to bring together enthusiasts into communities that are passionate about their Peloton experience.

What are the most important secondary networks? Can they enable additional network or learning effects?

Now that we understand the basics of our core network, we should start examining the business to analyze the characteristics of the many secondary networks. With the Parkinson's app, several networks are of interest. The most interesting is probably the network of physicians, because they can greatly benefit from having data on the patient's disease progression and from developing an additional channel of interaction with the patient. The app could even build functionality to help physicians or other medical staff provide additional coaching and advice. These services would add a substantial indirect network effect to the app, further improving its competitive position and business sustainability. There are a number of other interesting networks, such as researchers and insurers, who would benefit from the patient data, as well as pharmacies, which could use it to help trigger prescriptions and refills.

Do we have challenges with network clustering? Multihoming? Disintermediation?

Now we go a little deeper on the characteristics of the networks the business is focused on. The Parkinson's app business is inherently clustered on Parkinson's patients, so scale there is limited. When the app plugs in to related networks, however, it can truly deliver daily value to patients. Engagement is likely to be high, and disintermediation and multihoming appear unlikely because the value emerges from the integration of related networks. As the app accumulates an increasing amount of patient data and perhaps even engages the patient's physicians, the likelihood of multihoming and disintermediation is even more distant.

What are the best value capture opportunities?

To think seriously about value capture, one must first understand the characteristics of the networks in play. Now that we have examined the characteristics of the various networks plugging in to the Parkinson's app, what jumps out is the significant value that can be created at scale, to patients, physicians, researchers, and insurers. However, without critical mass, the value created by the app is limited, again because of the strong learning and network effects. This suggests a strategy *not* to charge patients or physicians for using the app, because we want to do everything we can to encourage adoption and engagement.

However, there are many other ways to monetize the app. One is simply to provide it for free and gather the benefits in increased branding and exposure to the complementary pharmaceutical business, whose revenues are already in the billions of dollars. Any noticeable increase in those revenues would easily pay for the app, with plenty to spare. We could also consider targeted ads (useful and tactfully designed), physician referrals, insurance subsidies, and anonymized data monetization opportunities. All in all, this app would make quite a good business and would add a ton of value to the treatment and management of the disease.

Are there network bridging opportunities? Considering the data you can accumulate from your core network, is it of value to another network?

Finally, we should ask what kinds of previously separate networks this business could bridge to for additional value creation or capture opportunities. The Holy Grail for the Parkinson's app would be to transcend disease classes, but these are highly clustered, so the points of connection are few. Insurers could push for the adoption of similar apps in different environments, or even serve as a distribution channel, after the app is well established and successful in Parkinson's treatment. Physicians and other health-care providers could also enable bridging into other disease networks.

This chapter has examined some of the more important approaches to crafting strategy in an age driven by data and AI and dominated by digital networks. In the next chapter we illustrate the broad strategic implications of these ideas and examine the resulting competitive dynamics observed in various sectors of the economy.

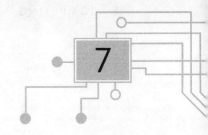

Strategic Collisions

Can anyone catch the cell phone king?

—*Forbes* cover story about Nokia, November 12, 2007,
    half a year after the iPhone was introduced

In chapter 6, we explored how digitizing key elements of the firm's operating model can open new strategic options and transform the way a firm creates and captures value. This chapter examines some of the broader competitive implications and explores what happens as firms featuring a digital operating model encounter and collide with more traditional firms.

A *collision* occurs when a firm with a digital operating model targets an application (or use case) that has traditionally been served by a more conventional firm (see figure 7-1). Because digital operating models are characterized by different scale, scope, and learning dynamics from those of traditional firms, collisions can completely transform industries and reshape the nature of competitive advantage.

Note that it can take quite a while for digital operating models to generate economic value that comes anywhere near the value generated by traditional operating models. This explains why executives ensconced in the traditional model have a difficult time at first believing that the digital model will ever catch up. But after the digital operating model scales beyond critical mass, the value delivered can be truly impressive, and firms operating with digital models can easily overwhelm traditional firms. The implications are increasingly felt across our entire economy.

FIGURE 7-1

The collision between a digital and a traditional firm

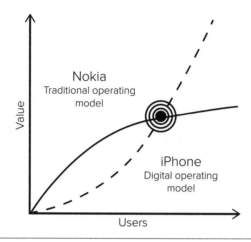

Take the global travel industry, where Airbnb is colliding with hotel companies like Marriott and Hilton. Airbnb serves similar needs but is built on a completely different kind of operating model. While Marriott and Hilton own and manage properties, with tens of thousands of employees in separate organizations devoted to enabling and shaping customer experiences, Airbnb's lean organization sits on top of a virtual AI factory, aggregating data and using carefully crafted algorithms to match users to its digitally tracked and managed community of property owners. And where both Marriott and Hilton are a cluster of groups and brands, each with its own siloed business units and functions equipped with their own information technology, fragmented data, and organizational structure, Airbnb's lean and agile organization sits on top of its integrated data platform, accumulating customer and process information, mining analytic insights, running rapid experiments, and producing predictive models to inform key decisions.

Airbnb accumulates network and learning effects, rapidly driving scale, scope, and learning, while Marriott's growth and responsiveness are limited by its traditional operational constraints. In barely a decade, Airbnb has scaled to offer an inventory of more than 4.5 million rooms, three times as much lodging capacity as Marriott managed to accumulate in its one hundred years.

As with Amazon's supply chain or Ant Financial's credit scoring process, Airbnb moves human labor from the core of the operating model to the edge, in this case even outside the company boundaries (the hosts). Airbnb constantly mines its data to acquire new customers, identify new traveler needs, optimize experiences, and analyze risk exposure. As it does so, it accumulates even more data on hosts and travelers, and it uses artificial intelligence and machine learning to provide new insights, confirmed through frequent experimentation. Airbnb is also rapidly expanding in scope to offer a broad variety of experiences, from concerts to flight lessons. This drives new network and learning effects and multiplies opportunities for both value creation and capture.

Airbnb isn't the only digital firm agitating the global travel market. Booking Holdings is another formidable force, whose brands— Booking.com, Kayak.com, and Priceline.com—offer 30 million listings in more than 150,000 destinations built over a lifetime slightly longer than Airbnb's. As with Airbnb, Booking is architected to enable a software- and data-centric operating model, increasing scale, scope, and learning without running into traditional operational constraints. And as with Airbnb, Booking's only real growth bottlenecks sit outside the company, in ensuring a growing inventory of travel accommodations and experiences. Booking's valuation is already twice Marriott's.

The industry is transforming in front of our eyes. In only a few years, Airbnb and Booking have dramatically increased the number of room nights sold and have catapulted into leadership positions, while increasing the bundle of services offered to consumers. Market concentration is also increasing, with M&A activity on a high boil.

Marriott has responded by merging with Starwood, aiming to exploit synergies across loyalty programs and related data assets. In a race against time, Marriott is working hard to operationalize the merger and rearchitect its operating model to remain competitive against Airbnb's and Booking's data-driven growth machines. The hotel industry is in the midst of a collision.

The Competitive Dynamics of Collision

The collision between digital and traditional travel companies shows what happens when traditional user needs are met in new ways by a different kind of operating model that digitizes some of the most critical tasks in the delivery of value. The market needs are very similar—travelers need accommodations and experiences—but unlike traditional hotel chains, Airbnb and Booking have built systems to satisfy those needs without relying on massive traditional organizations, armies of hotel managers and sales employees, and cumbersome operating processes.

Airbnb and Booking are effectively adding a software layer to the travel industry; think of it as an operating system for travel. If Marriott is the IBM mainframe company of the travel industry, Airbnb and Booking are vying to be Microsoft Windows. In doing so, they push traditional operational bottlenecks outside their organizations and remove constraints on their own scalability, scope, and learning potential.

As with computer operating systems companies, digital operating companies like Booking and Airbnb amplify the value they create by leveraging network and learning effects. Network effects are central to their model. More demand for lodging by travelers will induce more hotels and homeowners to offer their properties online, and the more properties that are offered, the more travelers who are likely to come.

Learning effects further amplify the value delivered, as data trains machine learning algorithms to recognize patterns and improve operational decisions. Both Airbnb and Booking.com accumulate all kinds of data on user behavior, such as the types of content that a certain user will be more likely to click on, linger on, or mouse over. This data is used by an algorithm to select and prioritize the content to be steered to a user's app. As the app accumulates varied data, the learning analytics can amplify the impact of network effects as they're trained to increasingly engage the user.[1] The more data, the more refined the optimization, and the more the typical user will engage with the content.

Travel industry examples, once again, show how AI and learning and network effects can go hand in hand to build a rapidly growing value proposition for a digital operating model in a series of self-reinforcing loops. As the operating model develops more connections, it also develops increased opportunities to generate and accumulate data. The more data that is generated, the better the services the organization can provide and the more incentive there is for third parties to plug in. The better the services it provides, the more users it will attract, and the more users, the more data, and so on, in turn increasing the impact of any learning and network effects. In general, the larger the networks and the more data that is generated, the better the algorithms, and the better the algorithms, the sharper the increase of value delivered because of scale and scope.

These self-reinforcing loops in network and learning effects make a big difference in the nature of competition. The value delivered by traditional operating models becomes saturated as the organization grows. This implies that traditional operating models tend to allow for competition, enabling entrants to threaten incumbents, because the advantages of scale are significant but not insurmountable. New companies can be competitive by offering interesting, innovative solutions even on a smaller scale; think of a country inn taking room nights away from a Marriott resort. But as network and learning effects drive more of the value delivered, traditional constraints go away, and the value delivered will continue to increase, possibly at an increasing rate. If network and learning effects are strong, and if multihoming and disintermediation are rare, the viability of competitive alternatives is diminished, and markets are driven toward concentration.

As value delivered increases for digital operating models, the space left for competitors at lower scale, scope, and learning continues to shrink, making it difficult for a traditional company to sustain a profitable offering. Although hotel companies will not cease to exist, their profits are moving to the "operating system" layer. The immense scalability of the new AI-centric "travel experience operating system" model is altering competitive dynamics, forcing Marriott, Hilton, Hyatt, and other traditional operators into the fight of their lives.

The next decade will witness an epic battle for control of the multitrillion-dollar global travel market. To get a better sense of how this battle, as well as many similar collisions, might evolve, let's revisit the collision between traditional and digital phone providers. The story is old news, but it offers interesting insights when analyzed through our new lens.

The Classic Case

Nokia was founded in 1865 as a paper mill and eventually grew into the world leader in mobile communications. Only five years after *Forbes* featured Nokia's industry leadership on its November 2007 cover, the company had completely collapsed. Sold to Microsoft for $7 billion, less than one-tenth its 2007 value, Nokia's mobile phone business was resold a couple of years later for only a few hundred million dollars. From a position of industry dominance, Nokia tumbled into irrelevance.[2]

How could this have happened to a company that seemed to do everything right? A marvel of product innovation, design, and usability, Nokia invented most of the new features we still use on phones today, from touch screen interfaces to the first mobile internet browser. Its designs won prizes for style and usability. Its marketing organization was second to none in its relentless focus on the user. Its manufacturing processes were renowned for their high quality, low costs, and generous operating margins. In many ways, Nokia was the quintessential product company.

Nokia was architected like all other large, traditional product companies: a siloed, geographically separated, multidivisional business unit structure, dedicated product teams, and multiple R&D centers around the world. Nokia ran hundreds of simultaneous R&D projects and introduced thousands of products across more than a dozen major geographies. Its product development teams optimized integrated hardware and software features to match specific customer needs and create great designs. Supporting its product strategy was a vertically integrated manufacturing process and a dedicated and responsive supply chain. Nokia's competitive advantage increased with the variety of differentiated models and designs—each tuned to a different geography or market segment. All this was complemented by investments in technical capabilities, patents, and branding and marketing.

But as product companies often do, in order to optimize each product and tailor it to the unique needs and context of each market and organization, Nokia sacrificed digital consistency. Even though Nokia invested heavily in the Symbian operating system, that OS was only one of several the company used. And even within Symbian products, each phone's software was fine-tuned to a different user interface design, form factor, or customer features. The developer interface, moreover, was unstable, inconsistent, and emphatically not user friendly. All this added to developers' headaches when they tried to create apps for Nokia's broad variety of models and operating system versions. Any app would have to be redesigned (by hand) for virtually every product Nokia offered. It's no surprise, then, that when Nokia opened an app store (Ovi) in 2008, the marketplace never attracted developers and never offered a critical mass of apps.

Nokia operated like any great product company would have, optimized to produce laser-focused, differentiated products. As such, it gathered no scale benefits from a standard digital foundation, no scope benefits from a successful platform ecosystem, and no learning benefits from a consistent data architecture or experimentation platform.

Then in 2007, Apple's iOS hit the market, rapidly followed by Google's Android. Rather than being built within a traditional, siloed product business featuring separate product units, iOS and Android phones were built on one software version, a single, consistent digital foundation. Although they could work like a phone and matched Nokia's in performance, the iPhone-iOS combination embodied a single digital platform, and soon Apple offered an elegant and consistent API, in a fashion very similar to the way PCs had been conceived since the 1980s. Android rapidly followed suit and also opened its architecture, thereby enabling a diverse set of smartphone original equipment manufacturers (OEMs).

In contrast with Nokia phones, iOS and Android phones attracted ever-expanding ecosystems of third-party app developers

and service providers, complementing the core functionality embedded in the phone. Unlike Nokia's fragmented product line, the
consistent iOS and Android platforms encouraged the formation of
large networks of app developers, spurring intense developer excitement. The positive reinforcement loops were remarkable: the
more iPhone and Android apps there were, the higher the levels of
user engagement; and the higher the levels of user engagement, the
greater the number of transactions and the greater the amount of
data and value that flowed to developers and advertisers.

As the developer and advertiser networks reached critical mass,
the value of iOS and Android increased rapidly. The slope of the value
curve grew steeper as the value delivered overwhelmed the value
delivered by traditional smartphones trying to serve the same
customers. With millions of deployed apps, iPhone and Android
took off and left Nokia's traditional, product-based business model
behind (see figure 7-2). Along with Nokia, other competitors, including BlackBerry, Sony Ericsson, and Motorola, fell off the map.

FIGURE 7-2

The Nokia and Apple value curves

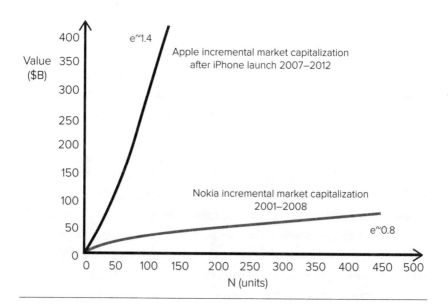

Beyond displacing traditional industry leaders, the collision in smartphones dramatically changed the structure of the industry. Virtually all profits migrated from the highly competitive hardware layer to the highly concentrated software layer, capturing value through complementary revenue sources such as bundled hardware, advertising, and app download fees. The battle is not over yet, but it looks as if the final victory is likely to go to Android, already powering more than 85 percent of global smartphones.

The irony is that Nokia invented and introduced many of the features we now associate with smartphones—touch screen functionality, integrated cameras, embedded search, even apps and app stores—well ahead of the iPhone introduction in 2007. Indeed, throughout the period it was losing ground to iOS and Android, Nokia was investing an impressive 8 percent to 15 percent of revenue in R&D. But iOS and Android were architected to build value in a profoundly different way. Just as Airbnb and Booking are becoming data-driven magnets for travel experience providers, both iOS and Android became magnets for app developers and advertisers. The market tipped, and Nokia and the nature of competition changed. All in all, it took less than five years. Nokia discovered that once digital network businesses reach critical mass, they can rapidly grow to dominate markets, and transform the economy.

To meet the new threat, Nokia had two options. First, it could have built its own digital operating model and competed head-on with Android and iOS. But to do this, it would have had to transition from a siloed, product-based operating architecture to a software-optimized operating architecture—standardizing on a single consistent digital framework and adopting a standard approach to software component design, ecosystem development, and data integration. Building Symbian technology was not enough. What was required was a deep-rooted transformation, the likes of which we discussed in chapters 4 and 5.

Nokia's second option would have been to acknowledge the newfound dominance of smartphone OS companies and focus on becoming the best possible complement to the new software-based entrants. This is essentially what Samsung has done, by conceding the software battle and focusing on hardware features and components. Although not approaching the kind of value and profitability captured by iOS and Android, Samsung has survived and, to some extent, prospered. Unique to its strategy is becoming one of the industry's very few strategic suppliers of high-quality screen displays—still a highly profitable (and significant) niche. For the rest of the smartphone hardware OEMs, it's been a different story, as profits have dwindled in the brutally competitive market. However, despite the adversity, many companies still survive.

Interestingly, Nokia did not execute either option, which may explain its rapid demise. Nokia at first simply refused to change and tried to answer the threat by building more products within its existing operating architecture. But even when the failure of this approach was patently obvious, Stephen Elop, the company's CEO, refused to acknowledge Android's clear advantage and committed to the Windows mobile operating system, which already lagged far behind in market share. Without harvesting the gains of digital scale, scope, and learning, Nokia took a nosedive into oblivion.

The Pattern Repeats

The smartphone story is threatening to repeat everywhere. We have argued that Airbnb and Booking are posing a similar challenge to Marriott and Hilton. And just as cloud computing services from Amazon and Microsoft are replacing traditional software and hardware providers, marketplace platforms like Alibaba and Amazon are replacing traditional retailers. Digital, over the top (OTT) video content delivery services (think Netflix, Hulu, and Amazon Prime Video) are threatening traditional pay TV providers. New fintech companies are competing with traditional banks and insurance companies by providing data-centered financial services over the internet. Across the economy, we see traditional firms colliding with highly scalable, data-driven, software-centric operating models, leveraging networks, data, and AI to drive personalization and to expand the range of services by using digital networks to plug in to service providers. The ensuing transformation in each of these industries is profound, and it cuts across value creation, capture, and delivery to change competitive dynamics and market structure.

Let's look at a few more examples, both past and present.

Computing

The computing sector has already witnessed a number of different collisions between operating architectures, each digitizing new aspects of the industry value chain. The most impactful transformation probably took place as far back as the 1980s, when mainframe and minicomputer providers collided with personal computer firms. For the first time we saw a digital platform structure having separate, modular operating systems like CPM, DOS, and later Windows and the Mac OS. CPM fell out of favor, but the Mac OS retained an integral structure for most of its history (with Apple contributing its own applications), and Microsoft established Windows—with its hundreds and later thousands of APIs and easy-to-use Visual Studio programming tools—as the OS of choice for the industry.

Windows thus used digital interfaces to modularize and distribute the creation of software applications, thereby building a large and powerful ecosystem; at its peak there were more than six million developers whose daily occupation was building software for Windows, working for a variety of application providers. The developer ecosystem generated strong network effects, and the dominance of Windows continued for more than a decade, with Microsoft's market share in PC operating systems peaking at greater than 90 percent. In many ways, Google's increasing dominance in smartphones simply revisits the old Windows playbook, with the addition of data, AI, and the massive revenues provided by tailored advertising services.

In recent years, cloud computing has led to yet another collision, in essence digitizing the process of software distribution. The cloud offers a new business and operating model for distributing a variety of computing services, with easy, network-based access to flexible computing capacity and consumption-based pricing for computing, storage, and other applications and services. The operating model for cloud computing providers is completely different from traditional software OS providers, as it hinges on the establishment of extensive data center infrastructure to efficiently deliver the services instead of either selling software in stores or deploying software on-premise in enterprises.

After losing out to Linux and other (primarily open source) alternatives, Microsoft is back in the game. Chasing Amazon Web Services, Microsoft has made great inroads in transforming business and operating models to be among the first to offer cloud services optimized for business applications. Gone are the software boxes available at Best Buy and Computer City, and soon to be gone are the massive on-premise deployments of products like Windows Server and SQL Server; all software is now available for easy digital download, on demand, from the cloud. Not surprisingly, leadership in the industry turned over again, with Amazon (primarily through AWS) and Microsoft (after its transformation) now alternating as the world's most valuable company.

Because this industry has been dealing with collisions for so long, firms have become good at transformation. Experience is one factor, but so is the fact that the operating architecture of firms in this industry is less siloed and fragmented than you see in traditional industries. After a firm is architected as a software and data platform company, it is comparatively easier to transform it to adopt new generations of technology.

Retail

Among the first online retailers was Amazon, founded in 1994 with the emergence of the World Wide Web. Early "e-tailer" operating models like those of Amazon, drugstore.com, JD.com, or even Pets .com digitized buying transactions and moved them online. Over time, online retailers grew into actual digital retail platforms, with Amazon launching and scaling its marketplace and connecting to thousands of third-party merchants that offered unprecedented scale and scope across thousands of product categories. As described in chapter 4, Amazon rearchitected its own operating model to aggregate data and share software components—designing a powerful, data-centric operating platform and driving a formidable transformation in the retail experience.

Traditional retailers stood up to the first generation of online retailers fairly well, because the transformation was relatively limited. Lacking extensive data and analytics and bottlenecked by a traditional supply chain, online retailers did not generate substantial network or learning effects. Ultimately, the likes of Pets.com and drugstore.com did not serve the unique needs of a customer any better than a traditional store. The extensive variety of goods that could be provided online was hard to navigate without personalization, and individual in-store clerks can be quite effective if well trained. The bigger threat was Amazon's rearchitected, data-centric, software-based operating model, which companies like JD.com and Wayfair emulated.

The transformation consisted of more than simply moving transactions online. It called for a fundamentally different operating approach based on a data- and AI-centric unified understanding of the customer, offering a way to personalize the retail experience not only online but also offline (as we see, for example, in Amazon's Whole Foods Market acquisition). Retail supply chains became software centric, deploying labor, not in the core of the process but on the edge (e.g., to pick odd-shaped products from shelves), an action that removed traditional bottlenecks and scale constraints. By the late 2010s, the retail apocalypse was in full force, taking down all manner of traditional players, including Toys "R" Us, Sports Authority, Nine West, and Brookstone, to name just a few.

The insight from retail is that putting a business online does not necessarily topple a traditional industry giant. The difference is having a software- and data-centric operating architecture. It was only after some of the online retailers figured this out that the industry truly transformed.[3]

Entertainment

The first organization to compete using a data- and software-centric operating model to collide successfully with the entertainment industry may have been Napster, which allowed people to digitize and share their music online for free—without any of the usual payments to the various players in the music industry. When it emerged in the late 1990s, it introduced music as a service. Despite its immense popularity, Napster was plagued by legal troubles and shut down in 2001. After Napster, Apple Music, Spotify, and others sparked new collisions with traditional music distribution companies, transforming the business and operating models for music distribution in the United States and beyond.

Collisions spread from music to video. Launched in 1997, Real-Networks was the first internet streaming video company.[4] By 2000, almost all of the video streamed over the internet was in the RealNetworks format. Its business model hinged on selling server software, however, and RealNetworks suffered in competition with established software providers such as Microsoft and Apple.

Streaming services truly took off with YouTube, founded in 2005, and Netflix, which transitioned from a DVD business into a streaming service starting around 2007. YouTube and Netflix offered a more compelling value proposition for consumers as well as scalable value capture models through advertising and subscription, patterned largely on the music streaming business.

However, there is a significant difference between the Netflix and YouTube operating models, with important implications for competition. By aggregating a huge community of small content providers, YouTube accumulates important network effects and essentially dominates its market. The kinds of video streaming services provided by Netflix, on the other hand, come from a much more concentrated set of content production studios, which routinely multihome and offer their content across various delivery platforms. Although Netflix's data and learning advantages are important, they do not add up to the kind of advantage enjoyed by YouTube at scale. This has enabled a number of companies to sustain competitive offerings, from Hulu to Amazon. Lacking strong network effects, each of these providers is attempting to differentiate itself by accessing unique content through special studio relationships and vertical integration. Digital firms now have huge content production budgets and are challenging traditional providers in most global markets.

As a group, Google, Netflix, Apple, and Amazon are colliding with traditional cable and satellite television providers, providing OTT internet-based video content distribution platforms that have rapidly scaled to hundreds of millions of users globally. Despite differences in the network effects accumulated, each of these firms competes on a data-centric operating model, driving extensive customization and personalization to cater each viewing experience to the needs of individual users. On alert after the devastation in music and retail, traditional media companies are scrambling to react, merging with content and internet service providers to spark transformation and rearchitecting operations around a digital core. Comcast and Disney have demonstrated important progress, from the development of the X1 platform to ESPN streaming services.

The transformation of entertainment reveals other interesting patterns. First, the original innovator in a given industry does not always win; Napster is long gone. Deploying a digital operating model is not enough. For a collision to threaten established players, the innovator needs an effective business model as well. Additionally, as they compete with traditional companies, digital firms compete with each other. As they do so, they may emerge as focused competitors like Netflix, or they may leverage synergies in assets and capabilities across industries, like Amazon and Apple. The winners and level of concentration in each market will be shaped by the resulting economies of scale, scope, and learning.

Automotive

Cars are becoming increasingly connected and digital, and this increased connectivity and functionality is threatening the traditional operating models of automobile companies. At stake is the enormous value of connecting to consumers while in transit—for example, during the work commute, which, on average, takes around one hour a day in the United States. The value of one hour of consumer access is high—hundreds of billions of dollars in the United States alone.

Exploiting opportunities to extract economic value from a moving, connected car will require a digital, data-centric operating model that delivers a marketplace of on-demand services or highly targeted ads that will be embedded in the cars themselves, through various screens or audio aimed at drivers and passengers. Car-sharing services like Uber, Lyft, and DiDi are starting to show the way, but the best opportunity lies in autonomous driving systems. When consumers no longer need to pay attention to driving, they'll want entertainment and social interactions—turning the car into a large smartphone on wheels. It's no surprise, then, that new and old companies are engaged in a fight for the incremental value created and captured.

Alphabet is first in line. Already at scale from its mobile business, Android is ready to shape automotive user behavior and value capture for its parent company. Google Maps and advertising networks are also already at scale and ready to create relevant local ads pinpointed to the car's location. The next step is literally driving users to commercial opportunities. Auto manufacturers, pressured by consumer demands, have given hub firms dashboard screen access in many cars, directly integrating their services into the driving experience. Adding to these already massive opportunities, Alphabet subsidiary Waymo is developing a driverless car as a service business, which, by itself, could one day earn hundreds of billions of dollars in revenue.

These changes will transform the industry. As the trends continue, transportation will become less about car ownership and experience, and more about the convenience and services offered by automobiles as they drive passengers around. Sure, some people will still want cars they can actually drive, but differentiation will lessen, and most car hardware might well become increasingly commoditized, just as with most Android OEMs.

Just as we saw in other examples, the effects of transformation in the auto industry won't be limited to auto manufacturers; they will upend a range of connected sectors, including insurance companies, repair and maintenance providers, road and construction companies, law enforcement, and infrastructure providers, as the digital dominos continue to fall. Even governments will be affected, because many local, state, and federal authorities rely on various forms of automotive taxes.

As the Nokia saga suggests, the auto manufacturers' core business will increasingly be commoditized as a more concentrated software layer emerges. Revenues and margins will erode as demand saturates and car utilization increases. As differentiation moves from hardware to software and networks, now largely outside the manufacturers' control, price premiums will plummet.

What can traditional auto manufacturers do? As with Nokia, they appear to have two options: either challenge hub firms like Alphabet and Apple, or work with them and become their chosen, best suppliers. Both strategies come with challenges. The first entails competing with the likes of Android and iOS, which are already at scale, and includes crucial services like maps and advertising platforms. The second involves resisting the commoditization of automotive hardware and its components as functionality and market power move to the software layer.

As the traditional automotive business appears to head toward commodity status, some auto manufacturers are attempting to participate in the emerging software and services layers of the automotive stack. Indeed, some automakers are preparing for a pay-per-use model for car usage, and several manufacturers have already acquired or partnered with major car-as-service providers, as with GM's investment in Lyft or Daimler's acquisition of car2go. Several manufacturers have also invested in their own driverless research or have partnered with external providers. The key issue is whether they will be able to gather enough scale, scope, and learning advantages to compete with the pros.

Beyond investing in digital transformation and experimenting with new, service-based business and operating models, automakers may need to play the way the digital hubs do. And to reach the scale required to be competitive, once fiercely competitive automotive companies will need to rearchitect their operating models and even join forces to aggregate enough scale.

HERE, a precision map and location service provider, is an interesting example. HERE has its roots in Navteq, one of the early online mapping companies, acquired first by Nokia and more recently by a consortium of Volkswagen, BMW, and Daimler. Providing a sophisticated set of tools and APIs to enable third-party developers to develop location-based ads and other services, HERE is an attempt by traditional auto manufacturers to work together to assemble a "federated" platform. In doing so, HERE neutralizes a potential competitive bottleneck and counterbalances clear threats from Google and Apple. The consortium could play a significant role in preventing automotive value capture from tipping completely toward existing digital firms.

The next decade will entail major changes and transformation for the automotive sector. Traditional manufacturers should not underestimate the competitive skill and scale, scope, and learning advantages exhibited by the digital firms that are entering the space. They have played this game before and obviously understand the new shape of competition.

Where We Are Heading

We are witnessing a new generation of digital operating models transforming the economics and nature of service delivery. Software, along with data- and AI-centric architectures, is removing traditional operational constraints and enabling a new generation of business models that cut across industries. This is transforming competition, and we already see evidence of a more concentrated, winner-take-all world emerging in some traditional markets. And as collisions multiply across the economy, different industries become increasingly connected to each other, through the new, ubiquitous digital fabric. Our entire economy is starting to resemble a vast, highly connected network coalescing around a small number of digital superpowers.

A generation of hub firms has emerged—the likes of Apple, Alphabet/Google, Amazon, Baidu, Facebook, Microsoft, Tencent, and Alibaba, including many of the examples covered in this book. Beyond challenging some traditional competitors, hub firms are enabled by their operating models to occupy increasingly central positions in our economy, reaching across to connect and orchestrate traditionally disparate industries. While creating real value for users, these companies also capture a large and expanding share of the value generated, and they're shaping our collective future.

Beyond influencing individual markets, hub firms are poised to create and control essential connections in key networks. The Android operating system is forming a competitive bottleneck well beyond the phone industry, owning access to billions of consumers that other product and service providers want to reach. Amazon's and Alibaba's marketplaces connect vast numbers of users with vast numbers of retailers and manufacturers. Tencent's WeChat messaging platform aggregates a billion global users and provides a critical source of consumer access for businesses offering online banking, entertainment, transportation, and other services. Alibaba is connecting e-commerce transactions with credit scoring, investment management, and loans, all at an unprecedented scale.

The more users join these networks, the more attractive (and even mandatory) it becomes for enterprises to offer their products and services through them. By driving increasing returns to scale, scope, and learning, these digital superpowers can control crucial competitive bottlenecks, extract disproportionate value, and tip the global competitive balance, as suggested in figure 7-3. The implications, as we are all witnessing, go well beyond the economy.

The speed with which traditional processes are being replaced by digital technology is increasing at what is starting to feel like an exponential rate. The introduction of software platforms provided an initial impulse, but the technologies are becoming sophisticated enough to rapidly transcend relatively simple software applications. The impact of data, analytics, and AI is just ramping up and has ways to go. And as digital technology increasingly collides with disparate aspects of our economy and society, Nokia's fate is threatening industries as diverse as media and banking, automotive and travel. After a hundred years of history, companies like Marriott and Hilton are investing in driving major transformation, integrating disparate data assets, developing capabilities in analytics and AI, and working hard to rearchitect their traditional operating models.

Beyond shaping the fate of leading firms, the impact of these collisions is being felt across our entire economy and into our social

FIGURE 7-3

The evolution of the modern economy

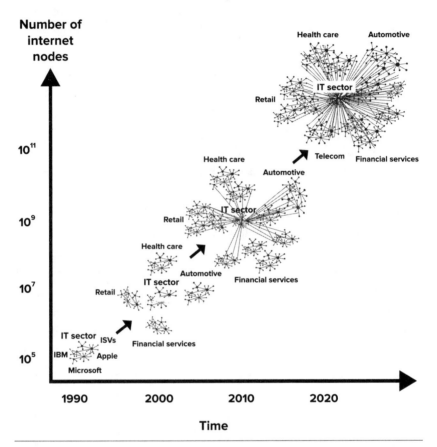

and political system. As disparate industries increasingly consolidate into one giant network, the concentration of value and
information not only creates opportunity but also introduces new
problems. From the erosion of consumer privacy to the emergence
of an increasing variety of cyber threats, and from disinformation
campaigns to economic disparity, the spread of digital operating
models is causing a range of new threats.

Managers will have their work cut out for them, as they reflect
on their evolving role in our increasingly digital economy. The next
chapter focuses on some of these considerations.

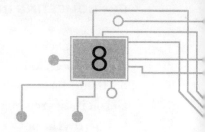

The Ethics of Digital Scale, Scope, and Learning

> As I have discussed with you in other contexts, and as you have acknowledged, the algorithms which power [your] services are not designed to distinguish quality information from misinformation or misleading information, and the consequences of that are particularly troubling for public health issues . . .
>
> As more Americans rely on your services as their primary source of information, it is vital that you take that responsibility with the seriousness it requires, and nowhere more so than in matters of public health and children's health. Thank you for your attention to this important topic.
>
> —Excerpts of letters from Rep. Adam Schiff (D-CA), Chairman of the House Select Committee on Intelligence, to Sundar Pichai of Google and Mark Zuckerberg of Facebook in February 2019. Jeff Bezos of Amazon received a similar letter from Schiff.

What prompted Rep. Adam Schiff to send these letters was the spread of anti-vaccination propaganda on Amazon, YouTube (owned by Google), Facebook, and Instagram (owned by Facebook). Schiff's concern is not an idle one: by April 2019 the incidence of measles in the United States was at its second highest since the disease was thought to be eliminated in 2000.[1] And false health information is not only a problem in the United States. Similar public health concerns are being raised in Europe and across Asia and South America. In China, for example, regulators came down hard on Baidu for allowing dubious medical information to spread via ads on its search engine.

Clearly, the power of platforms like YouTube and Baidu to propagate and target information is also what makes them an engine for weaponizing misinformation and stoking bias. The same factors that drive a digital firm's ability to get increasing returns to scale, scope, and learning can also have significant negative effects.

As a result, digital operating models are prompting new kinds of ethical considerations and transforming the issues confronted by managers. The learning algorithms at the heart of new digital systems can be misused to tailor, optimize, and amplify inaccurate and harmful information, from targeting and shaping misleading ads to creating highly realistic fake social personas that are used to extract personal information from users. And the enormous datasets needed to fuel AI are also vulnerable to cyberattack, threatening consumer privacy by putting all sorts of sensitive information at risk.

Although it's generally accepted that business leaders should always take into account the organization's responsibilities to its customers, employees, shareholders, partners, and the communities in which it operates, the potential for digitally enabled businesses to harm these stakeholders raises issues that test the limits of traditional business ethics frameworks and guidelines.

We group these challenges into five main categories: digital amplification, bias, security, control, and inequality. The problems created by these challenges apply to organizations as diverse as Tencent and Target, Facebook and Equifax—all businesses that are increasingly powered by data, analytics, and AI and connected to digital networks. When these factors come together, new ethical challenges multiply. In new as well as old firms, leaders should be aware of how their newly deployed digital capabilities can be used and misused in ways they never intended—or possibly even imagined.

More to the point, because the challenges we describe in this chapter affect all of us—as managers, leaders, and citizens—it's no longer OK to plead ignorance. To ensure the health of our organizations and our political and social systems, every one of us must understand the nature of the problems that digital operating models can generate. And every one of us must be prepared to act when we see them emerge.

Digital Amplification

Rep. Schiff's letters to Amazon, Facebook, and Google take aim at the algorithms that are used to optimize views, purchases, ad clicks, and personal engagement. But even a simple learning algorithm that is rewarded based on clicks and money earned can quickly become dangerous by serving content that reinforces biases and other kinds of flawed thinking, and it can efficiently find users likely to be influenced by content that reinforces their views. The vast scale, scope, and learning potential of the operating models that embed these algorithms means that harmful messages can be tailored and targeted to, literally, hundreds of millions of people.

The grassroots anti-vaccination movement relies on the efforts of a community of individuals who believe that certain kinds of inoculations cause severe illness. The movement dates back as far as the eighteenth century, but its impact has been vastly amplified in recent years by social networks, video streaming sites, and ad-targeting technology. A 2017 study of 2.6 million Facebook users over seven and a half years found that consumption of anti-vaccine content was boosted by *echo chamber effects*: users looked only at posts that affirmed their beliefs, ignored dissenting information, and joined groups reinforcing their biases.[2]

The scale of the impact is striking. In Texas alone, at least 57,000 schoolchildren were exempted from vaccination for nonmedical reasons in 2018, a twentyfold increase since 2003.[3] And health officials in Europe and the United States blame the "anti-vax" movement for outbreaks of dangerous diseases like measles and pertussis over the past ten years.[4]

The anti-vax movement is by no means isolated. The same methods and mechanisms that have made it potent are being used to systematically create echo chambers of all sorts—especially political, social, and religious. In some ways, these echo chambers are similar to those that have long characterized cable TV and radio. But traditional media does not easily reach the same kind of scale as digital networks. And, unlike social networks, traditional media does not allow a message to be tuned in real time: the algorithm serving a Google search result or a Facebook social ad can automatically personalize the information seen by a user to maximize her engagement. Additionally, traditional media does not enable the kind of active user engagement that promotes sharing of content at zero marginal cost to like-minded individuals.[5]

Digital scale, scope, and learning can amplify the impact of any bias, even without systemic intent to do harm or sway views. Our colleagues Mike Luca, Ben Edelman, and Dan Svirsky were among the first scholars to find examples of this: their work on Airbnb shows that people with names that sound distinctively African American were 16 percent less likely than those with European-sounding names to be accepted as guests by Airbnb hosts. Subsequent research by other scholars has found that Airbnb hosts similarly discriminate against people with Islamic-sounding names, people with disabilities, and members of the LGBTQ community.[6]

The same sort of bias afflicts financial services. Even microlending platforms like Kiva, which are explicitly designed to provide financial opportunity to disadvantaged communities, have been found to exacerbate bias.[7]

There was no organized effort to promote discrimination on Airbnb or Kiva. The digital systems simply amplified the impact of the implicit, or subconscious, bias of homeowners and even progressive lenders. Even if the percentage of individuals who are truly bad actors is small or almost nonexistent, the amplification potential of digital operating models means that many people may be adversely impacted.

The intensifying of human bias, discord, and misinformation is not, unfortunately, the only new ethical challenge. Our considerations need to be extended by examining the intrinsic bias embedded in digital algorithms.

Algorithmic Bias

Generally speaking, the quality of the data inputs and the assumptions made in constructing an algorithm will determine the quality of the algorithmic predictions it generates. As the saying goes, "Garbage in, garbage out." Let's examine two common types of algorithmic bias that can lead to seriously flawed AI-driven decisions.

Selection Bias

Selection bias is introduced when the input data does not accurately represent the population or context being analyzed. Amazon, for example, found in 2018 that an internal HR system used to screen job applicants based on internal employee performance devalued the potential of female job candidates, because the underlying data that powered the predictions was based primarily on résumés of male engineers.[8] According to Reuters, "It penalized résumés that included the word 'women's,' as in 'women's chess club captain.' And it downgraded graduates of two all-women's colleges." Similar issues occur in a range of activities such as finance, insurance, and law enforcement. Imagine being turned down for a loan by an algorithm that explicitly (or implicitly) includes gender (or race) in its training data.

The problems created by selection bias go well beyond routine business decisions. For example, in a 2017 study, Joy Buolamwini of the MIT Media Lab and Timnit Gebru of Microsoft Research found that AI-based facial recognition software (from Microsoft, IBM, and the Chinese company Face++) correctly identified gender nearly all of the time (99 percent) for white men, but only 65 percent of the time for darker-skinned women.[9] (The authors noted that the three companies failed to describe their training data—a lapse that is common in the industry.) As Buolamwini argued in her TED Talk, training datasets composed primarily of white faces may have caused the discrepancies: "If the training sets aren't really that diverse, any face that deviates too much from the established norm will be harder to detect."[10]

In 2016, a Russian company called Youth Laboratories, which staged an international beauty contest judged by AI, fell into the same trap. The contest, called Beauty.AI, got support from such companies as Microsoft and Nvidia.[11] It included thousands of contestants from Africa and India, but the forty-four winners were predominantly white; a few were Asian, and only one had dark skin. Youth Laboratories' CTO and the contest's chief science officer blamed the results on a lack of diversity in the training dataset. As *Vice* editor Jordan Pearson noted, Beauty.AI trained its algorithms on off-the-shelf, open source datasets—a common means by which bias can spread.

Labeling Bias

Bias may also result during the exercise of labeling or tagging data (see chapter 3), a task that is often crowdsourced. In a 2016 paper, Emiel van Miltenburg studied the Flickr30k dataset, composed of more than thirty thousand images labeled by crowdworkers. He found that many of the crowdsourced labels exhibited bias; an image of a woman and a man, for example, was tagged as a conversation between a woman and her boss. In van Miltenburg's view, "Crowdsourced descriptions of images *are* biased."[12]

Examples of labeling bias are numerous. In 2017, computer scientists at Princeton and the University of Bath found that after what appeared to be a sensible tagging process, a commonly used machine learning model associated the words "female" and "woman" with pursuits like homemaking and occupations in the arts and humanities, while "male" and "man" were associated with work in math and engineering.[13] The model, according to a report in the *Guardian*, was also "more likely to associate European American names with pleasant words such as 'gift' or 'happy,' while African American names were more commonly associated with unpleasant words like 'abuse' and 'evil.'"[14]

And in another 2017 study, this one by Vicente Ordóñez at UVA and Mark Yatskar at the University of Washington, research-image collections supported by Microsoft and Facebook were shown to demonstrate gender bias: cooking images were linked to women, and sports images were linked to men.[15] The researchers found that human bias was effectively increased by the tagging process. As described in *Wired*, "Machine-learning software trained on the datasets didn't just mirror those biases, it amplified them. If a photo set generally associated women with cooking, software trained by studying those photos and their labels created an even stronger association."

Bias can also plague data tagged by specialists. Studies have shown how a bias in medical diagnoses, such as overtreatment bias, is easily translated into labeling bias.[16] Bias is a particular problem in medical imaging, where datasets are labeled by expert doctors to help algorithms identify various pathologies. Our own work at the Laboratory for Innovation Science at Harvard has shown that maxillofacial MDs and dentists have a rate of approximately 50 percent false negatives in detecting dental diseases using X-rays, so the datasets they label not only capture their mistakes but also amplify them. In using expert-labeled data, objective measures of outcomes (sometimes known as *ground truth*) are essential but can be very difficult to obtain.

Some form of algorithmic bias is virtually unavoidable. In selection, no training data can ever be infinite and cover every possible situation. In labeling, the process intrinsically simplifies the interpretation of an observation and is limited by the knowledge and perspective of the person doing the labeling. More generally, algorithms are designed for a purpose, and that, by itself, introduces a kind of bias.

Take a newsfeed-type algorithm, which shapes the content displayed on a social network. What purpose should this algorithm be designed to achieve? To maximize engagement? To optimize ad spend? To avoid using sensitive data and protect consumer privacy? To guarantee the accuracy of the information displayed? To minimize reliance on sensitive data? These criteria, along with many others, are important, and they require the algorithm designer to make thoughtful decisions and confront excruciating ethical challenges and trade-offs in the specific way the algorithm is designed. When the algorithm makes these kinds of trade-offs in real time and steers content to millions and even billions of people, the potential for far-reaching mistakes is high.

The study of algorithmic bias is in many ways still in its infancy. Although it is impossible to remove bias entirely, it is important to understand its pervasiveness and to work to reduce it. It is thus crucial for managers to understand the phenomenon and to support important countermeasures. First, the choice of model is critical and should match carefully chosen objectives. Second, the dataset chosen to train the algorithm should be carefully selected, come from a transparent source, and be fully appropriate for and representative of the problem the algorithm is designed to solve.

These considerations show that ethical challenges involved in algorithmic operating models are complex enough even when all actors involved are trying to do the right thing. But unfortunately, reality is not so benign.

Cybersecurity

Every day Alibaba Cloud blocks 200 million brute force attacks, 20 million web hacking attacks, and 1,000 DDoS attacks.[17] That's only one of many, many examples. The scale, frequency, and impact of cyberattacks is daunting; the growth of AI—and the accumulation of the massive datasets required to feed it—will only compound the problem. Additionally, a whole new kind of cyberattack is emerging, as the power of digital operating models is effectively hijacked for rogue purposes.

Breaches

Let's begin with more traditional breaches. Consider the case of Equifax. In September 2017, the company revealed a breach that exposed the names, Social Security numbers, driver's license numbers, credit card numbers, birth dates, and addresses of 147.9 million Equifax consumers—nearly half the US population.[18] Putting all that sensitive personal data in one place opened the door to what one former Equifax manager called "a nightmare scenario"—one that, as the *Wall Street Journal* reported, could have been avoided: "When Richard Smith took over as CEO in 2005, Equifax was a staid, slow-growing credit-reporting company," says the story. "He set about to transform the company by expanding the amount of data it stored about consumers and monetizing it."[19] Smith retired after the disclosure.

As it turns out, the group responsible for the attack did not specifically target Equifax. According to the US Government Accountability Office, the Equifax breach occurred during a wide-ranging search for sites that contained a specific vulnerability; the attackers used an open source framework named Apache Struts, which is used to create enterprise applications.[20] The vulnerability allowed for remote code execution, which let third parties install programs, view, change, or delete data, or even create new accounts.

The problem had actually been identified by the National Cybersecurity and Communications Integration Center (NCCIC) two days before the attackers found the vulnerability in one Equifax website. (Smith blamed a single employee for failing to update the software in response to the NCCIC warning.)[21] When the group found the hole, it rapidly gained access to the Equifax systems and identified a database containing a number of unencrypted usernames and passwords. Equipped with Equifax credentials, the attackers gradually found and queried more than fifty databases behind the Equifax firewall. They masked their attack to make it look like normal network activity and remained undiscovered for seventy-six days.[22]

In the wake of the breach, Equifax's leaders behaved poorly. The company found out about the hack in late July 2017 and delayed announcing it for more than a month, even after they discovered that the hack had gathered extensive personal customer information. During that period, Equifax's CFO and two other executives sold shares together worth about $2 million.[23] Consumers and investors, meanwhile, remained unaware that all that data had

186 COMPETING IN THE AGE OF AI

been compromised in one of history's largest breaches of private information.

Equifax is obviously not alone. Over the past ten years many companies have acknowledged going through cybersecurity breaches. Microsoft, Marriott, Under Armour, Sony Pictures, FIFA, Anthem (the health insurance company), and the US Postal Service are among the many organizations that have been successfully targeted by hackers. The breaches released private consumer information, bug tracking data, credit card numbers, patient records, employee details, even the family health records of the Sony Pictures CEO. In a famous quote, sometimes attributed to John Chambers, but apparently originally spoken by Robert Mueller back in 2012, "There are two kinds of companies: those that know they have been hacked, and those that don't know they've been hacked."[24]

It is now abundantly clear to organizational leaders that they have a fundamental legal and ethical duty to protect the information they obtain from customers, employees, and partners. But that challenge is getting tougher as our reliance on data continues to rise—a trend that shows no signs of slowing given the data needs of both analytics and AI. There is certainly no lack of consultants offering solutions to protect companies from cyberattacks. And more companies are adopting best practices, such as two-factor authentication and formal IT security governance frameworks— unquestionably important moves.

But beyond general investments in security technologies, governance, and training, executives must recognize that they have a responsibility to safeguard data. As for Equifax, the company is currently awaiting punishment from both the Consumer Financial Protection Board and the Federal Trade Commission.[25]

The Equifax breach occurred because of its antiquated systems, arcane security procedures, confused organizational processes, and overall lack of leadership emphasis on cybersecurity.[26] But the widespread nature of these breaches underscores the fact that cybersecurity is a common challenge. Investing in prevention is essential, from spending the money on upgrading antiquated IT systems and on various technologies and services to prevent and detect cyber threats, to building the right culture and organizational capabilities. Additionally, when a breach is detected, a slow response or delayed communication can dramatically exacerbate the damages for the company and consumers. Companies should therefore also invest in understanding, simulating, and deploying cyber response mechanisms, both as a real-time operating challenge and as a legal and ethical responsibility.

Hijacking

It's important also to recognize that security challenges are not limited to traditional cyberattacks. We're now seeing the emergence of a different kind of attack—one that effectively hijacks digital operating models for a rogue purpose. Consider this example: the shooter who killed fifty people in two mosques in Christchurch, New Zealand, in March 2019 captured the events on a bodycam and shared them on Facebook Live. About two hundred people are believed to have viewed the original video stream, but apparently none of them flagged it.

About forty-five minutes after the seventeen-minute live stream ended, the police alerted Facebook, which promptly shut down the feed. But by that time, the video had been viewed about four thousand times. And despite the feverish efforts to remove the video over the next twenty-four hours, it continued to be shared across social media, often with posts inciting even more violence against Muslims.

According to Facebook, there were more than 1.5 million attempts to upload copies of the video on its network, of which 1.2 million were found and removed. But many managed to bypass Facebook's controls by making changes to the video—recutting it, altering its audio feed, or adding watermarks or logos. YouTube faced many of the same challenges and, despite its extensive efforts, also could not keep variants of the video from being distributed. In the words of Neal Mohan, YouTube's chief product officer, "This was a tragedy designed for the purpose of going viral."[27]

Recently, we have also seen evidence of Russian-sponsored digital hijacking to influence political campaigns in the United States, the United Kingdom, and elsewhere. Indeed, on February 16, 2018, the US Department of Justice indicted thirteen Russian citizens and three Russian companies for a broad set of criminal activities designed to spread bias, "sow discord in the US political system," and support the Trump campaign in 2016.[28] The activities centered on a company, suspected of being a front for a Russian intelligence operation, called the Internet Research Agency LLC, which allegedly "engaged in operations to interfere with elections and political processes."

According to the indictment, the Internet Research Agency employed hundreds of people in its online operations, which included analytics and search engine optimization. The indictment also alleges that the group dedicated eighty or so people to "operations" on YouTube, Facebook, Instagram, and Twitter that included generating and buying ads on social media, creating fake accounts and personas, and posting content and videos that were optimized and targeted with data and analytics to promote the Internet Research Agency's agenda.

Although the range and impact of these activities is still under debate, it appears the group was especially effective in suppressing the African American vote in key states, and in alienating Bernie Sanders supporters.[29] Perhaps most staggering is the scale of the operation. It appears that the efforts reached at least 126 million Facebook users, not to mention more than 2,700 Twitter accounts via 36,000 bots tweeting 1.4 million times.

Marshaling a Response

As digital operating models amplify an organization's scale, scope, and learning capabilities, society is becoming increasingly exposed to a new range of cybersecurity challenges. These threats begin with traditional breaches of private information and extend to systematic and increasingly sophisticated campaigns that take aim at the foundations of American social and political institutions. Critically, this is not only about Google and Facebook; the challenges extend to all sorts of new and old firms, from Sony Pictures to Equifax.

Many firms are deploying massive efforts to fight this new generation of criminals, but as the Equifax example shows, all we need is one weak link for the problems to begin. It took a call from the police to bring the first Christchurch video to Facebook's attention, but if more viewers had raised the problem earlier, its massive redistribution could have been reduced. Every one of us must take part in defending against these perils. Individuals, managers, and business and government leaders alike need to work together as the scale and scope of the challenges continue to increase.

It's important to note that not all harmful incidents are easily identified, or even necessarily illegal. There's a lot of gray area between full-fledged cyberattacks and the authorized and transparent use of customer data by third parties. These gray areas are routinely created by the many interfaces that connect digital operating models to one another, enabling the business networks that our digital economy critically depends on. This brings us to the related issue of platform control.

Platform Control

Across the board, we have a responsibility to not just build tools, but to make sure that they're used for good.
—**Mark Zuckerberg, Facebook CEO, during US Senate hearings, 2018**

Facebook, like most platform companies, seeks to shape and control its ecosystem and make sure that its tools and technologies do not cause harm. But how to properly exercise such control is not at all obvious. People argue about how to define the "good" Zuckerberg invokes in a way that doesn't harm free speech, and about how to trust an organization like Facebook—which has its own unique culture and political leanings—to make the decisions for the rest of us. However, without *some* control, a data-rich digital platform can spawn all kinds of problems.

In December 2015, the *Guardian* reported that a "little-known data company"—Cambridge Analytica—had provided funding for Aleksandr Kogan, a lecturer in psychology at Cambridge, to harvest Facebook user data in order to assess the psychological attributes of individual Americans.[30] Kogan, the *Guardian* revealed, had started working with Cambridge Analytica's parent company, SCL Group, in 2014.

With funding from SCL, Kogan used the crowdsourcing platform Amazon Mechanical Turk to pay people to take a survey and download an app that compromised both their Facebook data and the data of all their Facebook friends. As the *Guardian* later pointed out, "Kogan had something SCL wanted: an [older] Facebook application that worked under the social network's pre-2014 terms of service, which allowed app developers to harvest data not only from the people who installed the app, but from their friends."[31] After 2014, the terms of service forbade this sort of data collection.

Based in the United Kingdom and funded by American hedge fund billionaire Robert Mercer, Cambridge Analytica offered its clients the opportunity to influence voters by using psychological profiles constructed from Facebook data to micro-target potential voters.[32] In 2015, the company was working for both the Brexit campaign and the Ted Cruz presidential campaign.[33] When the Cruz campaign ended in May 2016, the company began working for the Trump campaign, and, as reported by the *Intercept*, Trump adviser Steve Bannon served as an officer at Cambridge Analytica.[34]

In March 2018, more than two years after the initial revelations, the *New York Times* and the London *Observer* published the results of a joint investigation: Kogan had given Cambridge Analytica the data of more than 50 million people, and Cambridge Analytica had created profiles of some 30 million of them. The 270,000 people who downloaded Kogan's "personality profile" app had inadvertently enabled bad actors to access sensitive information on significant portions of the US population. (Kogan claims that he is being used as a scapegoat in this matter.)[35] There is evidence that Cambridge

Analytica had used similar tactics on the British population to aid the Brexit campaign.[36]

What went wrong, and whose fault was it? Since its launch in 2007, the Facebook platform has enabled developers to launch applications—games, news apps, and others—that interact with the features of the social network. Very quickly after the launch, tens of thousands of apps were introduced, written by hundreds of thousands of developers. Over time the platform evolved, with the introduction of a variety of additional apps, including Facebook Connect (which allows users to sign on to an external site using their Facebook account) and Open Graph (a protocol that enables external sites to post user activity to their Facebook accounts, such as what a user is listening to on Spotify). Within five years, the Facebook platform was supporting more than nine million apps, offering a huge scope of services to Facebook's massive social network community. None of this seemed obviously problematic—at least at first.

Things started to go wrong as the platform allowed developers to collect data from users' friends without the friends' knowledge or permission—a problem Facebook had already addressed when Kogan's app gathered its trove of data and sold it to Cambridge Analytica. When the 2015 *Guardian* story came out, Facebook responded immediately that Cambridge Analytica had violated the Facebook terms of use. The terms gave researchers access to user data for an academic purpose—with the user's consent (users could opt out when they created an account). Facebook prohibited the sale or transfer of the kind of data used by Kogan "to any ad network, data broker or other advertising or monetization-related service."[37]

Facebook immediately suspended Cambridge Analytica's access to the platform and demanded the company delete the data. Cambridge Analytica confirmed it had indeed deleted its data, which apparently it had not done. What happened—and didn't happen—next is harder to judge. Facebook did not insist on an audit of the company, something it could also have demanded per the terms of the agreement. Failing to do so might have been a mistake, but the rationale may have been that performing audits is notoriously difficult with any degree of thoroughness.[38]

The Cambridge Analytica story is a fascinating example of the control challenges that can plague organizations that have adopted digital operating models. Much of the power of digital scale, scope, and learning comes from the openness and connectedness of digital platforms. In almost any digital model, each system plugs in to a variety of networks through powerful, relatively open interfaces. These connections greatly amplify the functionality of a digital system, but they also open it up to use in ways the original designers may never have imagined. Even when these unimagined uses are detected and understood, it may be difficult if not impossible to control them. Well beyond the challenges in cybersecurity, platform control involves the mandate to design systems that, as Zuckerberg states, are "used for good." But defining "good" is not only problematic but also almost impossible to enforce.

The power of digital platforms to foster unimagined invention among an ecosystem of innovators is also the platforms' vulnerability. And how to defend against unintended platform harm is not always intuitively obvious. The more open the platform, the greater the risk. For example, some observers have criticized Apple for keeping the iOS and the App Store platforms relatively closed; they have strict rules and require formal approval before an app is listed on the App Store for public download. On the other hand, the more open Google Android and Google Play Store have been distributing many more malicious apps, often unbeknownst to Google itself, spreading malware infections to millions of users.[39] How should a platform company maintain the balance between too much and too little control?

Clearly, a platform's control problems are further complicated when it contains and shares assets that relate to third parties, most notably consumer data. Operating models that include ad platforms are therefore especially tricky. Google Ads (formerly Adwords) and Facebook ads, to name two, form full-fledged software platforms, with sophisticated APIs that use data to aid advertisers in finding the right consumers. We note that much of this targeting is valuable not only to advertisers but also to consumers, who may appreciate receiving relevant ads instead of random commercial messages.

But where do you draw the line between offering relevance and violating privacy? The same ad may be appreciated by one consumer but found invasive or even offensive by another. Additionally, who should decide this question? Should the ad platform itself have the editorial authority to judge the appropriateness of each ad? Google's quality-scoring process, for example—which helps position an ad on the search-results page based on click-through rate, relevance, landing-page quality, and a variety of other factors—has been the subject of much discussion over the years. Although some people feel it's a necessary control on ad quality, others find it intrusive and anticompetitive.

These questions, at least in the United States, also run up against constitutional protections of free speech. For many content platforms that are open to anyone, the question of control and curation gets uncomfortably close to censorship. Executives and company stakeholders will increasingly face the issue of private actors governing public action, and few are equipped to deal with these questions or generate appropriate solutions.

Or consider the case of Ant Financial. The kinds of consumer data it assembles—data that integrates daily user engagement on a variety of tasks and services with commerce transaction data, location data, credit data, and even financial investment and risk preferences—is unprecedented. So far, there is no evidence that public harm has occurred, but the potential damage in case of a cyber breach could be highly significant. Amplifying these challenges is the common use of APIs by the company, a practice that exposes its data and functionality to an ecosystem of third-party providers.

As with amplification, bias, and security, the challenge of platform control highlights new ethical considerations for everyone. But another dynamic is making each of these challenges all the more pressing: as digital operating models drive network and learning effects, the asymmetries across organizations will tend to grow, and markets will become more concentrated. This asymmetry increasingly emphasizes differences among firms, communities, and consumers, prompting a range of concerns regarding equity. What is an equitable distribution of value, and even of decision rights, across the economy? And how should this allocation affect income and value sharing?

Fairness and Equity

Spotify is preparing for an antitrust battle with Apple and its music streaming business, Apple Music. The Swedish company filed an antitrust complaint in March 2019, arguing that Apple's 30 percent fee on every in-app purchase on the iPhone makes it impossible for Spotify to compete against Apple Music. Additionally, Spotify is protesting the restrictions that Apple puts on apps downloaded from its App Store, in an effort to control and shape the impact of its platform's ecosystem. Spotify is thus pushing back on Apple's platform control strategy, which, Apple argues, has led to consistently high quality in iPhone software and avoided viruses and malware.

Spotify is not the only firm to be upset about Apple's "tax" on app providers. Netflix and video game developers Epic Games and Valve Corporation have complained about its cost or have tried to bypass the App Store altogether. The problem stems from another fundamental challenge created by digital operating models: the kinds of network effects discussed in previous chapters can lead to increased market concentration. Network effects in mobile platforms are notably strong, leading to significant concentration. Multihoming among consumers is low, and so Apple effectively controls access to iPhone customers—just as Google controls access to Android smartphone users—in most countries. If Spotify wants access to the valuable community of iPhone consumers, it has little choice except to abide by Apple's rules and pricing conventions.

Amazon's retail marketplace, which enables millions of partners to sell products to Amazon's online customers, presents a similar challenge. Although everyone acknowledges that Amazon provides ample opportunity for a great variety of small businesses, store owners in the most attractive segments have complained that Amazon enters the segment and competes with them directly. Feng Zhu of Harvard Business School and Qihong Liu of the University of Oklahoma have found substantial evidence supporting these claims in a systematic study of more than 150,000 product offerings in twenty-two product subcategories.[40] And our own research has revealed the existence of difficult trade-offs when powerful platforms compete with their own complementors.[41]

The phenomenon is complex. We have seen how platform or hub firms may wield excessive market power and shape competition. However, we also discuss in chapter 6 how phenomena like multihoming and network clustering can work as substantial pushback against dominant behavior. Ultimately, Walmart's online marketplace may provide an important alternative for online sellers and a check on Amazon's behavior. In the case of ride-sharing, widespread multihoming in the rider and driver networks has curtailed the ability of firms like Uber, Lyft, and DiDi to raise prices and gather profits. Network clustering makes competition even more effective, because any ride-hailing or taxi service with local scale can become an effective alternative to the larger ride-sharing firms.

Companies like Uber and Lyft have worked tirelessly to reduce multihoming and clustering in their markets. They have implemented global features in their apps and services, such as the ability for a user to select music in any ride. They have worked to tie drivers to their service by designing specific app features, pricing discounts, bonus structures, and even financing schemes that provide powerful incentives for drivers to stay committed to one service. And when these operational tactics fail, they even buy their competitors—as Uber did just before its IPO in 2019 when it acquired Careem, the leading ride-sharing service in the Middle East.[42]

Each case is unique and fraught with subtleties, but it is hard to argue against the general trend that as we tie the economy together, the firms that shape and control these economic networks play an increasingly essential role, wield unprecedented impact, and typically harvest the profits to prove it. The broad deployment of AI-powered and data-centric operating models reinforces this dynamic. The concentration that is already a reality in industries from smartphones to messaging may soon shape industries as diverse as automotive and agriculture. Regulators and lawmakers are taking note and are insisting on increased scrutiny of digital firms, at both the federal and the local level.

However, while the problem is real, it is also important not to fall in love with simplistic solutions. Breaking up a winner-take-all business makes little sense: one of the resulting organizations would simply emerge as the winner, and the old problem would re-surface. Instead, we should work to fix and improve digital operating models, and not destroy them. When the conduct of firms is problematic, as for example with Facebook's privacy challenges, what is needed is an effective and responsive regulatory framework, as Zuckerberg himself has advocated.[43] Communities should be able to help and to play an active role.

The issues are subtle and the trade-offs are difficult, but if we all work together on the issues, solutions will be found. Most critically, we need the new generation of leaders to acknowledge new responsibilities and work proactively to solve the new challenges.

New Responsibilities

The leaders of modern firms cannot afford to ignore this new generation of ethical challenges. A variety of practical, implementable technical and business solutions is needed. Clearly, we are not alone in thinking this way. Google and Microsoft are investing heavily in research on algorithmic bias, and Facebook is devoting massive resources to tackling the problems of fake news and harmful posts.[44] And even the leadership of traditional organizations like Equifax and the Democratic National Committee—having been stung by hackers—is investing in remedies.[45] Navigating the ethics of digital scale, scope, and learning has become a universal management imperative.

The greatest responsibility lies in the organizations that wield the most power and occupy the central network positions in our economy and society. A helpful analogy may be found in biological ecosystems. Like the modern economy, biological ecosystems are highly connected networks of species, which collectively depend on the behavior of their most critical agents. In an ecosystem, so-called keystone species are especially critical to the sustainability of the whole. From providing nesting areas to channeling rainwater, these species perform especially critical functions, maintaining ecosystem health through specific, evolved behaviors that have effects much beyond their own species to impact the entire ecosystem. Removing keystone species will critically harm the sustainability of the whole.

In a similar fashion, companies like Facebook and Equifax effectively regulate the health of their business networks. Their activities propagate to all network nodes or community members, whether they post video content, apply for loans, sell advertisements, or share messages. As these central firms occupy richly connected network positions and provide the foundation for networkwide value creation, they have become essential to the economy and social system. In each case, they provide services and technologies on which many of us depend. Their removal or even their problems can lead to potentially catastrophic events.

But as leaders in many firms already understand, the role of a network hub comes with responsibilities. Building on the biological analogy, the authors of this book defined the concept of a keystone strategy many years ago.[46] A *keystone strategy* aligns the objectives of a hub firm with those of its networks. By improving the health of its network (or business ecosystem), a keystone strategy also benefits the long-term performance of the firm.

The central feature of this strategy is its focus on aligning internal and external needs to shape and sustain the health of the networks a firm depends on. When Google invests in technologies that remove bias from its algorithms, it's deploying a keystone strategy. When Facebook removes harmful videos from its networks, it's doing the same thing. The point here is that sustaining a business network is not only an ethical responsibility but also the only way to preserve a networked business for the long term.

The keystone concept is related to the idea of *information fiduciary* proposed by Jack Balkin and Jonathan Zittrain:[47]

> In the law, a fiduciary is a person or business with an obligation to act in a trustworthy manner in the interest of another. For example, financial managers and planners are entrusted to handle their clients' money. Doctors, lawyers, and accountants are

*examples of information fiduciaries—that is, a person or busi-
ness that deals not in money, but in information. Doctors and
lawyers are obligated to keep our secrets and they cannot use the
information they collect about us against our interests.*[48]

Controlling hubs in important economic networks, firms like
Google and Facebook acquire extensive consumer information. As
information fiduciaries, they have important responsibilities not
to harm the communities they collect information from. Again, we
quote Balkin and Zittrain:

*There is an opportunity for a new, grand bargain organized
around the idea of fiduciary responsibility. Companies could
take on the responsibilities of information fiduciaries: They
would agree to a set of fair information practices, including security and privacy guarantees, and disclosure of breaches. They
would promise not to leverage personal data to unfairly discriminate against or abuse the trust of end users. And they would
not sell or distribute consumer information except to those who
agreed to similar rules. In return, the federal government would
preempt a wide range of state and local laws.*[49]

Zittrain and Balkin further argue that state legislators and common law, particularly with the threat of class-action suits, might
provide enough additional incentive for hub firms to adopt the idea.
Microsoft has already indicated that it is open to comprehensive
privacy legislation, in part in an attempt to preempt state-level restrictions.[50] Facebook has also indicated similar preferences.[51]

Ultimately, the responsibility to sustain the (digital) economy
rests in large part with the leaders who are poised to control it. By
occupying central positions of power and influence, hub firms have
become de facto stewards of the long-term health of the economy.
In part in response to public pressure, leaders of firms like Apple,
Alibaba, Alphabet, and Amazon are increasingly aware of their impact on tens of thousands of other firms and on the economic health
of billions of consumers. The same hub firms that benefit from the
ecosystems they control have important reasons to sustain the eco-

nomic health of not only their shareholders but also the broader communities they are organizing and serving. These digital firms should thus pursue a consistent set of actions that enables the long-term sustainability of the networks they (and all of us) depend on. Many leaders already understand this, at least in theory. Now the rest of us need to nudge them into action.

We have already seen how digital networks and AI are prompting the development of new operating capabilities, strategic principles, and ethical dilemmas. But beyond these immediate changes, we must also think through the broader long-term patterns and gather the wisdom required to deal with our newfound challenges. We turn to this topic in the next chapter.

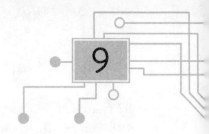

The New Meta

Nothing but absolute want could have driven a large, and once honest and industrious body of the people, into the commission of excesses so hazardous to themselves, their families, and the community.

—Lord Byron, speech in the House of Lords addressing
   the Luddite movement, February 27, 1812

In gaming, a *new meta* is a new reality that transcends the existing game rules or goes beyond traditional game limits and constraints. A new meta is like changing the moves allowed on a chessboard or the rules of bridge halfway through a game.

The age of artificial intelligence is changing the game for all of us. But this new meta isn't characterized by robots acting like humans. It's all about the emergence of a new type of firm, one that uses AI in a much subtler way to break down age-old operational constraints, driving new value, growth, and innovation. Embedded in digital networks, operating models, and AI factories, the software-driven firm is enabling a new way to produce value and changing the rules of our economy and society.

Our new meta is generating enormous opportunity, as evidenced by economic growth, thriving tech stocks, and even improvement in some of the best traditional firms. But it's also leaving us struggling to understand the full implications of the new rules, dealing with a new range of problems, and coping with increasingly complex consequences.

A glance at history can provide some hints.

A Kind of Déjà Vu?

This kind of fundamental change in the rules has happened before. It began around the turn of the eighteenth century, with the dawn of the Industrial Revolution. Technological change in the means of production drove a transformation in the means of value creation and capture. Indeed, early industrialization marked a profound shift in operating models toward the increased specialization of work, the componentization of organizations, and the creation of carefully designed and engineered production processes.

What had traditionally been handcrafted by artisans increasingly became produced with much greater efficiency by specialized, mass production methods. Where highly skilled workers once had meticulously crafted and fitted every part of a manufactured product, each part was now created separately by workers using specialized skills and equipment, later to be assembled in yet a different specialized process. This transformed the skills and capabilities required and redefined industry boundaries and competitive dynamics, with a great impact on wealth creation and distribution. The repercussions were felt around the globe in successive waves of economic, social, and political change, as society gradually internalized the implications.

One early response to the change was the Luddite movement, which emerged near Nottingham in 1811 and spread rapidly throughout England. The Luddites railed against the new coal-powered automated handlooms and high-volume factories that were replacing traditional textile production methods. Weavers, croppers, and cotton spinners had traditionally worked from home and enjoyed good pay along with plenty of leisure. They did not take kindly to being replaced by specialized equipment, which required a much smaller number of less-skilled workers to operate in large, often squalid factories. Just as we are seeing now, the Industrial Revolution upset the status quo, driving the obsolescence of traditional capabilities and manufacturing strategies and creating new ethical dilemmas.

Some workers first tried bargaining, asking for a fair share of the increased factory profits. Others demanded a new tax on cloth that could help support the workers who had lost their jobs. Still others tried to slow down the deployment of the new machinery and the construction of textile factories to allow more time for workers to adapt to new trades. The mill owners refused to meet any of these demands.

In November 1811, half a dozen men, their faces blackened with coal, marched into the home factory setup of master weaver Edward Hollingsworth and destroyed six framing machines. The men came back a week later and burned down Hollingsworth's house. The attacks spread to other towns, destroying almost two hundred machines each month.

The attackers had a kind of twisted humor. As they sent warning notes to manufacturers, they made up a mysterious General Ludd (or King Ludd) as the instigator. The name appeared to be inspired by the myth of Ned Ludd, an apprentice who was beaten by his master and who had retaliated by destroying his stocking frames.

The Luddites were especially upset by the new concentration of wealth among the industrialists, which they believed came at the expense of the working class. The movement became increasingly violent, with the Luddites taking responsibility for several assassinations and attempts, until the British army sent more than fourteen thousand soldiers to the Luddite counties.[1] Two dozen Luddites were hanged; another fifty-one were shipped off to Australia.

The Luddite movement epitomizes the kind of unrest we see when a new meta emerges. The modern firm at the outset of the Industrial Revolution was characterized by a revolutionary operating architecture that drove increased specialization, enabled by new production technology that subdivided production methods into clearly specified, specialized work components and organizational subdivisions—all of which rendered obsolete the traditional artisanal methods of production. We can track this fundamental shift to standardization and specialization across industries, from apparel manufacturing to automobile production and assembly, and even across services, from banking to the fast food industry.

From the early 1800s until the mid-twentieth century, the waves of transformation brought about by the emergence of the modern firm were deep, disruptive, and pervasive, eventually touching most of the world economy. Overall, Europe and North America enjoyed a marked increase in the average standard of living. But the Industrial Revolution also brought an increase in the disparity in overall wealth between the few who owned the means of production and the many who did not. In addition, the displacement caused by the transformation created enormous uncertainty and exacerbated social and political tensions.

The New Age

The rules of the game are changing again. As we enter the age of AI, we should pay careful attention to these emerging principles.

Rule 1: Change Is No Longer Localized; It Is Systemic

The age of AI is driven by a relentless and *systemic* driver of change. Rather than a number of separate waves of technological innovation, gradually spreading the Industrial Revolution across different industries and geographies, our new engine of change appears to be tackling all industries, globally, at just about the same time. Our entire economy is now effectively subject to Moore's law.

In 1975, Gordon Moore speculated that the density of transistors in integrated circuits would double every year, with a corresponding increase in the power of computing. Transistor density trends have slowed, but general computing performance has continued to increase. Indeed, the most powerful insight from Moore's law may be the simple idea that digital machines continue to improve and increase in capability over time. Gradually, relentlessly, digital technology keeps getting better, more powerful, and more broadly applicable—with no slowdown in sight. Accelerated by advances in software technology, AI and ML algorithms, and computing architecture, successive generations of digital technology will continue to enable improvements in performance across a broad range of application areas. Digital technology has become an inexorable engine of systemwide transformation.

Inventions during the Industrial Revolution pertained to individual industries or at least clusters of industries—even the steam engine, which possibly had the broadest reach, had more impact in manufacturing and transportation than, say, in banking or health care. In contrast, digital transformation cuts across every industrial environment at the same time. Digital technology and AI are meeting an increasing variety of needs and enabling an incredible variety of use cases. We can already see them producing music, crafting email responses, targeting ads, interpreting X-rays, making pricing decisions, trading stocks, connecting passengers with vehicles or enabling predictive maintenance on mining equipment.

Moreover, we see no sign that the current systemwide trend will slow its pace, as the human, technical, and financial resources devoted to AI and computing technology continue to expand. In fact, most indications are that we are only at the beginning. Thus, the challenge is for us to recognize that transformation is happening at an accelerated pace across all industries, with a massive wave of change across the entire economy and society.

The digital engine of change is driving both opportunities and challenges. Even if artificial intelligence never fully catches up with human thinking, it is clear that an increasing number of operational tasks now performed by humans will be enhanced by or automated by digital systems. This provides an unprecedented opportunity for starting new ventures. But as many traditional tasks are digitized, we will also inevitably see dislocation. Several studies point to a very large impact, with as much as *half* of current work activities being replaceable by AI or software-enabled systems.[2] Erik Brynjolfsson, Tom Mitchell, and Daniel Rock (of MIT, Carnegie Mellon, and MIT, respectively) offer one of the more provocative insights as they show that the impact of machine learning will reach across virtually *all* occupations, transforming the nature of every job, regardless of income level and specialization.[3]

We shouldn't be too surprised by these striking predictions. After all, for at least a century, operating models have been designed to standardize many human tasks and make them predictable and repeatable. From scanning products at a cash register to making the perfect latte, and from performing a heart transplant to designing a house, many operating tasks benefit from accepted methods and standardized procedures and do not always benefit from the kind of creativity that can truly distinguish human intelligence. Unquestionably, AI improvements will enrich many jobs and will generate a variety of interesting opportunities. However, at the same time, it seems inevitable that AI will also drive widespread dislocation across many occupations.

Just as in the Industrial Revolution, the age of AI is transforming the economy. However, the speed and breadth of the impact appear to be many times as great. It will not take a hundred years for digital transformation to pervade every sector of the global economy. This is generating unprecedented entrepreneurial opportunity and all kinds of new consumer surplus, from medical breakthroughs to instant deliveries. But not everyone is coming out a winner. Labor augmentation and displacement are already on the rise.[4] And even if all jobs threatened by digital automation are replaced with other jobs, social dislocation is likely to become increasingly challenging, and do so as soon as this next decade.

Rule 2: Capabilities Are Increasingly Horizontal and Universal

As we saw in the Industrial Revolution, technological change is transforming the nature of capabilities. However, the adoption of AI is doing so in a fundamentally different way. In almost every setting, AI-powered, network-centric organizations are taking on companies that have highly specialized capabilities and skills. But what is needed to compete in an AI-driven world has less to do with traditional industry specialization and more to do with a *universal* set of capabilities. In a dramatic reversal from the trajectory started in the Industrial Revolution, the age of AI is gradually making many vertical, siloed organizations and specialized capabilities less relevant and less competitive.

As algorithmic models target an increasing variety of tasks, competitive advantage is shifting away from vertical capabilities toward universal capabilities in data sourcing, processing, analytics, and algorithm development—building AI factories and implementing operating models that can make many decisions in an automated way. As this transition continues, we are witnessing a marked erosion of traditional differentiation strategies and the emergence of a new breed of universal competitors. This erosion is not only changing the balance of economic power but also contributing to the gradual demise of traditional specialization.

This new universality of capability reshapes a variety of operating tasks and reaches into strategy, business design, and even leadership. Strategies in various digital and networked settings look similar, as do the drivers of operating performance. Similarly, the characteristics of each market respond more to new drivers like network and learning effects than to traditional industry-specific knowledge and expertise. When Uber looked for a new CEO, the board hired someone who had previously run a digital firm (Expedia) and not a large transportation services company.

We are moving from an era of core competencies, differing from firm to firm and embedded deep in each organization, to an age shaped by data and analytics, powered by algorithms and hosted in the computing cloud for anyone to use. This is why Amazon and Tencent are able to compete in industries as disparate as messaging and financial services, video gaming and consumer electronics, health care and credit scoring. Each of these sectors now requires a similar technological foundation, along with common methods and tools, all powered by massive computing capacity that is available on demand. Emphasis on primary differentiation on the basis of cost, quality, and brand equity is shifting from specialized, vertical expertise to the firm's position in the network, its accumulation of differentiated data, and its deployment of a new generation of analytics.

Rule 3: Traditional Industry Boundaries Are Disappearing; Recombination Is Now the Rule

Industries originally evolved from traditional trades to support the increasingly vertical specialization demanded by the Industrial Revolution. These clear boundaries are going away as widespread digitization drives ubiquitous connections across previously separate industries.

We saw it when Google entered the auto industry and when Alibaba launched a bank. Digital interfaces easily allow operating models to cut across old verticals and enter new industries with new, highly connected business models. Industries are thus merging with each other, as capabilities become more universal, as data and analytics refined in one environment can be useful in other contexts, and as digital machines connect easily into massive networks. Digital networks are simply not constrained in the same ways that human-centered organizations are.

While traditional organizations suffer from diminishing returns to scale or scope, many digital networks enjoy increasing returns, not only as they grow in size but also as they connect to other networks.[5] We have seen how Ant Financial leveraged networks and AI to supercharge its business in a variety of markets. A similar playbook is in effect at Amazon, through its Prime membership model, and at Tencent, as its messaging and gaming platform extends into financial services and health care. This kind of evolution poses dramatic challenges to many incumbent firms.

The advice to executives in search of excellence was once to stick to their knitting and stay with businesses they knew. However, in the age of AI, organizations that cannot leverage customers and data across markets are likely to be at a disadvantage. From telecommunications service providers to automobile manufacturers, firms are finding themselves competing with companies from different sectors, using different business models, and integrating, bundling, and cross-subsidizing products and services. Leaders are finding their business and operating models at risk if they do not understand the dynamics of scope expansion.

Creating new value through recombination is not without its costs, however, and the impact on existing actors is not always positive. Expanding an exclusive community to new participants will upset some old members. Expanding the Uber network to more drivers or the Amazon marketplace to more sellers can reduce the economic opportunity available to long-standing members. And adding a new node to an existing network can introduce cyber threats.

As more tasks are digitized and networked, value is indeed generated. However, not all participants are affected in the same way. Some will benefit, but others will not.

Managers increasingly need to understand the dynamic of recombination. Some firms may benefit from figuring out their own network bridging strategies and find new opportunities to leverage their own data and relationships across traditionally separate industries. Other firms instead need to move quickly to defend themselves, anticipating potential threats to their products and services, perhaps by focusing on increasing loyalty and differentiation.

Rule 4: From Constrained Operations to Frictionless Impact

As digital operating models continue to displace traditional industrial processes, they also remove traditional operating constraints. This is why a new generation of firms has grown to unprecedented scale at unprecedented rates. Ant Financial is serving an order of magnitude more customers than the largest traditional bank. Facebook is providing news and information services to an order of magnitude more people than are served by the US postal system.

Moreover, digital scale is driving an increasing *variety* of important processes, influencing not only operating efficiencies and economic returns but also social and political activities. From Amazon to WeChat, digital operating models are shaping a remarkably diverse range of human interactions. Relevant information moves instantaneously at nearly zero marginal cost via networks to infinite numbers of recipients and is processed rapidly by boundless cloud-based computing capacity. From pinpointed product recommendations to personalized advertisements, many enablers of economic, social, and political activity are running in an effectively frictionless fashion.

However, as many engineers will recognize, removing friction is not always a good thing. Frictionless systems are prone to instability and have difficulty finding equilibrium. Think of a car without brakes, or a skier who can't slow down. Once in motion, frictionless systems are hard to stop. A similar intuition applies to a viral meme.

Once it gets going, a digital signal can reach networks with virtually infinite scale and scope and do so rapidly. After it goes, the signal is almost impossible to stop, even for the organization that launched the signal in the first place, or the organization that controls the key hubs in the network. Think of the millions of videos posted, despite frantic efforts by Facebook and Google, after the Christchurch shooting.

It's clear that frictionless processes can create major problems. A phony headline can spread with infinite speed to billions of people on a variety of platforms and can morph to optimize impact and click-through. And as with the Christchurch videos, even if the specific content is flagged by a social network, multiple variants can still be communicated, "liked," and retransmitted across the internet. This vast reach and impact was inconceivable in the days of good old friction-heavy newspapers. Thus, frictionless, AI-driven processes can work as powerful amplifiers of information, opinion, and, of course, bias and aggression. If you have a message to send, there is no better way to do it, reaching billions of people with tunable, customizable content, tested to reach your goal. But the marketer's paradise can be the citizen's nightmare.

Frictionless operating models enable companies to scale new businesses at unprecedented rates. After product-market fit is ensured, traditional boundaries to organizational scalability are bypassed, and users, engagement, and revenues can grow at unprecedented rates. But as they create unprecedented valuation multiples, digital scale, scope, and learning also create a slew of new leadership and governance challenges. And often, these challenges are not well met by current institutions, which struggle not only with a rapidly changing knowledge base but also with the greater responsiveness that is needed.

Rule 5: Concentration and Inequality Will Likely Get Worse

As in the Industrial Revolution, transformation drives the redistribution and concentration of wealth. But this time, the phenomenon is exacerbated by the dynamics of digital networks. The evolution of these networks leads to the concentration of the flow of transactions and data, and from that to increased concentration of power and value.

As digital networks carry more transactions, we are witnessing the expanding importance of network hubs. We have already discussed hub firms like Google and Facebook, WeChat and Baidu, which connect consumers, firms, and whole industries to each other. And once a hub is already highly connected in one sector of the economy (such as Airbnb in home rentals or Alibaba in peer-to-peer retail), it can gain important advantages as it links to a new sector (e.g., Airbnb in travel experiences or Alibaba in financial services). These trends are not new, but in recent years, the high degree of digital connectivity has dramatically accelerated the rate of transformation and increased the importance of digital hubs beyond our wildest expectations. Consider how industry after industry is consolidating around a few hubs and being utterly reshaped.

This pressure toward increased power and wealth accumulated in network hubs adds to the challenges of digital labor replacement, erosion of capability, and skill obsolescence. The pattern toward concentration creates increased inequality, not only across workers but also across firms, which further segments wealth, power, and relevance across markets, industries, and geographies. This naturally builds to a general sense of inequity, frustration, and anger, especially in certain segments and geographical regions. Many of these reactions were seen during the Industrial Revolution, but one is left to wonder whether the potential impact could be even greater now that the scale, speed, and impact of current trends appear truly unprecedented.

Vulnerabilities, New and Old

The rise of the industrial firm provides an interesting contrast to the current patterns of transformation. It does not take much imagination to envision how our new age might drive economic and social changes that are at least as significant as those seen in the Industrial Revolution. And—thanks to lightning-fast communication speeds and tight linkages across the global economy—they're happening much faster and more comprehensively.

The digitization of our economy appears to have moved past an inflection point. And as the digital firm continues to amplify its impact, we are starting to see a marked drop in public trust and cohesion. Significant signs of fracture have been apparent for years—the Occupy and Yellow Vest movements are two such signs—suggesting that we may have been too smitten with digital innovation and its immense value. Mesmerized by booming stock markets, voice-controlled homes, and driverless cars, we may enjoy the stunning potential of the new age. But the challenges created by relatively unconstrained digital operating models are also becoming clear, from amplifying economic disparities to reinforcing extreme political views, to opening us all to attack by rogue actors. The sometimes uninformed responses of politicians, regulators, and even some tech leaders add to the strains.

These trends are converging to uncover deep-seated vulnerabilities that are threatening some of the most important institutions in society. As the nature of work is redefined by software and algorithms, reshaping the strategic dynamics of industries and markets, we are starting to see widespread implications. When we combine increasing economic disparity with widespread news bias and outright political manipulation, add the challenges of job loss and transformation to the specter of cyber warfare, it's clear that we are dealing with a possibly explosive combination.

These vulnerabilities require new sensitivities. Thankfully, many of the best leaders have already moved beyond a single-minded focus on increasing shareholder value to take in the concerns of employees, customers, partners, and the community at large. As digital transformation accelerates, these considerations will need to be extended. It's not enough to retrain workers, to cite one important example of smarter stakeholder management. We are once again facing the social dislocations that come with the transformation of the means of value creation, capture, and delivery. Addressing these changes—along with the resulting redistribution of income, influence, and power—will require a much broader range of managerial and policy considerations, from creative, targeted investments to generate work opportunities for depressed specialties or geographic areas, to consideration of a universal basic income. As leaders' decisions increasingly shape the evolution of our collective community, they may be judged less by Wall Street and more by Main Street.

Here Lord Byron's speech can provide useful guidance:

> *Yet had proper meetings been held in the earlier stages of these riots, had the grievances of these men and their masters (for they also had their grievances) been fairly weighed and justly examined, I do think that means might have been devised to restore these workmen to their avocations, and tranquility to the country.*[6]

Luddites emerged just as the template for the modern company was being established. Now, most of us in developed economies live and work within the context of the modern corporation. The age of AI is once again creating new rules, and it is, once again, a time for wisdom.

In chapter 10, we offer some recommendations to leaders for meeting these new challenges.

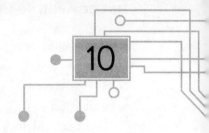

A Leadership Mandate

What is all your studying worth, all your learning,
all your knowledge, if it doesn't lead to wisdom?
—Beychae, *Use of Weapons*, by Iain Banks

In contrast with the current wealth of data, analytics, and AI, we still appear to be suffering from a shortage of managerial wisdom. The reason could be that the new rules of the age of AI are redefining the impact of firms, and we are still trying to figure out the implications. Old assumptions no longer seem to apply. The assets and technologies wielded by organizations, as well as the tools and capabilities required to manage them, are changing drastically, expanding their reach and scope. The very concept of the firm is evolving as processes become embedded in software, and as data, analytics, and AI drive an increasing proportion of operating activities and managerial decisions. This has transformed managerial tasks and created all kinds of opportunities. But despite many great successes, it is clear that we still have some things to learn.

The age of AI defines a clear mandate. Simply stated, we must find wiser ways to lead the increasingly digital firm. Engineering feats are not enough. We have already reengineered the economics of business and subjected the rate of transformation to Moore's law. But while we approach the many opportunities, we must find better ways to manage the new assets and capabilities that are being created and deployed, every day, across every organization.

This mandate is not limited to any particular class of firm, old or new. When it comes to leading our increasingly digital organizations, we have some things to work on—whether we work in incumbent enterprises, small startups, digital hubs or platforms, or regulatory bodies, or we participate in the communities that surround these organizations.

We highlight four arenas in which this leadership mandate is playing out.

Transformation

We have talked a lot about transformation. It starts at the top, with motivating and grooming a generation of leaders to do the hard work involved. There is no longer a rationale for staying behind, doubling down on old strengths and capabilities, and ignoring the emergence of a new operating model that is overwhelming every major sector of the economy. A better collective outcome hinges on each enterprise and its management team doing its part. No organization should be standing still.

The wise path forward in managing enterprise transformation should be clear. The technologies are available for everyone to use as a service from the cloud, with plenty of experts to help with their deployment. There are plenty of articles, books, and online courses describing how to use them. The most difficult work is in changing the organization, transforming its operating architecture, and building the right skills, capabilities, and culture to drive an increasingly digital operating model. We have highlighted some of the most critical transformation steps. We recognize that theory does not equal practice, but still, there is no effective plan B as digital transformation moves rapidly across every industry. Wisdom requires managerial action, despite its obvious difficulties.

But even if we understand the managerial tasks involved, developing the wisdom to act is a serious leadership challenge. It's easy to talk about change. But as traditional silos are broken down, power relationships will shift, and some functions and skills will lose their importance. It becomes critical to be committed to leading the transformation, to be all in.

Often, we have found that traditional firms dabble in transformation and set up pilots or demonstration projects but then can't pull the trigger on the real thing, especially when the threat to the status quo becomes clear. Even when they do, the transformation is sometimes slowed by those who don't see an immediate benefit. Failures arise when managers cannot diagnose the architectural shift occurring in their industries, or when they are not willing to challenge the status quo; we've seen it with incumbent phone manufacturers (Nokia, Motorola, BlackBerry), video distribution and production companies (Blockbuster, Viacom), and retailers (shopping malls, big box retailers).

Even when managers recognize the architectural shift needed and are ready to provide a sustained commitment and spend the required resources, they may still face significant headwinds. The challenges at General Electric provide a sobering example. Although the company invested billions to set up its GE Digital unit and even though the group's early successes impressed many people (including the two of us), it did not lead to sustainable or widespread transformation.

The GE Digital unit was hobbled by a variety of problems. For one thing, its technology was perceived as lacking the reliability, stability, and openness necessary for widespread implementation, both by customers and by other GE business units. The situation was not helped when GE Digital grew into a separate profit center (a top-tier SBU) and was increasingly seen as competition by several other GE businesses, which did not adopt its technology nor provide the support needed, especially in sales. In addition, the giant Alstom acquisition, along with the major financial problems faced by the GE Power unit, proved a huge distraction and diverted resources.

After enterprise transformation begins, its success requires leaders to inspire a full, ongoing commitment. Even spending billions of dollars will not bring cohesion to a fractured organization. This is when enlightened and committed leadership will make the difference—in finding ways to build bridges across the inevitable fractures, in making the hard calls to understand where alignment won't happen, and in acting to make the necessary changes. Vittorio Colao, who was CEO of Vodafone during much of its digital transformation efforts, puts it well:

> *There are big new winds blowing—in data analytics, automation and artificial intelligence—and they will not blow exactly in the same way across all of the organization. In my fleet some boats will gain speed, while others have smaller sails and won't capture the same momentum. The question is whether you allow each boat to go at its own cruising speed—as we did in the beginning—or if you want to align the fleet and wrap it into a big program, as we are now trying to do. Aligning the boats is helpful for the organization, but you also risk forcing them into a linear speed that ends up being blown away by disruptors.[1]*

We emphasize that the leadership challenge in transformation does not apply only to traditional firms. As we have seen repeatedly in this book, every hub company must transform to survive and must do so repeatedly. Given the remarkably high risks inherent in their business models—the privacy of assets in Facebook's social communities or in Ant Financial's networks, to name two examples—leaders of digital organizations need to transform to build a deep foundation of safety, security, and sustainability in their business models as well as their operating models.

Also, we emphasize that the concept of leadership should not be limited to the top of an organization. The opportunities and challenges are so great that anyone and everyone should be inspired to contribute, especially those who are building and shaping the systems that form the core of the firm. It takes only a few great people to improve the Facebook algorithms that we all depend on, or to install the software patches that make our data at Equifax secure. Obviously, we cannot ignore the impact of the most senior people in an organization, but it is important to understand that anyone can rise and play a crucial leadership role.

These considerations motivate the education, mentoring, and selection of a generation of leaders as transformers of new and old companies. Many of the best managers will have to retool and learn both the foundational knowledge behind AI and the ways that technology can be effectively deployed in their organization's business and operation models. They do not need to become data scientists, statisticians, programmers, or AI engineers; rather, just as every MBA student learns about accounting and its salience to business operations without wanting to become a professional accountant, managers need to do the same with AI and the related technology and knowledge stack.

Qualifications for leaders should start with an understanding of the digital systems they are creating and leading, and with a full appreciation of the organizational, ethical, economic, and political consequences of getting these systems wrong. We emphasize that good leaders of digital firms must also understand the softer issues. They still need to master the human side and understand the critical issues that inevitably come up as workers interact with increasingly digital operating models. Managers need to have a feeling for the inspiration, capabilities, and culture needed to drive continued, ongoing evolution. An integrated perspective is key, and a little knowledge of history. A leader deep in technology and driven by a strong sense of entrepreneurship, but less well rounded on the human nature of leadership and its impact on people, organizations, and institutions, may be as poorly qualified as a great traditional manager with no understanding of digital operating models, agile methods, or AI.

Entrepreneurship

The emergence of the age of AI has possibly created the greatest entrepreneurial opportunity in the history of civilization. The extent of digital transformation is vast, and one only needs to look at traditional processes, scenarios, and use cases to get a sense of how each might be better performed by a digitally enabled, AI-based solution. Whether one looks at how content is crafted and distributed, how health care improvements are being developed, how equipment is being developed, manufactured, deployed, and maintained, or how news reports are being generated, the world is literally jammed with entrepreneurial opportunity.

Many of the challenges identified in this book provide additional opportunities for innovation and entrepreneurship. From ensuring cybersecurity to avoiding algorithmic bias, and from fighting fake news to creating good jobs, real technological breakthroughs and innovation will be a big part of the many solutions required. Thankfully, as we discussed, innovation costs have dropped significantly. The ubiquity of digital technology, the ability to get on-demand computing power to virtually anyone anywhere, and the wide availability of open source software and hardware tools have democratized the power of invention.

However, as opportunities are examined and evaluated, it is crucial to not only examine the technological feasibility of the innovation required or the scalability of the venture's operating model. Deeper analysis is often needed to fully comprehend and evaluate the venture's business model, including its often subtle competitive implications. The classic example must be Uber, which has been plagued with losses for years—its IPO prospectus even warns investors it may *never* be profitable—and all this after attracting almost $25 billion in investment capital.[2]

We have discussed how Uber's competitive outlook is challenged by the extensive competition it will likely always face because of the extensive multihoming and network clustering its business model enables (see chapter 6). Uber and other ride-sharing companies present a paradox: the service provided has increased consumer surplus (who does not want a ride on demand within five minutes?) and has enabled employment flexibility for more than a million drivers, and yet it's difficult to find wisdom in money being invested in a business model that likely makes no money while providing only marginal employment to large communities of people and potentially even causes environmental and traffic externalities due to increased congestion in urban cores.

To scale opportunities beyond initial financial gains and to sustain their success into actual improvement in the life of the many constituencies they touch, the wiser leaders will better appreciate how their increasingly digital firms impact the communities around them, and consider more difficult social and ethical implications. But while many invest in research and engineering, few have so far committed the same attention and resources devoted to understand the more subtle implications of their business and operating models. The challenge is to fully internalize the long-term impact of a newly launched digital firm on the reality that surrounds it.

Blockchain ventures are a great example. With their foundational impact, blockchain-based or -inspired architectures may well be an important part of the solution to many of the problems caused by the waves of digitization and AI.[3] The blockchain space embodies a range of useful methods and technologies, from distributed ledgers to smart contracts, and from cryptocurrencies to peer-to-peer networks. But to work within the context provided by complex industries and institutions, blockchain-based *business* models need to reflect new thinking. Despite its enormous promise, the impact of blockchain so far—beyond financial speculation—has been spotty at best.

Sustainable impact will be achieved only if its leaders shape technology to fit our complex norms and institutions, or to at least help them transform. As the blockchain matures, the variety of technologies may increasingly be unbundled and may be tailored to fill a range of institutional needs, from immutable smart contracts to news tracking and supply chain monitoring. Significant business model innovation will thus increasingly drive the success of each blockchain technology. And if blockchain technology ever really does help reduce the dramatic inefficiencies of traditional bureaucracy, it will certainly not be a moment too soon.

Gone are the days when competitive advantage could be based on unique, static assets and capabilities, often going decades without disruption. Today's leaders will need to deal with continuous change and with frequent collisions threatening the very nature of the organizations they lead and the nature of the markets they compete in. Along with transformation, innovation and entrepreneurship will provide an important way through. And the greater the entrepreneurial wisdom, the better the outcomes for all of us.

Regulation

Regulators are racing to catch up with the evolution of technology. Current efforts in fields as different as antitrust and privacy have made important contributions to the increased scrutiny and accountability of digital firms. In addition, local governments are getting involved, as with Uber and Airbnb. As the impact of AI continues to increase, we will see widespread regulation, at many levels of government, shaping spaces as different as traffic safety and racial bias.

Regulators have focused much of their attention on the increased need for privacy regulation. Europe has led the way with the 2018 introduction of the General Data Protection Regulation system, or GDPR, which helps individuals control how their personal data is used by organizations. Most critically, GDPR introduces fundamental data protection principles, such as pseudonymization and right of access and erasure, which give individuals some ownership over their data.

The regulation puts in place strict controls by default, so that consumers must opt out in order for any of these controls to be relaxed. This naturally enables at least some level of protection for everyone. However, there is also significant worry that the companies that can respond most effectively to the GDPR system will be the large technology companies, thus raising the costs for entrepreneurial startups and reinforcing the domination of the large firms.

In addition, debate is heating up around antitrust, especially in the context of digital hub firms. A number of major antitrust efforts, most of them in Europe, have targeted several firms: Microsoft during the late 1990s and early 2000s, and Google more recently. In the past few years, Google has been fined in Europe for anticompetitive behavior in search services and with the Android operating system. Although the European competition authority may have achieved many of its original goals, it is not clear whether exacting fines is the most effective remedy for an economy that is increasingly fraught with new kinds of deep-rooted issues. The crafting of appropriate and impactful remedies for violations in both the privacy and antitrust spaces is highly challenging, and a crucial, open issue worthy of extensive debate.

These activities shouldn't proceed in isolation. Hub companies are recognizing that they must work with governments to shape regulations and policy. We doubt we'll again see anything like Microsoft's unambiguously adversarial relationship with antitrust enforcement agencies during the 1990s. Tech firms, including Apple, Microsoft, Alphabet (Google), Facebook, and Alibaba are developing sophisticated capabilities to help shape the outcome. Despite a significant emphasis on political lobbying and positioning, the importance of real collaboration is being felt. Just as companies can make mistakes, government regulators cannot have a perfect crystal ball to modify systems and organizations they don't fully understand.

But collaboration is only the first step. The reality is that many of the problems defining our newly digital economy are truly difficult to fix. Inequality, privacy, and bias are hard enough to define, let alone resolve. Moreover, these challenges provide moving targets, and they morph on both short and long time lines. Beyond individual regulations, therefore, the most important solution may be to set up collaborative structures and approaches that, while exhibiting regulatory power, also benefit from sustained expert involvement to monitor the situation, motivate necessary changes, create potential solutions, and drive serious regulatory innovation.

Community

Communities are an increasingly important complement to regulation in providing checks and balances to digital firms.

The impact of community on the software industry has a long history. The ongoing development and evolution of the Linux operating system was a true breakthrough in the history of technology. Unlike other major, widely deployed software programs, Linux was architected, developed, deployed, and supported entirely by a global community of engineers. The organization was (and still is) highly structured, with clear governance provided by clear roles and responsibilities and with clear accountability for contributions as well as mistakes.

All this is embedded in an exhaustive, distributed testing process, powered by tens of thousands of community members. The software was (and is) available for free and licensed under the GNU Public License, or GPL, which guarantees that any product derivative of the free software will also be made available for free. Open source software has attracted the enthusiasm and imagination of millions, who join forces to improve software globally and are motivated by incentives as different as skills development, explicit corporate assignments, intrinsic enjoyment, reputation building, and basic community and common cause.

Linux today is by far the most popular cloud operating system, broadly supported by enterprises and available at any capacity on demand from all the main providers: AWS (Amazon), Azure (Microsoft), and Google Cloud. In addition, variants of the open source software approach have been used to power a variety of projects ranging from web servers like Apache to browsers like Firefox. The latter was originally built by Netscape as Navigator, subsequently open sourced, and now managed by the Mozilla Corporation. Open source software powers a huge variety of popular products, from databases like MySQL to user interface libraries like REACT (originally built by Facebook), to the now almost ubiquitous machine learning framework TensorFlow, originally built by Google and now part of the open domain.

The open source approach has also been effective well beyond the development of software infrastructure. For many years, Craigslist, an open approach to online listings, dominated a broad range of categories, later imitated by countless focused websites ranging from Uber to Airbnb. But perhaps the most important example might be Wikipedia. Launched in 2001 by Jimmy Wales and Larry Sanger, Wikipedia is a universal online encyclopedia featuring millions of articles in three hundred languages and available to its almost one billion users every day.

Wikipedia's governance resembles that of many open source projects, with a clear organization, clear roles and responsibilities, and a clear process of accountability. While becoming the most commonly used encyclopedia in the world, Wikipedia has consistently avoided inaccuracy and bias. The great thing about the system is that if you think an entry is incorrect, you are welcome to fix it and subject your improvements to its open and transparent editing process.

The process works, as has been repeatedly established by research studies. Our Harvard colleagues Shane Greenstein, Feng Zhu, and Grace Gu, for example, measured the evolution of Wikipedia political bias over thousands of articles on politically sensitive topics, and they showed that bias tends to erode over time as multiple contributors make corrections. The researchers even found that the editors themselves tended to become less biased over time, as they internalized community-based feedback.[4] Complementing this work, our Laboratory of Innovation Science at Harvard colleague, Misha Teplitskiy, and coauthors showed that diversity of political views in Wikipedia articles produced higher quality content.[5] The polarization and diversity combined with a distributed process in which anyone can participate enabled higher quality content.

The potential for a community to lead in solving new generations of problems is enormous. Communities can be immense assets in the push to master the challenges created by digital operating models. In all its years of history, Linux has proved relatively resilient to manipulation and cyberattack. TensorFlow is powering machine learning efforts in hundreds of countries. Wikipedia bias is typically corrected in a matter of days, if not hours. This kind of robustness, global reach, transparency, and responsiveness is now critical, and delivering it is hard for regulators through traditional bureaucratic organizations. New kinds of organizations modeled after the open source community, but perhaps with an even broader and more powerful mandate, could play a critical role in solving many of the problems confronting our digital economy and society, from algorithmic bias to fake news. As open source champion Eric Raymond wrote, "Given enough eyeballs, all bugs are shallow."

The community ethos is not limited to active individuals. As the collective work and effort of the Apache, Linux, and Mozilla foundations show, companies of all sizes, within and across a range of industries, can collaborate with other companies, nonprofits, and individuals to create, maintain, extend, and preserve a variety of important software products and technologies. This model has been emulated in many settings, including content and AI research. The wisdom of the community is an asset we cannot ignore.

We believe that it is essential for the health and vigor of the economy that the crucial leadership roles played by communities be safeguarded and improved. Community considerations should seriously influence future thinking regarding regulatory checks and balances on hub firms and should connect closely with any new policy and regulation. It would make a lot of sense for us to increase investments in shaping crowds and innovation communities, leveraging the kind of fair and dynamic governance systems enacted by open source projects to drive the kind of monitoring, instant response, and long-term improvements that have been demonstrated for many years. Ultimately, crowds and communities can dramatically improve and extend the impact of regulatory and policy-making bodies, bringing enforcement and response systems to new levels of response and innovation.

The Leadership of Collective Wisdom

Understanding the impact of digital transformation has become critical, not only to sustain the performance of firms but also to safeguard institutions. The new kinds of operating models characterizing firms in the age of AI are binding us together across industries, countries, markets, and political affiliations. The many resulting interdependencies have become much too important to ignore and are motivating the need for a new kind of collective wisdom.

As the digital firm reduces human friction and erases traditional internal bottlenecks, the complex interrelationships across communities and organizations have become crucial. All too often, the only constraint left appears to be a new kind of sudden, collective failure. We have seen the sudden destruction of value from Facebook's and Twitter's fake news and privacy crises, as well as from massive data breaches, such as those at Equifax and Yahoo!, each affecting hundreds of millions, if not billions, of consumers. Ant

Financial's investment accounts capture the savings for a huge portion of the Chinese population. The responsibility this creates for the leaders of a relatively small organization is immense.

The collective dynamics of AI-enabled social and economic networks change the perspective on management and on leadership. As collective effects become increasingly important, the performance of digital firms will increasingly hinge on their impact on the rest of us, well beyond traditional drivers of managerial effectiveness. This demands a new look at traditional notions of management and suggests that we should pay more attention to its impact beyond the single firm to the vast economic and social networks it depends on and contributes to. Consequences on the broader community have all too often been treated as a second-order effect—a discussion that usually takes place after the fact.

As digital firms increasingly shape our global economy, their management will be held accountable to a different standard. Despite competing as individual businesses, each will benefit or suffer from collective accomplishments, such as improving privacy, removing news bias and manipulation, or even creating effective systems to encourage and retrain displaced labor.

Managers frequently abandon the common perspective when facing critical business decisions. Even when executives embrace the idea of an AI-driven and digitally connected economy on the surface, they often stop short of making decisions that go beyond the optimization of individual firm performance. They often insist on arguing that "their" system is better than their competitors', ignoring the fact that both systems are connected and can drive jointly toward collective improvement. For example, Facebook, Google, and Twitter would be better off (along with the rest of us) if their leaders found ways to establish a common and consistent approach to monitoring and addressing concerns in such areas as truth and bias. Communities and regulators can also help, not only by establishing common principles but also by developing open digital technologies and platforms. Organizations—such as the Partnership on AI, a consortium to help realize the collective promise of artificial intelligence—provide a promising model for research and collaboration going forward.[6]

If we take the concept of an economic network seriously, the analogy should carry us beyond traditional notions of competition to a more progressive understanding of interfirm dynamics. We have outlined how individual organizations should move to better leverage and shape their networked competitive settings. We have discussed key assets and capabilities and have depicted an operating model to deploy them.

But to reach the full potential of these ideas, we feel that a deeper philosophical shift is needed. Individual firms will live and die by the collective health of their ecosystems, and they should make common cause to take these fundamental considerations deeply into account when making business decisions. As CEO Mark Zuckerberg well understands, Facebook will not sustain its success if the members of the networks on which it depends are increasingly frustrated and alienated. The notion of a firm's network health, and the responsibilities it underlines, effectively defines a new wisdom of leadership in competition.

The greatest part of this increased burden will fall on the small number of firms that serve as network hubs. Alphabet, Microsoft, Facebook, Alibaba, Amazon, and Tencent are performing an enormously important role in our society, with a disproportionate impact on our economy and social system. It is remarkable to think that a few thousand people have shaped the destiny of the billions that shop on Amazon and Alibaba, pay through Alipay and PayPal, or communicate on WeChat and Facebook. Despite some setbacks, these organizations have succeeded by making their networks into strong and resilient ecosystems and deserve great credit for what they have accomplished so far. But crucially, what started as an opportunity and continued as a clever and effective strategy, has now become a fundamental leadership responsibility.

———————

We live in an important moment in the history of our economy and society. As digital networks and AI increasingly capture our world, we are seeing a fundamental transformation in the nature of firms. This removes historical constraints on scale, scope, and learning and creates both enormous opportunity and extraordinary turbulence. But despite all this newfound digital automation, it seems that we can't quite do away with management just yet. The challenges are just too great, too complex, and too amorphous to be solved by technology (or technologists) alone. But leading through these changing times will require a new kind of managerial wisdom, to steer organizations from full-scale firms to new ventures, and from regulatory institutions to communities.

We hope that the frameworks presented in this book will generate new thinking and inform the debates on these crucial dynamics. The implications are important for a wide range of domains, most of all in shaping the thinking of a generation of leaders. The best is, hopefully, still to come.

Notes

Preface

1. World Health Organization, "Archived: Who Timeline—COVID-19," April 27, 2020, https://www.who.int/news-room/detail/27-04-2020-who-timeline—covid-19.

2. Moderna, "Moderna's Work on a COVID-19 Vaccine Candidate," 2020, https://www.modernatx.com/modernas-work-potential-vaccine-against-covid-19.

3. All the quotations attributed to Moderna executives are from interviews with the authors conducted in May and June 2020.

4. All the quotations attributed to MGH executives are from interviews with the authors conducted in May and June 2020.

Chapter 1

1. For more on the video, see https://nextrembrandt.com/.

2. Blaise Aguera y Arcas, "What Is AMI?" Medium, February 23, 2016, https://medium.com/artists-and-machine-intelligence/what-is-ami-96cd9ff49dde.

3. Jennifer Sukis, "The Relationship Between Art and AI," Medium, May 15, 2018, https://medium.com/design-ibm/the-role-of-art-in-ai-31033ad7c54e.

4. Clayton M. Christensen, *The Innovator's Dilemma: When New Technologies Cause Great Firms to Fail* (Boston: Harvard Business Review Press, 1997; 2013).

5. Bret Kinsella, "Amazon Alexa Now Has 50,000 Skills Worldwide, Works with 20,000 Devices, Used by 3,500 Brands," Voicebot.ai, September 2, 2018, https://voicebot.ai/2018/09/02/amazon-alexa-now-has-50000-skills-worldwide-is-on-20000-devices-used-by-3500-brands/.

6. The title of this section is inspired by a quote by Walmart president and CEO Doug McMillon, "We are becoming a more digital company."

7. Lauren Thomas, "Sears, Mattress Firm and More: Here Are the Retailers That Went Bankrupt in 2018," CNBC, December 31, 2018, https://www.cnbc.com/2018/12/31/here-are-the-retailers-including-sears-that-went-bankrupt-in-2018.html.

8. EDI, "electronic data interchange," is a standard communication protocol used in supply chain management. RFID stands for "radio frequency identification" and is used to track objects, often used in supply chains.

9. "JD.com to Launch 1,000 Stores per Day," *Retail Detail*, April 17, 2018, https://www.retaildetail.eu/en/news/g%C3%A9n%C3%A9ral/jdcom-launch-1000-stores-day.

10. Liberally translated as "WeChat, thank you."

11. Jonathan Jones, "The Digital Rembrandt: A New Way to Mock Art, Made by Fools," *Guardian*, April 6, 2016, https://www.theguardian.com/artanddesign /jonathanjonesblog/2016/apr/06/digital-rembrandt-mock-art-fools.

12. Vipin Mayar, interview with the authors, January 2019.

13. Keystone Strategy is a technology and consulting firm focused on the strategy and economics of digital transformation.

14. Carliss Y. Baldwin and Kim B. Clark, *Design Rules, Vol. 1: The Power of Modularity* (Cambridge, MA: MIT Press, 2000).

15. Carl Shapiro and Hal R. Varian, *Information Rules: A Strategic Guide to the Network Economy* (Boston: Harvard Business School Press, 1998).

16. See Jean-Charles Rochet and Jean Tirole, "Platform Competition in Two-Sided Markets," *Journal of the European Economic Association* 1, no. 4 (2003): 990–1029; Annabelle Gawer and Michael A. Cusumano, *Platform Leadership: How Intel, Microsoft, and Cisco Drive Industry Innovation* (Boston: Harvard Business School Press, 2001); Geoffrey G. Parker, Marshall W. Van Alstyne, and Sangeet Paul Chaudhuri, *Platform Revolution: How Networked Markets Are Transforming the Economy—and How to Make Them Work for You* (New York: W. W. Norton and Co., 2016); Michael A. Cusumano, Annabelle Gawer, and David B. Yoffie, *The Business of Platforms: Strategy in the Age of Digital Competition, Innovation, and Power* (New York: Harper Business, 2019); F. Zhu and M. Iansiti, "Entry into Platform-Based Markets," *Strategic Management Journal* 33, no. 1 (2012); M. Rysman, "Competition between Networks: A Study of the Market for Yellow Pages," *Review of Economic Studies* 71 (2004); A. Hagiu, "Pricing and Commitment by Two-Sided Platforms," *RAND Journal of Economics* 37, no. 3 (2006); K. Boudreau and A. Hagiu, "Platform Rules: Multi-sided Platforms as Regulators" in A. Gawer, ed., *Platforms, Markets, and Innovation* (London: Edward Elgar, 2009); Eric von Hippel, *Democratizing Innovation* (Cambridge, MA: MIT Press, 2005); Shane Greenstein, *How the Internet Became Commercial: Innovation, Privatization, and the Birth of a New Network* (Princeton, NJ: Princeton University Press, 2015).

17. Erik Brynjolfsson and Andrew McAfee, *The Second Machine Age: Work, Progress, and Prosperity in a Time of Brilliant Technologies* (New York: W. W. Norton and Co., 2016); Kai-Fu Lee, *AI Superpowers: China, Silicon Valley, and the New World Order* (New York: Houghton Mifflin, 2018); Ming Zeng, *Smart Business: What Alibaba's Success Reveals about the Future of Strategy* (Boston: Harvard Business Review Press, 2018); Ajay Agrawal, Joshua Gans, and Avi Goldfarb, *Prediction Machines: The Simple Economics of Artificial Intelligence* (Boston: Harvard Business Review Press, 2018).

Chapter 2

1. We are extremely grateful to both Feng Zhu and Krishna Palepu, who originally wrote about Ant Financial and introduced us to its remarkable business and operating model. This chapter draws heavily from their case study series: Feng Zhu, Ying Zhang, Krishna G. Palepu, Anthony K. Woo, and Nancy Hua Dai, "Ant Financial (A), (B), (C)," Case 9-617-060 (Boston: Harvard Business Publishing, 2018).

2. Lulu Yilun Chen, "Ant Financial Raises $14 Billion as Round Closes," *Bloomberg*, June 7, 2018, https://www.bloomberg.com/news/articles/2018-06-08 /ant-financial-raises-14-billion-as-latest-funding-round-closes.

3. According to *Forbes*, in June 2018 the market cap of American Express was $87 billion, and Goldman Sachs was $92 billion. Ant Financial raised almost as much money in 2018 as did all the fintech startups in the United States and Europe.

4. Alfred D. Chandler, *Scale and Scope: The Dynamics of Industrial Capitalism* (Cambridge, MA: Belknap Press, 1990).

5. See, for example, David J. Teece, Gary Pisano, and Amy Shuen, "Dynamic Capabilities and Strategic Management," *Strategic Management Journal* 18, no. 7 (1997): 509–533.

6. Robert H. Hayes, Steven C. Wheelwright, and Kim B. Clark, *Dynamic Manufacturing: Creating the Learning Organization* (New York: Free Press, 1998).

7. Zhu et al., "Ant Financial."

8. Eric Mu, "Yu'ebao: A Brief History of the Chinese Internet Financing Startup," *Forbes*, May 18, 2014, https://www.forbes.com/sites/ericxlmu/2014/05/18/yuebao-a-brief-history-of-the-chinese-internet-financing-upstart/#68523023c0e1.

9. Don Weiland and Sherry Fei Ju, "China's Ant Financial Shows Cashless Is King," *Financial Times*, April 13, 2018, https://www.ft.com/content/5033b53a-3eff-11e8-b9f9-de94fa33a81e.

10. Ming Zeng, "Alibaba and the Future of Business," *Harvard Business Review*, September–October 2018, https://hbr.org/2018/09/alibaba-and-the-future-of-business.

11. Ibid.

12. Alexander Eule, "Wearable Technology with Pedals and Wheels," *Barron's*, December 13, 2014, https://www.barrons.com/articles/wearable-technology-with-pedals-and-wheels-1418445513.

13. Zoe Wood, "Ocado Defies the Critics and Aims to Deliver a £1bn Flotation," *Guardian*, February 21, 2010, https://www.theguardian.com/business/2010/feb/21/ocado-flotation.

14. Anne Marie Neatham, speech and Q&A with authors, January 2019.

15. James Vincent, "Welcome to the Automated Warehouse of the Future," *The Verge*, May 8, 2018, https://www.theverge.com/2018/5/8/17331250/automated-warehouses-jobs-ocado-andover-amazon.

16. Stephanie Condon, "Google I/O: From 'AI First' to AI Working for Everyone," ZDNet.com, May 7, 2019, https://www.zdnet.com/article/google-io-from-ai-first-to-ai-working-for-everyone/.

Chapter 3

1. We are truly grateful to Vladimir Jacimovic, who energized us to study many of these ideas and provided invaluable help and advice.

2. "CineMatch: The Netflix Algorithm," *Lee's World of Algorithms* (blog), May 29, 2016, https://leesworldofalgorithms.wordpress.com/2016/03/29/cinematch-the-netflix-algorithm/.

3. "Netflix, Inc. History," Funding Universe, accessed June 6, 2019, http://www.fundinguniverse.com/company-histories/netflix-inc-history/.

4. David Carr, "Giving Viewers What They Want," *New York Times*, February 24, 2013, https://www.nytimes.com/2013/02/25/business/media/for-house-of-cards-using-big-data-to-guarantee-its-popularity.html.

5. Todd Spangler, "Netflix Eyeing Total of About 700 Original Series in 2018," *Variety*, February 27, 2018, https://variety.com/2018/digital/news/netflix-700-original-series-2018-1202711940/.

6. Nirmal Govind, "Optimizing the Netflix Streaming Experience with Data Science," Medium, June 11, 2014, https://medium.com/netflix-techblog /optimizing-the-netflix-streaming-experience-with-data-science-725f04c3e834.

7. Xavier Amatriain and Justin Basilico, "Netflix Recommendations: Beyond the 5 Stars (Part 2)," Medium, July 20, 2012, https://medium.com/netflix -techblog/netflix-recommendations-beyond-the-5-stars-part-2-d9b96aa399f5. For more on this topic, see Josef Adalian, "Inside the Binge Factory," *Vulture*, https://www.vulture.com/2018/06/how-netflix-swallowed-tv-industry.html.

8. Ming Zeng, *Smart Business: What Alibaba's Success Reveals about the Future of Strategy* (Boston: Harvard Business Review Press, 2018).

9. To us, one of the most astonishing examples of datafication is an AI-based system that tracks student attention and learning outcomes through facial recognition cameras in classrooms, as pioneered by China's Face++—naturally a personal favorite of professors who want to ensure that every participant is fully engaged in the class session.

10. Ajay Agrawal, Joshua Gans, and Avi Goldfarb, *Prediction Machines: The Simple Economics of Artificial Intelligence* (Boston: Harvard Business Review Press, 2018).

11. For an excellent treatment of the six main types of algorithmic design, see Pedro Domingos, *The Master Algorithm: How the Quest for the Ultimate Learning Machine Will Remake Our World* (New York: Basic Books, 2018).

12. The outcome can be a category (dog or cat), in which case a logistic regression is used. Or the outcome can be a numerical value (the score of English proficiency), in which case a linear regression is used. Other, fancier approaches—depending on the depth and breadth of data you have and the kind of problem you are trying to solve—include support vector machines, K-nearest neighbor, random forests, and neural networks.

13. Ashok Chandrashekar, Fernando Amat, Justin Basilico, and Tony Jebara, "Artwork Personalization at Netflix," Medium, December 7, 2017, https:// medium.com/netflix-techblog/artwork-personalization-c589f074ad76.

14. Ibid.

15. "It's All A/Bout Testing: The Netflix Experimentation Platform," Medium, April 29, 2016, https://medium.com/netflix-techblog/its-all-a-bout-testing -the-netflix-experimentation-platform-4e1ca458c15.

16. Zeng, *Smart Business*. See chapter 3 for more details on how Alibaba has implemented APIs and a data infrastructure.

17. R. H. Mak et al., "Use of Crowd Innovation to Develop an Artificial Intelligence–Based Solution for Radiation Therapy Targeting," *JAMA Oncol,* published online April 18, 2019, doi:10.1001/jamaoncol.2019.0159.

Chapter 4

1. API Evangelist, "The Secret to Amazon's Success—Internal APIs," January 12, 2012, https://apievangelist.com/2012/01/12/the-secret-to-amazons -success-internal-apis/.

2. Melvin E. Conway, "How Do Committees Invent?" *Datamation* 14, no. 5 (1968): 28–31.

3. One of us (Marco) did some research on this topic a couple of decades ago and showed this to be empirically true. Marco Iansiti, "From Technologi-

cal Potential to Product Performance: An Empirical Analysis," *Research Policy* 26, no. 3 (1997).

4. Lyra Colfer and Carliss Y. Baldwin, "The Mirroring Hypothesis: Theory, Evidence, and Exceptions," HBS working paper no. 10-058, January 2010.

5. Rebecca M. Henderson and Kim B. Clark, "Architectural Innovation: The Reconfiguration of Existing Product Technologies and the Failure of Established Firms," *Administrative Science Quarterly* 35, no 1 (1990): 9–30.

6. This is not particularly surprising given that both Rebecca Henderson and Kim Clark were on Christensen's thesis committee at the Harvard Business School.

7. Clayton M. Christensen and R. S. Rosenbloom, "Explaining the Attacker's Advantage: Technological Paradigms, Organizational Dynamics, and the Value Network," *Research Policy* 24, no. 2 (1995): 233–257.

8. If we include armies and governments, we can find examples of componentized organizations going back thousands of years. The ancient Roman military organization is only one example.

9. See Marco Iansiti and Roy Levien, *Keystone Advantage: What the New Dynamics of Business Ecosystems Mean for Strategy, Innovation, and Sustainability* (Boston: Harvard Business School Press, 2004), chapter 7.

10. Despite its clever operating architecture, the company also engaged in a number of disturbing activities, from slavery to the opium trade, which we emphatically do not endorse.

11. R. P. Wibbelink and M. S. H. Heng, "Evolution of Organizational Structure and Strategy of the Automobile Industry," working paper, April 2000, https://pdfs.semanticscholar.org/7f66/b5fa07e55bd57b881c6732d285347c141370.pdf.

12. Robert E. Cole, "What Really Happened to Toyota?" *MIT Sloan Management Review*, June 22, 2011, https://sloanreview.mit.edu/article/what-really-happened-to-toyota/.

13. Amazon Inc. v. Commissioner of Internal Revenue, docket no. 31197-12, filed March 23, 2017, p. 38 (148 T.C. no. 8).

Chapter 5

1. Richards is Keystone Strategy's CEO and cofounder.

2. Microsoft, "Satya Nadella Email to Employees: Embracing Our Future: Intelligent Cloud and Intelligent Edge," March 29, 2018, https://news.microsoft.com/2018/03/29/satya-nadella-email-to-employees-embracing-our-future-intelligent-cloud-and-intelligent-edge/.

3. Satya Nadella, interview with authors.

4. It is ironic (but exciting!) to us and underlines the deep transformation at Microsoft to note that it has become a leading contributor to open source software. One of us (Karim) became an academic researcher to understand the open source phenomenon, and at that time Microsoft was viewed as the nemesis of the open source community. The company's executives during the 1990s and 2000s called the open source movement "un-American" and a destroyer of intellectual property. Quite the transformation! See, for example, Charles Cooper, "Dead and Buried: Microsoft's Holy War on Open-Source Software," CNET, June 1, 2014, https://www.cnet.com/news/dead-and-buried-microsofts-holy-war-on-open-source-software/.

5. Interview with authors, January 2019.

6. Microsoft, "Microsoft AI Principles," https://www.microsoft.com/en-us/ai/our-approach-to-ai.

7. The benchmarking analysis was a collaboration with Keystone Strategy LLC, funded in part by Microsoft Corporation, and focused on the impact of data and analytics on a company's business and operating models. See Robert Bock, Marco Iansiti, and Karim R. Lakhani, "What the Companies on the Right Side of the Digital Business Divide Have in Common," HBR.org, January 31, 2017, https://hbr.org/2017/01/what-the-companies-on-the-right-side-of-the-digital-business-divide-have-in-common.

8. Interview with authors, January 2019.

Chapter 6

1. See, for example, Albert-László Barabási, "Network Science: The Barabási-Albert Model," research paper, http://barabasi.com/f/622.pdf.

2. Marco Iansiti and Roy Levien, *The Keystone Advantage: What the New Dynamics of Business Ecosystems Mean for Strategy, Innovation, and Sustainability* (Boston: Harvard Business School Press, 2004); David Autor et al., "The Fall of the Labor Share and the Rise of Superstar Firms," NBER working paper no. 23396, May 2017, https://www.nber.org/papers/w23396; Marco Iansiti and Karim R. Lakhani, "Managing Our Hub Economy," *Harvard Business Review*, October 2017, https://hbr.org/2017/09/managing-our-hub-economy.

3. Feng Zhu and Marco Iansiti, "Entry into Platform Based Markets," *Strategic Management Journal* 33, no. 1 (2012); Feng Zhu and Marco Iansiti, "Why Some Platforms Thrive and Others Don't," *Harvard Business Review*, January–February 2019, https://hbr.org/2019/01/why-some-platforms-thrive-and-others-dont.

4. Note that *network analysis* is a general term that is also applied to the analysis of people (social), computers, the electric grid, software modules, proteins, and the like. The essential components are nodes in the networks and the links (edges) connecting them.

5. Hal R. Varian, "Use and Abuse of Network Effects," SSRN paper, September 17, 2017, https://papers.ssrn.com/sol3/papers.cfm?abstract_id=3215488.

6. Harold DeMonaco et al., "When Patients Become Innovators," *MIT Sloan Management Review*, Spring 2019, https://sloanreview.mit.edu/article/when-patients-become-innovators/.

7. This section draws extensively from Zhu and Iansiti, "Why Some Platforms Thrive."

8. Sadly, the US health care system still relies heavily on fax machines for most of its interoffice and interorganizational communications.

9. This section also draws extensively from Zhu and Iansiti, "Why Some Platforms Thrive."

10. Ibid.

Chapter 7

1. As we discuss in detail in chapter 8, in doing so, these learning analytics almost inevitably introduce some sort of bias. The more the algorithms customize the content to encourage user engagement, the more they will suffer from bias. Users will inevitably click on, engage with, and watch more of what they are interested in.

2. We are grateful to our Harvard colleagues Tarun Khanna, Juan Alcacer, and Christine Snively for their excellent case on Nokia (Juan Alcacer, Tarun Khanna, and Christine Snively, "The Rise and Fall of Nokia," Case 714-428 [Harvard Business School, 2014, rev. 2017]).

3. Ming Zeng's book on Alibaba's journey, *Smart Business: What Alibaba's Success Reveals about the Future of Strategy* (Boston: Harvard Business Review Press, 2018), provides an instruction manual on how traditional retail businesses can be dismantled by competitors using a digital operating model.

4. RealNetworks has its origins in Progressive Networks, founded by Rob Glaser in 1994.

Chapter 8

1. Centers for Disease Control and Prevention, https://www.cdc.gov /measles/cases- outbreaks.html.

2. A. L. Schmidt et al., "Polarization of the Vaccination Debate on Facebook," *Vaccine* 36, no. 25 (2018): 3606–3612; *Infectious Disease Advisor*, "Social Medicine: The Effect of Social Media on the Anti-Vaccine Movement," October 31, 2018, https://www.infectiousdiseaseadvisor.com/home/topics/prevention /social-medicine-the-effect-of-social-media-on-the-anti-vaccine-movement/.

3. Peter Hotez, "Anti-Vaccine Movement Thrives in Parts of the United States," *Spectrum*, November 19, 2018, https://www.spectrumnews.org/news /anti-vaccine-movement-thrives-parts-united-states/.

4. Lena Sun, "Anti-Vaxxers Face Backlash as Measles Cases Surge," *Washington Post*, February 25, 2019, https://www.washingtonpost.com/national /health-science/anti-vaxxers-face-backlash-as-measles-cases-surge/2019/02/25 /e2e986c6-391c-11e9-a06c-3ec8ed509d15_story.html?utm_term=.e8a7bf2286c7; A. Hussain, S. Ali, and S. Hussain, "The Anti-Vaccination Movement: A Regression in Modern Medicine," *Cureus* 10, no. 7 (2018).

5. Vyacheslav Polonski, "The Biggest Threat to Democracy? Your Social Media Feed," World Economic Forum, August 4, 2016, https://www.weforum .org/agenda/2016/08/the-biggest-threat-to-democracy-your-social-media-feed/.

6. B. Edelman, M. Luca, and D. Svirsky, "Racial Discrimination in the Sharing Economy: Evidence from a Field Experiment," *American Economic Journal: Applied Economics* 9, no. 2 (2017): 1–22.

7. See, for example, Robert Bartlett, Adair Morse, Richard Stanton, and Nancy Wallace, "Consumer-Lending Discrimination in the Era of FinTech," Berkeley research paper, October 2018, http://faculty.haas.berkeley.edu/morse /research/papers/discrim.pdf.

8. Jeffrey Dastin, "Amazon Scraps Secret AI Recruiting Tool That Showed Bias Against Women," Reuters, October 9, 2018, https://www.reuters.com /article/us-amazon-com-jobs-automation-insight/amazon-scraps-secret-ai -recruiting-tool-that-showed-bias-against-women-idUSKCN1MK08G.

9. Joy Buolamwini and Timnit Gebru, "Gender Shades: Intersectional Accuracy Disparities in Commercial Gender Classification," *Proceedings of Machine Learning Research* 81, no. 1 (2018): 1–15.

10. Joy Buolamwini, "How I'm Fighting Bias in Algorithms," TED, https:// www.ted.com/talks/joy_buolamwini_how_i_m_fighting_bias_in_algorithms ?language=en.

11. Sam Levin, "A Beauty Contest Was Judged by AI and the Robots Didn't Like Dark Skin," *Guardian*, September 8, 2016, https://www.theguardian.com

/technology/2016/sep/08/artificial-intelligence-beauty-contest-doesnt-like
-black-people; see also Jordan Pearson, "Why an AI-Judged Beauty Contest
Picked Nearly All White Winners," Motherboard, *Vice*, September 5, 2016,
https://motherboard.vice.com/en_us/article/78k7de/why-an-ai-judged-beauty
-contest-picked-nearly-all-white-winners.

12. Emiel van Miltenburg, "Stereotyping and Bias in the Flickr30K Dataset," *Proceedings of the Workshop on Multimodal Corpora*, May 24, 2016, https://arxiv.org/pdf/1605.06083.pdf.

13. Adam Hadhazy, "Biased Bots: Artificial-Intelligence Systems Echo Human Prejudices," Princeton University, April 18, 2017, https://www.princeton.edu/news/2017/04/18/biased-bots-artificial-intelligence-systems-echo-human-prejudices.

14. See Aylin Caliskan, Joanna J. Bryson, and Arvind Narayanan, "Semantics Derived Automatically from Language Corpora Contain Human-Like Biases," *Science* 356, no. 6334 (2017): 183–186.

15. Tom Simonite, "Machines Taught by Photos Learn a Sexist View of Women," *Wired*, August 21, 2017, https://www.wired.com/story/machines-taught-by-photos-learn-a-sexist-view-of-women/.

16. Tristan Greene, "Human Bias Is a Huge Problem for AI. Here's How We're Going to Fix It," *TNW*, April 10, 2018, https://thenextweb.com/artificial-intelligence/2018/04/10/human-bias-huge-problem-ai-heres-going-fix/.

17. A *brute force* attack is a trial-and-error method to discover a user password or personal identification number; a *web hacking* attack is a cyber threat designed to steal data assets, such as credit card details; a *distributed denial of service* (DDoS) attack is an orchestrated attempt to make an application unavailable by overwhelming it with a massive amount of fake traffic from many hijacked sources. Rosa Wang, "How China Is Different, Part 3—Security and Compliance," Medium, March 13, 2019, https://medium.com/@Alibaba_Cloud/how-china-is-different-part-3-security-and-compliance-3b996eef124b; "Safeguarding the Double 11 Shopping Festival with Powerful Security Technologies," Alibaba Cloud, November 9, 2018, https://www.alibabacloud.com/blog/safeguarding-the-double-11-shopping-festival-with-powerful-security-technologies_594163.

18. Brian Fung, "Equifax's Massive 2017 Data Breach Keeps Getting Worse," *Washington Post*, March 1, 2018, https://www.washingtonpost.com/news/the-switch/wp/2018/03/01/equifax-keeps-finding-millions-more-people-who-were-affected-by-its-massive-data-breach/?noredirect=on.

19. AnnaMaria Andriotis and Emily Glazer, "Equifax CEO Richard Smith to Exit Following Massive Data Breach," *Wall Street Journal*, September 26, 2017, https://www.wsj.com/articles/equifax-ceo-richard-smith-to-retire-following-massive-data-breach-1506431571.

20. Tara Siegel Bernard and Stacy Cowley, "Equifax Breach Caused by Lone Employee's Error, Former C.E.O. Says," *New York Times*, October 3, 2017, https://www.nytimes.com/2017/10/03/business/equifax-congress-data-breach.html; United States Accountability Office, "Data Protection: Actions Taken by Equifax and Federal Agencies in Response to the 2017 Breach," https://www.warren.senate.gov/imo/media/doc/2018.09.06%20GAO%20Equifax%20report.pdf.

21. Bernard and Cowley, "Equifax Breach Cause by Lone Employee's Error."

22. US Accountability Office, "Data Protection."

23. Chris Isidore, "Equifax's Delayed Hack Disclosure: Did It Break the Law?" CNN, September 8, 2017, https://perma.cc/WB44-7AMS.

24. Tao Security, "The Origin of the Quote 'There Are Two Types of Companies,'" December 18, 2018, https://taosecurity.blogspot.com/2018/12/the-origin-of-quote-there-are-two-types.html.

25. Jen Wieczner, "Equifax CEO Richard Smith Who Oversaw Breach to Collect $90 Million," *Fortune*, September 26, 2017, http://fortune.com/2017/09/26/equifax-ceo-richard-smith-net-worth/; Ben Lane, "Equifax Expecting Punishment from CFPB and FTC over Massive Data Breach," Housingwire, February 25, 2019, https://www.housingwire.com/articles/48267-equifax-expecting-punishment-from-cfpb-and-ftc-over-massive-data-breach.

26. Suraj Srinivasan, Quinn Pitcher, and Jonah S. Goldberg, "Data Breach at Equifax," case 9-118-031 (Boston: Harvard Business School, October 2017, rev. April 2019).

27. Elizabeth Dwoskin and Craig Timberg, "Inside YouTube's Struggles to Shut Down Video of the New Zealand Shooting—and the Humans Who Outsmarted Its Systems," *Washington Post*, March 18, 2019, https://www.washingtonpost.com/technology/2019/03/18/inside-youtubes-struggles-shut-down-video-new-zealand-shooting-humans-who-outsmarted-its-systems/?utm_term=.b50132329b05.

28. United States Department of Justice, https://assets.documentcloud.org/documents/4380504/The-Special-Counsel-s-Indictment-of-the-Internet.pdf.

29. Ibid.; Elaine Karmack, "Malevolent Soft Power, AI, and the Threat to Democracy," Brookings Institute, November 29, 2018, https://www.brookings.edu/research/malevolent-soft-power-ai-and-the-threat-to-democracy/.

30. Harry Davies, "Ted Cruz Using Firm That Harvested Data on Millions of Unwitting Facebook Users," *Guardian*, December 11, 2015, https://www.theguardian.com/us-news/2015/dec/11/senator-ted-cruz-president-campaign-facebook-user-data.

31. Julia Carrie Wong, Paul Lewis, and Harry Davies, "How Academic at Centre of Facebook Scandal Tried—and Failed—to Spin Personal Data into Gold," *Guardian*, April 24, 2018, https://www.theguardian.com/news/2018/apr/24/aleksandr-kogan-cambridge-analytica-facebook-data-business-ventures.

32. Nicholas Confessore and David Gelles, "Facebook Fallout Deals Blow to Mercers' Political Clout," *New York Times*, April 10, 2018, https://www.nytimes.com/2018/04/10/us/politics/mercer-family-cambridge-analytica.html; Davies, "Ted Cruz Using Firm That Harvested Data."

33. Robert Hutton and Svenja O'Donnell, "'Brexit' Campaigners Put Their Faith in U.S. Data Wranglers," *Bloomberg*, November 18, 2015, https://www.bloomberg.com/news/articles/2015-11-19/brexit-campaigners-put-their-faith-in-u-s-data-wranglers.

34. Mathias Schwartz, "Facebook Failed to Protect 30 Million Users from Having Their Data Harvested by Trump Campaign Affiliate," *Intercept*, March 30, 2017, https://theintercept.com/2017/03/30/facebook-failed-to-protect-30-million-users-from-having-their-data-harvested-by-trump-campaign-affiliate/.

35. Donie O'Sullivan, "Scientist at Center of Data Controversy Says Facebook is Making Him a Scapegoat," CNN, March 20, 2018, https://money.cnn.com/2018/03/20/technology/aleksandr-kogan-interview/index.html.

36. Jane Mayer, "New Evidence Emerges of Steve Bannon and Cambridge Analytica's Role in Brexit," *New Yorker*, November 17, 2018, https://www

.newyorker.com/news/news-desk/new-evidence-emerges-of-steve-bannon-and
-cambridge-analyticas-role-in-brexit.

37. Kevin Granville, "Facebook and Cambridge Analytica: What You Need to
Know as Fallout Widens," *New York Times*, March 19, 2018, https://www.nytimes
.com/2018/03/19/technology/facebook-cambridge-analytica-explained.html.

38. Nicholas Thompson and Fred Vogelstein, "A Hurricane Flattens
Facebook," *Wired*, March 20, 2018, https://www.wired.com/story/facebook
-cambridge-analytica-response/.

39. Robert Hackett, "Massive Android Malware Outbreak Invades Google
Play Store," *Fortune*, September 14, 2017, http://fortune.com/2017/09/14/google
-play-android-malware/.

40. Feng Zhu and Qihong Liu, "Competing with Complementors: An Empirical Look at Amazon.com," Harvard Business School Technology & Operations
Mgt. Working Paper No. 15-044, *Strategic Management Journal*, forthcoming.

41. Marco Iansiti and Roy Levien, *The Keystone Advantage: What the New
Dynamics of Business Ecosystems Mean for Strategy, Innovation, and Sustainability* (Boston: Harvard Business School Press, 2004).

42. Matthew Martin, Dinesh Nair, and Nour Al Ali, "Uber to Seal $3.1 Bil-
lion Deal to Buy Careem This Week," *Bloomburg*, March 24, 2019, https://www
.bloomberg.com/news/articles/2019-03-24/uber-is-said-to-seal-3-1-billion-deal
-to-buy-careem-this-week.

43. Jackie Wattles and Donie O'Sullivan, "Facebook's Mark Zuckerberg
Calls for More Regulation of the Internet," CNN, March 30, 2019, https://www
.cnn.com/2019/03/30/tech/facebook-mark-zuckerberg-regulation/index.html.

44. Cade Metz and Mike Isaac, "Facebook's A.I. Whiz Now Faces the Task
of Cleaning It Up. Sometimes That Brings Him to Tears," *New York Times*,
May 17, 2019, https://www.nytimes.com/2019/05/17/technology/facebook-ai
-schroepfer.html?action=click&module=Well&pgtype=Homepage&section
=Technology.

45. Tim Starks, "How the DNC Has Overhauled Its Digital Defenses,"
Politico, October 17, 2018, https://www.politico.com/newsletters/morning
-cybersecurity/2018/10/17/how-the-dnc-has-overhauled-its-digital-defenses
-377117.

46. Iansiti and Levien, *The Keystone Advantage*.

47. See *UC Davis Law Review*, "Information Fiduciaries and the First
Amendment," https://lawreview.law.ucdavis.edu/issues/49/4/Lecture/49-4
_Balkin.pdf; "Jonathan Zittrain and Jack Balkin Propose *Information Fiducia-
ries* to Protect Individual Rights," *Technology Academics Policy*, September 28,
2018, http://www.techpolicy.com/Blog/September-2018/Jonathan-Zittrain-and
-Jack-Balkin-Propose-Informat.aspx; and Jonathan Zittrain, "How to Exercise
the Power You Didn't Ask For," HBR.org, September 19, 2018, https://hbr.org
/2018/09/how-to-exercise-the-power-you-didnt-ask-for.

48. "Zittrain and Balkin *Propose Information Fiduciaries*."

49. Jack M. Balkin and Jonathan Zittrain, "A Grand Bargain to Make Tech
Companies Trustworthy," *Atlantic*, October 3, 2016, https://www.theatlantic
.com/technology/archive/2016/10/information-fiduciary/502346/.

50. Ibid.

51. Katie Collins, "Facebook Promises to Back US Privacy Regulation,"
CNet, October 24, 2018, https://www.cnet.com/news/facebook-promises-to-back
-us-privacy-regulation/.

Chapter 9

1. Clive Thompson, "When Robots Take All of Our Jobs, Remember the Luddites," *Smithsonian Magazine*, January 2017, https://www.smithsonianmag.com/innovation/when-robots-take-jobs-remember-luddites-180961423/.

2. Daron Acemoglu and Pascual Restrepo, "Robots and Jobs: Evidence from US Labor Markets," NBER working paper no. 23285, March 2017, https://www.nber.org/papers/w23285; McKinsey, "A Future That Works: Automation, Employment, and Productivity," January 2017, https://www.mckinsey.com/~/media/mckinsey/featured%20insights/Digital%20Disruption/Harnessing%20automation%20for%20a%20future%20that%20works/MGI-A-future-that-works-Executive-summary.ashx.

3. Erik Brynjolfsson, Tom Mitchell, and Daniel Rock, "What Can Machines Learn and What Does It Mean for Occupations and the Economy," *AEA Papers and Proceedings* 108 (2018): 43–47.

4. David Autor and Anna Salomons, "Is Automation Labor-Displacing? Productivity Growth, Employment, and the Labor Share," Brookings Papers on Economic Activities, March 2018, https://www.brookings.edu/wp-content/uploads/2018/03/1_autorsalomons.pdf.

5. In many cases, from fax machines to media platforms, networks have been shown to increase in value as N^e, with e>1, or as N log N.

6. The Luddites at 200, "Lord Byron's Speech," http://www.luddites200.org.uk/LordByronspeech.html.

Chapter 10

1. W. R. Kerr and E. Moloney, "Vodafone: Managing Advanced Technologies and Artificial Intelligence," case 9-318-109 (Boston: Harvard Business School Publishing, February 2018), 1.

2. "We have incurred significant losses since inception, including in the United States and other major markets. We expect our operating expenses to increase significantly in the foreseeable future, and we may not achieve profitability." US Securities and Exchange Commission, registration statement "Uber Technologies Inc.," https://www.sec.gov/Archives/edgar/data/1543151/000119312519103850/d647752ds1.htm, p. 12.

3. Marco Iansiti and Karim R. Lakhani, "The Truth about Blockchain," *Harvard Business Review*, January–February 2017, https://hbr.org/2017/01/the-truth-about-blockchain.

4. Shane Greenstein, Yuan Gu, and Feng Zhu, "Ideological Segregation among Online Collaborators: Evidence from Wikipedians," NBER working paper no. 22744, October 2017 (rev. March 2017), https://www.nber.org/papers/w22744.

5. Feng Shi, Misha Teplitskiy, Eamon Duede, and James A. Evans, "The Wisdom of Polarized Crowds," *Nature Human Behaviour* 3 (2019): 329–336.

6. See https://www.partnershiponai.org/.

Index

Disclosures

This book is based on both observations and actions. The insights and examples are derived from the actual experiences of the authors across a number of different firms. Whether individually or in association with Keystone Strategy, we have both been actively consulting for and shaping many of the companies in this book, including Microsoft, Facebook, Amazon, Alphabet, Fidelity, Marriott, General Electric, Uber, Roche, and Comcast. One of us (Marco Iansiti) has been involved as an expert in numerous legal matters on behalf of Microsoft, Facebook, Amazon, the Department of Justice, and the European Competition Authorities. Karim R. Lakhani and LISH received funding from NASA, the MacArthur Foundation, the Laura and John Arnold Foundation, the Schmidt Futures foundation, the Cook Foundation, and Linux Foundation. They have also been recipients of the Google Faculty Research Award. We have both taught extensively in Harvard Business School's Executive Education program and in private executive education settings where we have met and spoken with executives from many of the firms discussed in the book. As HBS faculty we also receive research funding support from the school's Division of Research and Faculty Development. Finally, we both serve on several boards. Karim serves as a director of Mozilla Corporation, Local Motors, Carbon Relay, and VideaHealth. Marco is a director of PDF Solutions (NASDAQ: PDFS), Module Q, and Keystone Strategy LLC, where he is also a cofounder and chairman of the board.

Acknowledgments

Knowing your own ignorance is the first step to enlightenment.
—Patrick Rothfuss, *The Wise Man's Fear*

This book emerged from old debates. We were both brought up on arguments about the impact of manufacturing on the competitiveness of firms, on whether a firm's strategy should be constrained by its capabilities, and about the threat of technological disruption to a firm's operating units. A little more than seven years ago, it started to dawn on us that these debates were losing steam. We were missing something. The challenge was not about any one firm losing out or being disrupted—all firms were experiencing essentially the same challenge, in industries as different as travel and agriculture. Something truly fundamental had changed in our economy: The nature of firms was evolving. The "digital firm" was born, powered by data, analytics, and artificial intelligence, leveraging the power of the digital networks that increasingly shaped, and even defined, our economy. These firms accomplished operating tasks differently, removing hundred-year-old bottlenecks to scale, to scope, and to learning.

We are grateful to the many mentors and colleagues who were instrumental in shaping this insight. Our understanding of the traditional world of operations was driven by the influence of great thinkers like Wick Skinner, Bob Hayes, Steve Wheelwright, and Kent Bowen, who spent much of their careers fighting for the importance of firm capability. Our understanding of the modern economy was sparked by the work of Carliss Baldwin and Kim Clark, expressed in

Design Rules. This book first demonstrated how information technology was restructuring the economy, from separate, monolithic industries into a clustered network of modular components. Our thinking on innovation, networks, and community was also shaped by Eric von Hippel, who mentored both of us and taught us how to look inside technology's "black box." Mike Tushman, Linda Hill, and Tsedal Neeley provided us with great insights on the organizational and cultural challenges inherent in achieving digital transformation. Jen Cohen, our coach, contributed important insights while keeping us grounded and ready to take on new challenges.

We are especially grateful to the Keystone Strategy team, which partnered with us to research and impact countless organizations, over hundreds of projects, while driving "transformative ideas" across a variety of industries. Greg Richards provided constant creative input, while Jeff Marowits gave us many insightful suggestions and all kinds of important comments. Ross Sullivan coached us and generated many thoughtful inputs and examples across many projects. A big thank you, too, to Rohit Chatterjee, Dan Donahue, and Sam Price for their critical input and feedback as we conceptualized and actualized the material, and to Tom Kudrle, Sean Hartman, Diane Prescott (from Microsoft), Henry Silva, and Seyla Azoz for many impactful ideas and contributions, as well as great energy and passion. We are also particularly grateful to Jack Cardwell and Jessica Solomon for great insights and examples, from Netflix to Walmart. The Keystone team made this book come alive.

Harvard Business School provided us with a unique platform on which to develop our ideas. Dean Nitin Nohria's ongoing support and encouragement of our work has been critical to its fruition. Youngme Moon was extremely helpful in the development of our ideas. A variety of senior associate deans and directors for research at HBS have enabled us to dive deep into the topic areas. They include Srikant Datar, Jan Rivkin, Leslie Perlow, Mike Norton, Cynthia Montgomery and Teresa Amabile. The HBS Case Research and Writing Group led by Carin Knoop and Kerry Herman provided extraordinary support in the development of the cases that have driven much of our research journey. Julia Arnous was our research assistant through the course of the book and made great contributions. Most of all, our intellectual agenda and impact were greatly stimulated by the extraordinary faculty of the Technology and Operations Management Unit at Harvard Business School. We are indebted to all of them. A special thank you goes to Feng Zhu, whose transformational research and insights on networks and platforms greatly informed our thinking and had a direct impact on many chapters of this book. Shane Greenstein was also particularly helpful across a variety of topics, from deepening our understanding of the history of the internet with his award-winning book to the development of several great case studies on various AI-based startups. Faculty, staff, and visitors engaged in Harvard Business School's Digital Initiative, of which we are codirectors, have also been an ongoing source of intellectual nourishment and have provided many leads to important aspects of the digital transformation occurring in the economy.

For the past decade, much of our research energy has been channeled through the Laboratory for Innovation Science at Harvard ("LISH") at Harvard's Institute for Quantitative Social Science. LISH and its various earlier forms (NASA Tournament Lab and Crowd Innovation Lab) enabled us to work with partners in solving innovation challenges while simultaneously conducting rigorous social science research. We are thankful to NASA colleagues Jason Crusan, Jeffrey Davis, William H. Gerstenmaier, Lynn Buquo, and Steven Rader for their partnership in our laboratory. Our early work with NASA showed us the power of AI-based algorithms in solving some of the toughest space sciences problems. We are also grateful for the partnership we've had with Topcoder (Jack Hughes, Rob Hughes, Mike Morris, Andy LaMora, and Dave Messinger), enabling us to solve AI innovation challenges through the incredible crowdsourcing community they have fostered. LISH is a unique partnership, with collaborators across Harvard University, and we are especially grateful to Eva Guinan (Harvard Medical School) and David Parkes (Harvard Paulson School for Engineering and Applied Sciences) for making our work technologically rigorous and practice focused. The staff, researchers, postdoctoral fellows, doctoral students, and visitors at LISH (including Jin Paik, Michael Menietti, Andrea Blasco, Nina Cohodes, Jenny Hoffman, Steven Randazzo, Rinat Sergeev, and Mike Endres) were a constant source of innovation, research insights, and powerful examples for our work, and we are very thankful to them for their dedication and hard work. We would also like to thank our assistants, Karen Short and Lindsey Smith, for keeping our work life organized, balanced, and productive.

Great credit goes to Melinda Merino and the Harvard Business Review Press for a great process and for encouraging us to focus the book on the rapidly changing field of AI. We also want to thank John Sviokla and Vladimir Jacimovic, and (again) Jeff Marowits who provided very helpful critical comments on the book and dramatically improved it. Vladimir was instrumental in helping us understand the AI factory concept and in getting us excited about its enormous impact on modern operating models.

Most of all we want to thank Amy Bernstein for her incredible impact on conceptualizing and writing the book. She was there through thick and thin, guiding us with a gentle but firm hand through the process of intellectual discovery and synthesis, helping us stay dedicated and energized, and truly bringing this book home. Amy has been our intellectual thought partner for the past eight years and has always helped us make our ideas better, sharper, crisper, and more relevant. We could not have done it without her.

Finally, we want to acknowledge the central role of our families in our intellectual agenda and in the writing of this book. They put up with our many days away from home and our many hours of solitude as we worked away on our computers. Karim is thankful for his wife and best friend Shaheen's patience and wisdom as he embarked on yet another "cool project." She provided the stability, the home base, and the encouragement to ensure that the explorations were fruitful and relevant. Karim's daughter, Sitarah, keeps him in awe of the future and inspires him to make the world a better place. Karim's mom, Doulat, made tremendous sacrifices to ensure that her son would have unbelievable opportunities, and she has been a constant pillar of support in his journey. Marco is grateful for his wife Malena's unbridled passion and enthusiasm, enlightening him with myriads of ideas, articles and posts, and constantly asking questions that kept the book relevant and focused on the truly important issues. Marco also thanks Julia, who questions and challenges and cleverly brings up "the other side" in all arguments, and Alexander, the book's "Chief Technology Officer," who kept the work grounded in real engineering and drove a number of insights about the actual impact of AI. Finally, he is grateful to Vanessa, Sua, and little SJ ("Where is Marco?"), who brought energy, passion, and many smiles into the process.

Marco Iansiti
Dover, MA

Karim R. Lakhani
Cambridge, MA

About the Authors

Marco Iansiti is the David Sarnoff Professor of Business Administration at Harvard Business School, where he also heads the Technology and Operations Management Unit and cochairs the Digital Initiative. In addition, Iansiti serves as faculty codirector of the Laboratory for Innovation Science at Harvard. His research examines the digital transformation of companies and industries, with a special focus on digital ecosystems, AI-centric operating models, and the impact of AI and network effects on strategy and business models. Iansiti is known for his research on the management of innovation, business ecosystems, and digital transformation. His work on business ecosystems and their impact on strategy has been widely recognized and quoted. More recently, his research on digital transformation has received broad attention among both academics and practitioners, and his writings on this subject made *HBR*'s list of top ten articles of the year for three of the last four years. Iansiti has authored or coauthored several books, including *Technology Integration*, *The Keystone Advantage*, and *One Strategy*.

Iansiti joined Harvard Business School in 1989 and taught extensively in the school's MBA, Executive Education, and doctoral programs. He developed courses on Managing Product Development, Starting New Ventures, and worked with Karim Lakhani to create the Digital Innovation and Transformation course. He is currently responsible for the Digital Transformation course module in the Executive Education Advanced Management Program, one of the world's oldest and most prestigious executive programs. He cofounded several companies, including Model N (NASDAQ:MODN) and Keystone Strategy LLC. In association with the Keystone

Strategy team, he has advised most of the largest technology companies, from Facebook to Amazon, and from Microsoft to Intel, as well as many more traditional Global 1000 firms. Iansiti currently serves on the boards of several companies, including PDF Solutions (NASDAQ: PDFS), ModuleQ, and Keystone Strategy, where he is Chairman.

Iansiti was awarded a PhD and an AB in Physics from Harvard University.

Karim R. Lakhani is the Charles E. Wilson Professor of Business Administration and the Dorothy and Michael Hintze Fellow at Harvard Business School and a Research Associate at the National Bureau of Economic Research. He is the founder and codirector of the Laboratory for Innovation Science (LISH) at Harvard, the principal investigator of the NASA Tournament Lab at the Institute for Quantitative Social Science, and the faculty cofounder of the Harvard Business School Digital Initiative. His research examines crowd-based innovation models and the digital transformation of companies and industries. Lakhani is known for his pioneering scholarship on how communities and contests can be designed and managed to achieve innovative outcomes and the origins and dynamics of open source software projects. His research on digital transformation has shown the importance of data and analytics as drivers of business and operating model transformation. His work with LISH researchers has yielded AI solutions in domains as diverse as space systems, life sciences, and online platforms. He has published over one hundred peer-reviewed journal articles, practitioner papers, and business cases. His research has been featured extensively in *Businessweek*, the *Boston Globe*, the *Economist, Fast Company, Inc.* magazine, the *New York Times*, the *New York Academy of Sciences* magazine, *Science*, the *Wall Street Journal*, the *Washington Post*, and *Wired*.

Lakhani joined Harvard Business School in 2006 and has taught extensively in the school's MBA, Executive Education, and doctoral programs. He codeveloped a new course on Digital Innovation and Transformation for the elective MBA curriculum and cochairs the executive program on Competing with Big Data and Business

Analytics. He is the cochair of the Harvard Business Analytics Program, an online executive-level course designed to train the next generation of data-savvy leaders. He has worked as a consultant with many companies on their innovation strategy, serves on the board of directors of Mozilla Corporation, and advises several AI startups. Previously he worked at GE Healthcare and the Boston Consulting Group.

Lakhani was awarded a PhD in Management and an SM in Technology and Policy from the Massachusetts Institute of Technology and a bachelor's degree in Electrical Engineering and Management from McMaster University.